D0217528

ETHNOGRAPHY AND VIRTUAL WORLDS

ETHNOGRAPHY AND VIRTUAL WORLDS

A Handbook of Method

TOM BOELLSTORFF
BONNIE NARDI
CELIA PEARCE
T.L. TAYLOR

PRINCETON UNIVERSITY PRESS
Princeton and Oxford

Published by Princeton University Press,
41 William Street, Princeton, New Jersey 08540
In the United Kingdom: Princeton University Press,
6 Oxford Street, Woodstock, Oxfordshire OX20 1TW
press.princeton.edu

Library of Congress Cataloging-in-Publication Data
Ethnography and virtual worlds : a handbook of
method / Tom Boellstorff ... [et al.] ; with a
foreword by George Marcus.
p. cm.
Includes bibliographical references and index.
ISBN 978-0-691-14950-9 (hardcover : alk. paper)
ISBN 978-0-691-14951-6 (pbk. : alk. paper)
1. Ethnology—Methodology. 2. Ethnology—Research.
3. Ethnology—Computer network resources.
4. Ethnology—Interactive media. 5. Virtual
reality. I. Boellstorff, Tom, 1969-
GN345.E745 2012
305.801—dc23
2012013805
British Library Cataloging-in-Publication Data
is available
This book has been composed in
Letter Gothic and Sabon
Printed on acid-free paper. ∞
Printed in the United States of America
10 9 8 7 6 5 4 3

To our informants, who make
our work possible

CONTENTS

ACKNOWLEDGMENTS

A number of individuals, whom we affectionately termed our "beta testers," read early drafts of the book and provided very helpful comments. We are grateful for their insights. In this regard we thank Donna Z. Davis, Grégory Dhen, Sharon Ding, Vrishti Gulati, Ben Koehne, Patricio Legras, Caitlin Lustig, Paul Manning, Israel Márquez, Sam Muhaidly, Ali Mushtaq, Russ Nelson, Stephen Rea, Jennifer Rode, Morgan Romine, Kalpana Shankar, Carl Symborski, Michael Tecson, Katie Vizenor, Martabel Wasserman, and Nic Watson. In addition, anonymous Princeton University Press reviewers provided thoughtful commentary and valuable suggestions.

Our editor Fred Appel at Princeton University Press offered sound guidance and strong support, as well as always being of good cheer and a pleasure to work with. We thank him for his advice, encouragement, and skillful management of the literary process. We thank as well Sarah David at Princeton University Press; Anita O'Brien, our copyeditor; Terri O'Prey, our production editor; Jason Alejandro, our designer; and J. Naomi Linzer, our indexer.

We also thank Melanie Richard for help in tracking down the history of the term "handbook."

Our thanks to the various foundations and funding agencies that have helped make possible our research over the years, including the National Science Foundation and Intel, and to our institutions for their support and the collegial environments they have fostered for us.

As always, we express our deepest appreciation and thanks to the many different communities, groups, and individuals, online and offline, among whom we conducted our research. We hope this handbook reflects the many things we have learned from them and will in turn support and inspire other researchers working in virtual worlds.

FOREWORD

George Marcus

> "This book is intended to help the trained anthropologist doing field work, and also to stimulate accurate observation and the recording of information thus obtained by anyone in contact with peoples and cultures hitherto imperfectly described."

So reads the inside cover copy of *Notes and Queries on Anthropology* (sixth edition, 1967; first edition, 1897!), revised and rewritten by a committee of the Royal Anthropological Institution of Great Britain and Ireland—the venerable handbook that has served generations of fieldworkers—professional and the curious amateur alike. Considerably more contemporary and addressed specifically to a new frontier of research, *Ethnography and Virtual Worlds*, a work by four authors writing also in an impressively seamless and collective voice, is offered nonetheless in the very same spirit. "Handbook" is one of the common labeling terms nowadays to dub contributions to the burgeoning literature on social research methods (in which ethnography is prominent), but few, if any, in my reading are as well designed as this work. It is meant to be used in advance of fieldwork as a clear and exhaustive introduction to the method; alongside it in its application to virtual worlds, in which each of the authors is deeply accomplished as a researcher; and in the crucial analytic-descriptive thinking about how to approach the collection and reporting of data.

Other than its well-crafted features as a manual and reference at hand, this work is distinctive for how it argues for the ethnographic method at a time when the reputation of ethnography and demand for it as the premier modality of qualitative research by all sorts of agencies, organizations, and design- and policy-driven projects have never been higher. With far more researchers adopting ethnographic methods than those who have been formally trained in those methods—in either its historic anthropological or sociological traditions—the irony is that its popularity threatens to undermine its validity and effectiveness. There is a tendency toward dilution, that is, for the data derived from subjects to lack a rich, critically developed context for interpretation, or toward fieldwork as the license to indulge speculation in a more authoritative guise. Direct engagement with subjects is the hallmark of fieldwork, and the minimal and perhaps Ur-modality of this, in the proliferation of ethnographic method, is the conversation or interview situation, or, as the authors remark, the function of elicitation. But without participant observation—or "being there," in recent tradecraft slang—interviews, even a series of layered interviews, lack the fabric and shell of the immersive experience of trying to live "inside," along with the patient, self-critical discipline of imposing objectivity on this experience by reflexive observational practices and their expression in intimate, constant recording of fieldnotes.

So while the authors provide a fine treatment of interviewing and elicitation techniques as well, they embed it in their considerable efforts to explain the demands and standards of sustained "being in fieldwork." They do so by a painstaking anticipation of both the misconceptions about the capacities of fieldwork (e.g., that it cannot be generalized beyond a specific observed instance) and the tendencies to shortcut it that are so ironically present in an era of social research that otherwise values what it purports to elucidate—the experiential, the practiced, and the understood among users and participants in the systems and organized projects of reason and technology that penetrate everyday life virtually everywhere and everywhere virtually.

And in this last phrase, the authors find their special agenda and mission: the overarching doubt that they address—that fieldwork methods, developed phenomenologically for "being there" in real-time, existential communities in the here and now, can be applied faithfully and with ingenuity to virtual worlds and communities enabled by contemporary information technologies. Indeed, ethnographies of virtual worlds—in the form of games and online communities (but not, or at least not yet, significantly, websites, platforms, email, databases, and networks like Facebook, which are outside their purview)—not only have been pioneered and achieved, by the Handbook's authors among others, but are now a manifestly vigorous, growing genre of research. Still the authors self-consciously choose to present their account of fieldwork by inflecting it with a certain tactical orthodoxy that is by no means stodgy. Their writing is in fact open-minded, filled with bright and lively ideas, advice, and innovative thinking about how fieldwork in online communities must change in order to remain the same (e.g., the domain of "textual listening" as a form of interviewing; their acute discussions and guidance about transcription; their brilliant and practical treatment of data-capturing methods). In presentation, however, it remains very important to establish the link with the achievements and capabilities of past ethnography—to reinforce its authority—as against commonsensical thinking that fieldwork in virtual worlds must somehow be different, must be less present or accessible to its subjects, that while connecting with its subjects, it cannot provide as thorough or deep knowledge of them as it could of its traditional physical world subjects. These authors do a masterful and convincing job of countering this common sense by the force and originality of their restatement of fieldwork as a method in the form of notes and queries oriented specifically to the study of virtual communities and social spaces.

Finally, since this account of method is strongly influenced by the specifically anthropological tradition of ethnography (three of the four authors having strong ties to it), it is worth reflecting on how engagements with virtual worlds in classic anthropological ethnography have morphed into its current field of study in the form of online cultures. After all, virtual worlds were in a sense the currency and intellectual challenge of much past ethnographic description and analysis in anthropology. Think of ethnographic efforts to grasp and descriptively report on the Dreamtime of Australian Aboriginal peoples. Think of the rich literature on shamanistic belief and ritual systems that mediate intimately the everyday lived realities of people with parallel, unseen worlds of beings and spirits that mirror and track everything that happens in the everyday.

During the pre-internet era of the late 1980s, in research on how wealth is constituted, virtually, as an unseen world that has authority over the everyday lives of the dynastic rich (in Marcus 1998), I tried to employ an ethnographic example of a Melanesian unseen or virtual world (of the Kaluli as brilliantly explored by Edward and Bambi Schieffelin, and by Steve Feld) as a contribution to an ethnographic understanding of a kind of fetishism in capitalist wealth accumulation and, in retrospect, as a waymark in my thinking that led to the postulation of the emergence of a distinctive trend of multi-sited research in the 1990s. The authors of this Handbook indicate that this postulation was in turn a kind of proto-stage in the development of ethnographic methods adapted to current internet-enabled virtual worlds. To quote Edward Schieffelin on Kaluli virtuality (in Marcus 1998:152):

> In talking about the people of the other world, the Kaluli use the term *mama*, which means shadow or reflection. When asked what the people of the unseen look like, Kaluli will point to a reflection in a pool or

> a mirror and say, "They are not like you or me. They are like that." In the same way, our human appearance stands as a reflection to them. This is not a "supernatural" world, for to the Kaluli, it is perfectly natural. Neither is it a "sacred world," for it is virtually coextensive with and exactly like the world the Kaluli inhabit, subject to the same forces of mortality. . . . In the unseen world, every man has a reflection in the form of a wild pig . . . that roams invisibly on the slopes of Mt. Bosavi. The man and his wild pig reflection live separate existences, but if something should happen to the wild pig, the man is also affected. If it is caught in a trap, he is disabled; if it is killed by hunters of the unseen, he dies. (1976:96–97)

While known by the Kaluli in everyday life in an episodic and commonsensical way, the unseen world is systematically imagined in ritual and discourse through mediums, who, roughly like ethnographers, have been to this other world and have seen what ordinary persons can only hear traces of. Communication with the unseen world and authoritative interpretation of events in the here-and-now world of the Kaluli thus depend on the coherent vision of mediums, who at certain moments give presence and order to Kaluli culture by creating primarily visualized representations of the unseen world within the fully sensed world of the here and now. While the ethnographer treats the unseen world respectively as if it were real, parallel, independent, yet implicated in constituting plainly observed Kaluli life, he or she has no apparent choice but finally to represent the unseen world as fully encapsulated by the here-and-now Kaluli cultural order, as fully present in the conventional category of ethnographic description, their "beliefs."

In that 1989 article I went on to evoke the engines of dynastic wealth, held and enjoyed by a family, as like the Kaluli unseen world, but whose virtuality (its constitution as facts and figures of ownership, investment, and practices of wealth management) could be materially investigated if the ethnographer, otherwise caught up in the dramas of dynastic family relations, would only move to the literal parallel sites of daily workshops of finance. Then emerges a project of multi-sited ethnography that makes literal what is otherwise empirically inaccessible and virtual in classic ethnography.

This is thus a personal parable of earlier research that I usefully understand now as a step between the virtual worlds encountered in, say, Melanesian ethnography, and the agile ways of thinking about them, as in the Kaluli research, and the kinds of virtual worlds that are now the subject of an ethnography, the methodology for which is so persuasively described for use in this Handbook. Virtuality that was empirically inaccessible to the ethnographer among the Kaluli, except through the second-order practices and interpretations of shamanistic paraethnographers of the virtual, is now directly accessible to the ethnographer through internet technologies and participations as a direct object of study by traditional fieldwork research methods.

While there is a vestigial sense that contemporary virtual worlds must somehow be related to everyday life, in the real-time, phenomenological here and now to apply ethnographic methods—not so different from the classic situation of incorporating peoples' dreamtimes and parallel existences into ethnographic accounts (to be sure, this kind of research on internet virtual worlds, anchored in the conventional real, remains important as a trajectory of research)—the authors of this Handbook show that fieldwork on virtual worlds need not be formulated or limited in this way. Virtual worlds are now directly accessible as "real" life for full ethnographic study as they were not, for example, among the Kaluli (*mama* could not be actually observed and their separate worlds engaged with by ethnographers, in the way that, for example, avatars in Second Life or games can be). This Handbook practically and persuasively makes such beings and worlds as accessible as physical world groups to the application of ethnographic methods at their highest standards of practice.

ETHNOGRAPHY AND VIRTUAL WORLDS

CHAPTER ONE

WHY THIS HANDBOOK?

1.1 BEGINNINGS

Virtual worlds are places of imagination that encompass practices of play, performance, creativity, and ritual. The social lifeworlds that emerge within them are very real. They represent a complex transaction between their designers, who have certain goals and desires about what people will do, and the denizens of virtual worlds themselves, who exercise individual and collective agency. They draw upon physical world cultures in multiple ways yet at the same time create possibilities for the emergence of new cultures and practices. Just as in the physical world, people within virtual worlds perform and cycle through different roles and identities. Virtual worlds make such shifts explicit, as well as introducing spaces for play and experimentation. How can we study these emerging cultural contexts?

Ethnography, an approach for studying everyday life as lived by groups of people, provides powerful resources for the study of the cultures of virtual worlds. As ethnographers, what interests us about virtual worlds is not what is extraordinary about them, but what is ordinary. We are intrigued not only by the individuals in a group, but by the sum of the parts. We aim to study virtual worlds as valid venues for cultural practice, seeking to understand both how they resemble and how they differ from other forms of culture. We do this by immersing our embodied selves within the cultures of interest, even when that embodiment is in the form of an avatar, the representation of self in these spaces. The goal of this handbook is to provide ethnographers with a practical set of tools and approaches for conducting successful fieldwork in virtual worlds.

Cultures, as shared systems of meaning and practice, shape our hopes and beliefs; our ideas about family, identity, and society; our deepest assumptions about being a person in this world. We now face a contemporary moment when the phrase "in this world" requires fresh inquiry. With the rise of virtual worlds, we find novel possibilities for human culture, even as we discover continuities with long-standing physical world conventions and practices.

We are four scholars who became intrigued by virtual worlds, impressed by the social life we saw emerging within them. We were enthusiastic about bringing the approaches used to study physical world cultures into these new online places of social life. In particular, we used ethnographic methods, originally designed for studying cultures in the physical world, to study cultures in virtual worlds. We were surprised and gratified that our approach paid off: in different virtual world contexts, we discovered places rich with social interaction, creativity, challenge, and history. This told us something important about virtual worlds themselves as vital places of social interaction and cultural activity (Hine 2005).

Between 2006 and 2010 each of us completed a book based on our individual research projects (Taylor 2006a; Boellstorff 2008a; Pearce and Artemesia 2009; Nardi 2010). Since publishing these books, all four of us have been surprised at how often we have been asked, "How did you study the virtual world you write about?" Our short answer is usually something like, "Well, as an ethnographer I observed social groups and conducted interviews, but I also participated in ongoing virtual world activities as much as possible." We add that participation entailed intense involvement and engagement, often to the point of mastery.

As ethnographers interested in immersive detail and rich context, we have been painfully aware of the inadequacy of such perfunctory responses and the growing need for better resources and discussion about how to conduct this kind of work. For a time we suffered our frustrations in relative isolation. However, in the early months of 2009, the four of us began a series of lively conversations in which we discovered that we shared this predicament and a desire to do something about it. Eventually we decided to put our heads together and write a text so that we could, in a principled and productive way, offload the question "How did you do it?"—by suggesting to our interrogators that they grab this short volume. Our intention is to elucidate as succinctly as possible what it means to ethnographically investigate a virtual world. As noted below, we discussed the genre of a "handbook" at length and concluded that our contribution would be a practical text to be stashed in a backpack, easily consulted, and kept "on hand" when doing fieldwork—even when the "field" in question is online.

As we plunged into writing, we realized that we wanted to do more than craft a guide to ethnography in virtual worlds. We also intend this handbook to serve as a primer on ethnographic research as a core social science methodology, and as a valuable mindset or approach to scientific inquiry. We hope our discussions resonate with virtual worlds researchers as well as those studying other online contexts, and even beyond. We discuss how ethnographic research requires immersion in a fieldsite using a palette of methods that always includes the central technique of participant observation. The goal is to grasp everyday perspectives by participating in daily life, rather than to subject people to experimental stimuli or decontextualized interviews. Ethnographers often speak of their work as "holistic." Rather than slicing up social life according to variables chosen for their contribution to variance in a statistically drawn sample, ethnographers attend to how cultural domains constitute and influence each other. We aim to discern broad patterns and meanings within what ethnographers often term "lifeworlds." Because of this focus, ethnographic research is predicated upon remaining in the field for a lengthy period, staying flexible in terms of what to study and how to study it, and avoiding deception. Ethnographic research is fundamentally distinct from experimentation; the goal is not to determine how controlled variables account for difference, but to trace and interpret the complex currents of everyday life that comprise our collective lived experience as human beings.

Ethnographic research has special resonance for anthropologists and sociologists, but it is also relevant for communication researchers and those inhabiting a loose coalition of computer science subdisciplines, including human-computer interaction, computer-supported collaborative work, computer-supported collaborative learning, and ubiquitous computing. The approach has long been of particular interest for those working in computer-mediated communication, social media, and game studies. While scholars outside of anthropology and sociology have reached out to ethnography in positive, generative ways, it is also true that they have sometimes misunderstood what ethnographic research demands. The four of us have, for example, reviewed manuscripts in which authors claimed they conducted an "ethnography" in only seven days, or labeled as "ethnography" a study in which the only data collection method was interviewing, or brought a game character to "level 85" and contended that voilà! an ethnography had (supposedly) been born.

The fact that we have independently encountered multiple instances of such confusions has motivated us even more strongly to clarify what ethnographic research requires. One powerful aspect of the approach is that ethnographers must be flexible in their techniques to make their methods sensitive to the contexts we study. We illustrate this flexibility by drawing on our experiences as ethnographers in a number of different virtual world environments. But this flexibility is not unlimited. Simply stating "this is ethnography" does not make it so. It is for this reason that we want to identify with the greatest possible precision the key tenets of ethnographic research, to avoid its being conceptually sucked into an inchoate mass of "qualitative" or "naturalistic" approaches within which its distinctiveness and specificity would no longer be discernible.

To delineate the fundamentals of ethnography, we return to its historical roots, exploring the research of foundational scholars such as Bronisław Malinowski, Margaret Mead, and Hortense Powdermaker. Even while we draw on classic formulations of ethnographic practice, we consider the impact of virtual world fieldsites on method. We have a good deal to say in regard to what ethnography in virtual worlds specifically entails. We consider critical aspects of what "virtual" means and examine how researchers are embodied in the field as they work through avatars. We analyze the forms of participation possible in virtual worlds and examine ethical issues such as the potential for researchers to disguise themselves in ways difficult in the physical world.

Like many scholars, on occasion we conversationally use phrases like "digital ethnography," "virtual ethnography," or "internet ethnography." However, we find these labels misleading overall because ethnographic methodology translates elegantly and fluidly to virtual worlds. We see ourselves as ethnographers conducting research in virtual worlds, not as "virtual ethnographers." While the specificities of these spaces prompt their own set of considerations, the ethnographic research paradigm does not undergo fundamental transformation or distortion in its journey to virtual arenas because ethnographic approaches are always modified for each fieldsite, and in real time as the research progresses. The successful deployment of ethnographic methods in virtual worlds is, for us, a ringing endorsement of their enduring power to illuminate novel dimensions of human experience.

This handbook is a compact and practical reference guide that provides the reader with a point of departure into conducting ethnographic research in virtual worlds. It is by no means comprehensive, nor should reading it be viewed as the only requirement to develop expertise in ethnographic methods. This book is not an analog to the famous scene in the movie *The Matrix* (itself a celebrated conceptualization of a virtual world) in which one character has the skills for flying a helicopter mentally "downloaded" into her brain in a few seconds. Instead, approach this handbook as an invitation to a journey, one that we hope will spur interest in ethnographic methods and help you engage effectively with other excellent ethnographic work.

A bit about us. Tom has the most traditional institutional background and affiliation, located in an anthropology department. During the writing of this handbook he served as editor in chief of *American Anthropologist*, the flagship journal of the American Anthropological Association, giving him a unique vantage point from which to encounter a wide range of ethnographic projects. His own research, however, has not been traditional in terms of method or topic; since 1992 he has conducted ethnographic physical world research on gay Indonesians. His virtual world ethnographic work in Second Life emerged from interests in globalization, identity, and power that were a direct result of his Indonesia research.

Bonnie, also trained as an anthropologist, has a long history of studying computer-mediated communication and collaboration. She conducted some of the first field studies of instant messaging, blogging, and collaborative video. Her interest in games emerged from her studies of social life on the internet in its manifold forms. Bonnie's work is accented by a strong interest in activity theory, a cultural-historical approach to the study of human consciousness with roots in early Soviet psychology. She coedits the MIT Press series "Acting with Technology," which publishes theoretical work directed toward social theory and technology.

Celia's background is as a game designer and game scholar. She came to ethnography from an interest in understanding how emergent behavior arises in multiplayer games through the interaction of large groups of players with specific software affordances. Her best-known ethnographic work concerns a group of "game refugees" from the game Uru who settled in other games and virtual worlds and created a "fictive ethnicity" around Uru tropes and culture. One of her most significant findings was identifying practices of "productive play" in which play parlays into creative practice.

T.L. was trained in ethnography as a sociologist, and her early work focused on embodiment in text-based virtual worlds known as MUDs (multi-user dungeons) and one of the first online graphical virtual worlds (Dreamscape). She then turned her attention to gaming spaces, writing a book about the massively multiplayer online game EverQuest and a number of articles on World of Warcraft where she has examined everything from play styles to forms of co-creation and governance. Her focus has been a critical sociocultural consideration of these worlds.

Each of us has thus conducted extensive ethnographic research in differing virtual worlds, exploring a wide range of topics. Our handbook builds on this background, and we will frequently illustrate conceptual points by turning to our own research.

1.2 WHY ETHNOGRAPHIC METHODS AND WHY VIRTUAL WORLDS?

We decided to focus on ethnographic methods in this handbook because in virtual worlds research (but more broadly as well), these methods are not always understood or valued. Some virtual world scholars still criticize ethnographic research by claiming it is anecdotal or unscientific—even doomed to irrelevance and extinction (e.g., Castronova 2006; Bloomfield 2009). Valuable empirical data obtained from ethnographic research are sometimes sidelined until "verified" by quantitative methods. Besides questioning the value of qualitative forms of inquiry, this kind of methodological partisanship does little to recognize the role that ethnographic methods play in building a rigorous and valuable scientific research corpus. As a result, we feel strongly that in addition to discussing ethnographic methods for virtual worlds as a set of research techniques, we must also discuss them in terms of the politics of knowledge production, examining these methods' importance to social science in the broadest sense.

We want to make clear that we advocate that the study of virtual worlds be driven by research questions, not a priori methodological dogmas or preferences. We may situate our study completely within a virtual world, and it is entirely legitimate and productive to do so if our research is so constituted. We may also fly across the globe to meet participants in physical world locales to conduct interviews and attend fan conventions. Our research will almost always include journeying to other online locales such as forums, blogs, and wikis. As we argue throughout this handbook, ethnography is a flexible, responsive methodology, sensitive to emergent phenomena and emergent research questions. There can be no argument for privileging certain locales or modes of study. Pertinent destinations and techniques issue from the aims of the research, and the choices of fieldsite and method should be based on the questions motivating inquiry.

Alongside our focus on ethnographic methods, we have worked to make our argument maximally concise and effective by focusing on the use of these methods to study virtual worlds. All four of us have research interests beyond virtual worlds, and we mean neither to privilege virtual worlds nor to imply that our scholarship is limited to them. Despite this fact, we see two reasons why texts that cover "internet methods" more broadly sometimes become unwieldy. One has to do with an overly diffuse focus on "methods." In our view this topic is too expansive to be a focus at all—thus our narrowing of the methodological discussion to ethnographic approaches. However, another source of the diffuse nature of many discussions of "internet methods" has to do with the first term in that phrase. A remarkably broad set of technologies and practices even in its early history (see Wellman and Haythornthwaite 2002), "the internet" now encompasses far too many contexts to serve as a reasonable topic for something of the scope of a handbook, a fate it shares with terms like "new media" and "digital media." While even "virtual worlds" encompasses a wide range of contexts (as the different character of our varied fieldsites indicates), we believe that the "virtual worlds" rubric is sufficiently focused to serve as an organizing principle for a handbook.

To frame our discussion, we describe virtual worlds as possessing the following characteristics. First, they are *places* and have a sense of *worldness*. They are not just spatial representations but offer an object-rich environment that participants can traverse and with which they can interact. Second, virtual worlds are multi-user in nature; they exist as shared social environments with synchronous communication and interaction. While participants may engage in solitary activities within them, virtual worlds thrive through co-inhabitation with others. Third, they are *persistent*: they continue to exist in some form even as participants log off. They can thus change while any one participant is absent, based on the platform itself or the activities of other participants. Fourth, virtual worlds allow participants to *embody* themselves, usually as avatars (even if "textual avatars," as in text-only virtual worlds such as MUDs), such that they can explore and participate in the virtual world. (For additional discussions of the definition of virtual worlds, see Boellstorff 2008a:17 and Pearce and Artemesia 2009:17–20.)

Sometimes networked environments are miscategorized as virtual worlds. For example, because of their lack of worldness and embodiment, we do not consider social networks like Facebook or Myspace in and of themselves to be virtual worlds in our definition (though we recognize that as platforms they can occasionally contain virtual worlds *within* them through third-party applications, such as YoVille, .Friends, or Farm Town). Nor do we consider online communities sustained via chat forums or other media virtual worlds. First-person shooter games, such as Counter-Strike or Halo, also do not qualify because they are not persistent: the world is only "on" as long as players are present. This is true as well for the single-player non-persistent worlds encountered in many non-networked console and computer games. For instance, we would not classify Bioshock or Myst as virtual worlds, although Uru, a networked instantiation of the Myst world, does meet the definition.

1.3 WHY A HANDBOOK?

Our decision to write a handbook was not capricious; the genre unifies questions of method and theory in a particularly effective manner. While texts terming themselves "handbooks" have appeared frequently in the social sciences and humanities, these sometimes resemble encyclopedias. For instance, the *Sage Handbook of Online Research Methods* weighs in at 2.7 pounds, with twenty-nine chapters across 592 pages of text (Fielding, Lee, and Blank 2008). Difficult to lift with a single hand, such volumes serve a valuable purpose but really belong to a different genre.

The notion of a "handbook" is not only specific but also ancient; for instance, Old English *handbōc* existed before the year 900 (Algeo 1993:282; see also Connors 1997), and the history of *manual* goes back at least five hundred years earlier. Historically handbooks were used by a range of persons, from clergy to military tacticians to students of Latin rhetoric during the first century B.C.E., and of Greek rhetoric four centuries earlier (Gaines 2010:163). The use of handbooks for teaching grammar seems to have been central to the term's reemergence in English in the 1800s. The enduring common thread uniting these notions of "handbook" across the centuries is the goal of capturing knowledge and making it accessible for practical use. In this sense a handbook is a guide to tools and procedures, a blueprint to things of the hand as much as the head.

The pivotal quality of a handbook is that you take it with you: it belongs as much in the field as in the library. In this sense a handbook ideally should be not just something you read before beginning a project, but something you keep at hand as you conduct research. We take this issue of portability seriously, in two key ways. The first concerns concision: we have labored to write a handbook that can actually be held in one hand. Of course, where virtual worlds are concerned the bookshelf and the fieldsite are often in the same physical room, so weight is not a direct concern. However, the handbook genre encourages concision not just for the sake of wrist muscles; concision is useful because it forces choices. No text can ever be everything to all readers, but the handbook form particularly demands conceptual triage, a focusing of one's scope and goals to the matters at hand.

A second way in which we have sought to make this handbook maximally portable is by abstracting key methodological insights from any particular fieldsite. In other words, our view is that a handbook should set forth generalized techniques that researchers can modify as they "carry" those techniques into fieldwork contexts that could not be imagined "beforehand." We have thus drawn from our varied research experiences, working to develop insights regarding portable ethnographic methods that can be useful for a broad range of virtual world contexts (and beyond).

1.4 AN ORIENTATION TO THE VIRTUAL WORLDS WE STUDIED

Because this text is a handbook about how to do ethnography, not an ethnography itself, we do not provide sustained explorations of the virtual worlds we studied. You will find many brief descriptions of our ethnographic experiences in these pages as they relate to questions of method, but for a full treatment of our fieldsites you will need to turn to our other publications, particularly our monographs (Taylor 2006a; Boellstorff 2008; Pearce and Artemesia 2009; Nardi 2010). One of the assets of this book is that our fieldsites vary greatly; as a result, we have produced a practical guide that transcends any one particular location. Even so, the worlds we studied are places of fascinating social interaction and technological transformation, and, as ethnographers, our instinct is to share our discoveries with you in all their amazing complexity and specificity. While we cannot go into all the details of these worlds, at the same time it may be helpful to provide a rough sketch of each we studied. With this in mind, we provide brief summaries of our virtual world fieldsites, knowing that readers interested in the details of these worlds can turn to our other publications and those of our colleagues.

In this handbook Tom draws from his fieldwork in Second Life, an open-ended virtual world that launched in 2003. In its early history it was subscription based, but after June 2006 it became possible to get an account for free. Second Life quickly became known for its graphical detail and ability to unleash resident creativity. During the time of Tom's fieldwork (and at the time we wrote this handbook), the business model undergirding Second Life was that residents had to pay to own virtual land, which allowed them to have persistent content inworld (for instance, a house, a store, or a park). The Second Life platform allowed residents to create objects inworld in real time, alone or in collaboration with others. Anything created (from a "script" that can animate an object to a virtual shirt, or a service like singing at a virtual club) could be sold for "Linden dollars" that were convertible with U.S. dollars or could be given away for free. When Tom began his research, Second Life had about 5,000 accounts and a maximum of about two hundred people inworld at any one time. From about 2008 to the writing of this handbook, the population had stabilized at around 1.5 million active accounts and around fifty thousand concurrent participants.

Bonnie draws from her research on the massively multiplayer online game World of Warcraft. Launched in 2004, the game had over eleven million players worldwide at the time of this writing. Available in nine languages, World of Warcraft was a truly global phenomenon. Players adventured in a medieval fantasy themed world, slaying monsters, practicing crafts, and trading at an auction house. World of Warcraft players communicated in text chat and often through voice. They came together in "guilds" or clubs that provided a cohesive social experience. The game was structured into several activities, among them raiding, in which ten to twenty-five people formed teams to engage in difficult battles. Players descended into dungeons to slay cunning raid bosses. These encounters required intense focus, communication, and coordination with other players. World of Warcraft has supported a plethora of game-related activities, including theorycrafting (the mathematical analysis of game mechanics), modding (the creation and distribution of player-created software extensions to the game, widely downloaded and used by players), machinima (videos of edited recordings of game action), the writing of games guides, and lively discourses about the game on blogs, forums, wikis, and social networking sites.

Celia's examples draw primarily from two environments—There.com and Uru: Myst Online. There.com opened in 2003, closed in 2010, and reopened in 2011. At the time of its 2010 closure, it was estimated to have 1.8 million users, 53 percent of whom were female. There.com had a cartoon aesthetic reminiscent of Disney's classic feature animation style. The emphasis was on avatar expressiveness rather than realism. There.com was an early virtual world to employ voice, accompanied by lip-sync and hand gestures, and text typed in cartoonlike bubbles triggered expressive animations, such as laughter (when you typed "laugh") or a pout (when you typed "sad"). Because There.com was an "all ages" environment, its player-created content, developed using external programs such as Gmax and Photoshop, was heavily monitored via a submission approval system.

Once approved, items were sold via an on-board auction system accessible through a browser within the There.com interface. There.com had its own online currency, Therebucks, and its real estate model was based on a system of community-owned "neighborhoods." Celia also studied Uru: Myst Online, a massively multiplayer game in the popular Myst series. The game consisted of a constellation of interrelated puzzles that slowly revealed the complex backstory of the now-uninhabited underground city created by the D'ni, a fictional race of people with the power to write entire worlds into being through magical books, when their own world was destroyed. Uru had a fairly realistic style but took place in a fantastical environment. Unlike many gaming-oriented virtual worlds, it had no levels and no combat. The gameplay focused on collaborative puzzle solving and unraveling the complex narrative (Pearce 2008b). Uru has opened and closed several times since it initially launched in 2003.

T.L. draws on her research across a variety of virtual worlds. Her original inworld ethnographic work, which looked at embodiment in these spaces, was focused on text-based worlds in the 1990s, as well as on one of the earliest graphical environments, Dreamscape (1995). Each of these worlds supported public spaces and private homes, made extensive use of virtual objects, and sustained rich forms of social life. She then turned her attention to primarily game-based worlds, in particular the massively multiplayer online games EverQuest (1999) and World of Warcraft (2004). Though more visually complex than the earlier worlds and reaching a broader mainstream audience, they shared many of the same properties, including forms of digital embodiment and emergent culture. They were also explicitly games, which shaped experience in specific ways. For example, coordinated collaborative activities like questing, fighting, and leveling up played a central role in organizing time and social lives. In all the worlds T.L. has studied, participants have engaged with them well beyond the confines of the software, including everything from websites to offline meet-ups. Because of this her work has tended to lead her to explore the ways communities construct their experience across diverse spaces and technologies well beyond the virtual world itself.

As these summaries indicate, the various virtual worlds we studied are diverse. Nonetheless, it should also be clear that this handbook was possible only because of many commonalities, parallels, and resonances among them. These commonalities represent the many ways in which virtual world ethnography shares fundamental tenets with ethnography in the physical world. Since its origins, ethnographers have worked to investigate cultural difference, the incredible range of ways to live a valid and meaningful human life. At the same time ethnographers have endeavored to show how these differences are not unbridgeable. These different pathways of life move across a shared terrain of the human. One of the many contributions of virtual world ethnography is to broaden this conversation by showing how forms of technologically mediated sociality shape and are shaped by the contemporary context.

CHAPTER TWO

THREE BRIEF HISTORIES

In this chapter we offer some background on the central topics of this handbook, ethnography and virtual worlds. We provide a history of ethnographic methods, a history of virtual worlds, and a history of ethnographic methods as used in virtual worlds. Each history is brief but points to key ideas shaping what we know about the development of ethnography as a scholarly practice and virtual worlds as important sites of human activity.

Why bother to elucidate these histories? In the hype-filled culture of technology research, it is easy to mislead oneself into thinking that everything is new: "too often internet researchers take the stance that, since the internet is new, old theory and methods . . . have nothing to offer in its exploration" (Baym 2009:180). More often than we would care to report, we have encountered scholarship weakened by authors overlooking previous work or making spurious claims of novelty. One of the most basic principles of scholarship is "standing on the shoulders of giants," building on the work of others. We thus feel it is critical to begin ethnographic inquiry with a sound understanding of how ethnography emerged and has been successfully used in the past, as well as how virtual worlds developed and have been studied ethnographically from their beginnings. Ethnographers of virtual worlds must "share a commitment to making sense of the new by understanding their research processes' and objects' continuity with the past" (Baym and Markham 2009:xv).

2.1 A BRIEF HISTORY OF ETHNOGRAPHIC METHODS

As far back as records go, it seems that humans have used the world-changing technology of writing to reflect on their cultures and the cultures of others. In the Western tradition, Greek classics such as Homer's *Odyssey* and Herodotus's *Histories* helped inaugurate genres of writing concerned with difference, displacement, and the social. Through myriad transformations and reconceptualizations, these forms of writing continue to the present day. But despite its Greek roots (*ethnos* "people," *graphein* "writing"), one would search in vain for "ethnography" in Homer or Herodotus. The term appears to have been coined only in 1767 by Johann Friedrich Schöpperlin, in the context of German Romanticism (Vermeulen 2008:276).

The notion of ethnography grew out of disillusionment with Enlightenment ideals of standardization, ideals famously exemplified in attempts during that period to create "encyclopedias" of all human knowledge. Indeed, the late eighteenth-century and early nineteenth-century studies by the geographer Wilhelm von Humboldt, working in a German tradition of *Geschichtswissenschaften* (historical sciences) that was shaped by thinkers like Herder and Goethe, played an important role in developing notions of culture, linked to the German Romantic notion of the *volk* or "people" (Bunzl 1996).

The distinction between "encyclopedia" and "ethnography" is instructive, revealing two distinct claims for the scientific conceptualization and presentation of knowledge. Authors of encyclopedias typically seek to produce comprehensive and comparative compendia. They subscribe to the theoretical standpoint known as "positivism" that originated with Auguste Comte (1798–1857), in the same nineteenth-century French environment in which the modern encyclopedia originated. Positivism, to oversimplify for brevity, is the view that the world (including human society) can be described in terms of generalizable laws. In contrast, authors of ethnographies typically seek to produce detailed and situated accounts of specific cultures in a manner that reflects the perspective of those whose culture is under discussion.

By the dawn of the twentieth century, there existed a range of writings that could be considered ethnographic in some sense. For the most part, these were produced by travelers without academic positions and with varied relationships to colonial and missionary projects. Frank Hamilton Cushing's work with Zuni communities in the 1880s and Baldwin Spencer and Francis Gillen's work in Australia in the 1890s are widely recognized examples of early ethnographic work (Cushing 1979; Spencer and Gillen 1899; for examples of contemporary discussions of this work, see Hinsley 1983; Povinelli 2002). These kinds of ethnographic reports, along with the writings of traders, explorers, and missionaries, became grist for ethnographic theorizing carried out by scholars who did not themselves work "in the field," in line with the broader mid-Victorian belief that "empirical data collected by gentleman amateurs abroad could provide the basis for the more systematic inquiries of metropolitan scholar-scientists" (Stocking 1992:18). During this period fieldwork was not prestigious, and "armchair scholars were accustomed to claiming the intellectual high ground" (Kuklick 2011:3). For instance, E. B. Tylor, who in 1896 became the first person to hold the position of professor of anthropology and was author of the influential *Primitive Culture* (1871), never conducted formal fieldwork (see Stocking 1995). Nor did James Frazer, whose book *The Golden Bough* (1915) was central to early twentieth-century anthropological thought.

In the history of ethnography, the single most pivotal figure is most likely Bronisław Malinowski (1884–1942), who taught at the London School of Economics from 1922 to 1938, training a whole generation of influential ethnographers (Kuper 1996). While Malinowski was not solely responsible for this new vision of ethnography, he may accurately be accorded a central role in its formulation and dissemination. The field research upon which Malinowski's best-known works were based was carried out primarily between 1914 and 1918 in the Trobriand Islands, near Papua New Guinea. After Malinowski, the norm in anthropology (and later in sociology and beyond) was that the hitherto largely segregated roles of "fieldworker" and "theorist/writer" were unified in the singular figure of the "ethnographer." This bringing together of method and theory is key to our understanding of ethnography. One reason for this is that "ethnography" is not a method narrowly defined; it is not part of the same categorical set as "interview," "survey," and so on. Rather, as its etymology suggests, ethnography is the written product of a palette of methods, but also a methodological approach in which participant observation is a critical element, and in which research is guided by experience unfolding in the field.

Some of Malinowski's ideas have not withstood the test of time, such as his linking of knowledge production to difference, resulting in an "entrenched design of fieldwork as an encounter between ethnographic Self and native Other" (Bunzl 2004:435). One still occasionally encounters this assumption that researchers cannot be objective if they "come from" the culture they study. This assumption persists despite the fact that it had been challenged by the work of anthropologist Franz Boas's students in the early twentieth century (see Hurston 1935), and also by ethnographers working in traditions of regions such as Eastern Europe, where long travel for fieldwork was never the norm (Hofer 1968; for discussions of national traditions in ethnography, see Gerlholm and Hannerz 1982; Restrepo and Escobar 2005).

One key insight that has taken root in ethnographic inquiry has been a distinction between "emic" and "etic" understandings of culture. These terms, coined by the linguist Kenneth Pike, were popularized in ethnographic research by Clifford Geertz (1983). For ethnographers, the outsider (etic) analyses of researchers are valid and informative—we do not expect that those we study will interpret their own lives exactly as we might in a scholarly context. However, ethnographers take insider (emic) analyses very seriously. We conduct research not just to mine data from informants, but to learn about their theoretical and pragmatic insights. An ethnographic approach thus implies drawing on both etic and emic forms of analysis. Above all, it implies keeping them distinct, for one of the clearest signs of a flawed or incomplete ethnographic study is confusion regarding which claims are the researcher's etic conclusions and which are the emic understandings of the informants themselves (although certainly at times emic and etic may overlap).

Another influential concept introduced to ethnographers by Geertz, derived from the work of philosopher Gilbert Ryle, is "thick description." This term refers to accounts of behavior that provide rich context. The argument is that without contextual embedding, it is not possible to meaningfully interpret what we see. Ryle illustrated this concept by contrasting three boys "rapidly contracting the eyelids of their right eyes"—in one case an "involuntary twitch," in the second a "conspiratorial signal to a friend," and in the third a parody of the first boy's wink (Geertz 1973:6). Ryle noted that a "thin description" of these three actions would term them all contractions of eyelids, but a "thick description" would account for their differing *meanings*. Building on this insight, Geertz noted that "the object of ethnography" is "a stratified hierarchy of meaningful structures in terms of which twitches, winks, fake-winks, parodies, rehearsals of parodies are produced, perceived, and interpreted" (Geertz 1973:7). This statement neatly encapsulates the goal of ethnographic research: an understanding of the cultural contexts in which human action takes place. These contexts exist in both physical and virtual worlds.

What do we call the people we study? In the early days of anthropology, researchers often referred to members of a culture as "natives." Although the term may now have ethnocentric or racist overtones in some contexts, it originally was keyed to cognates such as "nation" and "natal," connoting the integrity, legitimacy, and authenticity of the cultures early researchers encountered. As ethnographers grew increasingly self-conscious with respect to methodological development, they turned to the term "informant," which emphasized the knowledge ethnographers sought about unfamiliar cultures, their desire to be "informed." While the term was later critiqued as implying that culture members were voiceless without the ethnographer (the native informs, the ethnographer writes; see Clifford 1992), "informant" was the term of choice for an anthropological pantheon including Malinowski, Mead, Bateson, and Benedict, who wrote with humility and respect about the cultures they studied, appreciating their immense complexity and beauty. This respect for those we study and their authority on their own cultures is an enduring posture that virtual world ethnographers would do well to emulate.

Two other terms that are frequently used in contemporary ethnography are "interlocutor" and "study participant" or simply "participant." "Interlocutor" suggests an equality of conversational exchange between ethnographer and culture member. We have chosen not to use it because it is rather uncommon in daily conversation. The term can be seen as implying an overly optimistic equality between ethnographers and those we study. Additionally, it emphasizes speech, while ethnography is as much about doing—participating in everyday activities—as talking. The term "study participant" captures members' dual roles as participants in their own cultures and participants in the researcher's study.

In this handbook we primarily use the terms "informant" and "participant." We think these appropriate for our broad audience, although all of us have used other terms, and we recognize that no term is ever a perfect fit. "Informant" signifies that members of a culture inform ethnographers, sharing understandings about their lives through conversation and participatory activity. "Participants" suggests active sharing of knowledge between members of a culture and ethnographers participating within it. "Collaborator" is a term occasionally used in ethnographic projects with an explicit applied or activist component, to signal a shared set of goals. In certain cases the term can be effective, but in most cases we do not have the same goals as those we study, who also do not have a single unified goal among themselves.

The practices and meanings of ethnography have undergone a significant shift "through a series of transformations whose impetus can be traced to the 1960s" (Bunzl 2005:188), including debates over colonialism and conflict. These debates were accompanied by the increasing presence of women, people of color, non-Westerners, and queer persons as ethnographers. The varied positions of these persons as "native" ethnographers (Haniff 1985; Abu-Lughod 1991), particularly if they studied communities to which they in some sense belonged, troubled the distinction between Self and Other pivotal to classic assumptions about ethnographic research. The relational distance between researcher and subject, the belief in standing somehow neutrally "outside of" one's fieldsite, became problematized, offering the opportunity to reconsider principles of ethnographic research, including the possibility of "studying up" to explore "those who shape attitudes and actually control institutional structures" in one's own society (Nader 1969:284). From the 1970s through the 1990s, these varied shifts contributed to a rethinking of the practices of writing and representation that are at the core of ethnography as textual product (e.g., Geertz 1983; Clifford and Marcus 1986; Visweswaran 1994; Behar and Gordon 1995). While a detailed discussion of these developments lies beyond the scope of this short history, these interventions, as will be seen throughout this handbook, influenced our own thinking in various ways.

We point briefly to three other schools of thought that have shaped the history of ethnography—structuralism, postcolonialism, and feminism. Structuralism originated from linguistics, particularly in the work of Ferdinand de Saussure (1857–1913) and Roman Jakobson (1896–1982), and focused on the idea that one could study a language not just historically ("diachronically"), but in terms of the grammatical structures that make speech meaningful in a single slice of time ("synchronically"). Claude Lévi-Strauss (1908–2009) pioneered this approach to ethnography, viewing culture as a system of grammatical rules. By the latter half of the twentieth century, "poststructuralist" critiques asked if cultures really worked like languages, noting in particular the inability of a structuralist approach to account for power differentials within a culture, historical change, and phenomena like migration and globalization that made the argument that cultures are discrete entities difficult to sustain. This approach can be useful for researchers of virtual worlds as a way to approach coding, design, and ownership.

"Postcolonialism" refers to analyses by scholars skeptical of the "Orientalist" assumption that world history moves along a single path culminating in the West (Asad 1973; Gupta 1998; Said 1978). Much key scholarship in this field developed in relation to analyses of India and the legacy of British colonialism, but what "postcoloniality" means may differ in other contexts—for instance, Indonesia and the legacy of Dutch colonialism, Mexico and the legacy of Spanish colonialism, or former settler colonies like the United States and Australia that are in a sense postcolonial (Hall 1996). While virtual worlds are not colonies, questions of history, power, and global inequality are important for understanding them, and some scholars of virtual worlds have thus drawn on postcolonial theoretical frameworks. These foundations can be particularly useful when considering the underlying values embedded in the software of virtual worlds, which influence the cultures that emerge there, as well as unpacking the complex relations between physical and virtual world cultures. For instance, when Celia first introduced members of a collaborative of Canadian First Nations artists to Second Life, they were appalled by the Western capitalist notion of land ownership embedded in the software, and hence the culture.

Feminist ethnography has had a long presence in both anthropology and sociology (Visweswaran 1994; Maynard and Purvis 1994; Skeggs 1995, 1997), dating back to the work of early anthropologists in questioning the universality of gender roles (Mead 1935). In the 1970s a new wave of feminist ethnographic work, exemplified in the contributions to the key volumes *Woman, Culture, and Society* (Rosaldo and Lamphere 1974) and *Toward an Anthropology of Women* (Reiter 1975), explored the apparent universality of women's subordination and the cultural construction of gender itself. Since that time the field of ethnographic work on women, gender, and sexuality has become truly substantial. Feminist ethnography has particular relevance to the study of gaming-oriented virtual worlds because of their pervasive gender imbalance, a topic that both T.L. and Celia have tackled extensively in their work. The underlying gender politics of game design itself can create what T.L. has termed an "impoverished" sense of female embodiment that pervades the design of avatars in many online games (Taylor 2003b). Celia and her colleagues in the women's game collective Ludica have studied issues of instrumentalism, aesthetics, and gendered rhetorics of costuming, typically framed as "gear" in the context of combat-based games (Fron et al. 2007a). Thus feminist perspectives have influenced virtual worlds research by providing conceptual and practical tools not just for interrogating gender, but also for looking at processes of cultural construction and how virtual worlds come into being and change over time.

We often associate ethnography primarily with anthropology, but ethnography has a strong history within sociology as well, which some trace to de Tocqueville's travels in the United States in the 1840s (Gold 1997). While anthropologists spent decades forging theoretical frameworks that narrowed the divide between Self and Other, ethnographers within sociology from the beginning turned attention to contexts in which they were themselves nationally (even personally) located (Whyte 1943; Goffman 1961; Willis 1977; Fine 1993). Qualitative sociologists have thus used ethnography to produce rich accounts of everything from urban communities to medical work to sporting activities. Three powerful threads reappear in sociology's use of ethnography: a fundamental assertion of the valuable knowledge of participants as meaning-making actors, an attention to grounded (even mundane) practices, and a commitment to understanding the ways larger societal considerations or forms of social order shape everyday lifeworlds.

The realization that participants hold vital knowledge about their social worlds (and broader social processes) can be traced back to early sociological thought, most notably Weber's influential methodological considerations and his formulation of *verstehende sociologie*, which implied that one "could best understand society for what it is—not for what one thinks it might, should, or must be—by studying it from the points of view of its members. In effect, [Weber] required social researchers to become personally and deeply acquainted with their informants' experiences and views" (Gold 1997:389). This orientation provides sociologists a theoretical grounding for ethnographic work. In this view, those in the fieldsite can provide both data and core framings for those data, keeping in check assumptions and biases of the researchers themselves.

This attention to the fieldsite was echoed in some of the most influential early sociological ethnography, most notably the Chicago School associated with Robert E. Park and Ernest W. Burgess. Sociologists of this tradition produced a large corpus of ethnographic work dating back to 1917, perhaps best known from a body of mid-twentieth-century scholarship like *Street Corner Society* (Whyte 1943), *Outsiders* (Becker 1963), and *Asylums* (Goffman 1961). Such scholarship was based on a range of methods (e.g., participant observation, interviews, mapping, diaries) and often also drew on quantitative data like census information. Sociologists explored urban environments, deviance, race, and collective behavior, focusing on the "everyday life, communities, and symbolic interactions characteristic of a specific group" (Deegan 2001:11). Such a focus on the everyday was linked methodologically to "deep immersion." Park, for example, "exhorted students to 'go get the seat of your pants dirty in real research' " (Pollner and Emerson 2001:130). Yet for many researchers it was not simply about understanding experience, but about how structure is produced at the ground level. Paralleling how anthropologists sought to legitimize "native" cultures, Chicago School ethnographers often saw themselves as "giving voice to populations whose perspectives were ignored by institutions shaping their lives" (Katz and Csordas 2003:280).

In contemporary sociology ethnographic methods have remained important for weaving together grounded stories of everyday life with a broader social and often critical analysis. Building on pioneering work such as *The Sociological Imagination* (Mills 1959), this research has moved beyond a focus on urban poverty and "deviance" to explore a wide range of topics. For instance, this scholarship has examined the workplace, situating ethnographic research within a critical conversation about capitalism (Willis 1981; Burawoy et al. 1991). Other work has addressed the lived experience and institutional influences on gender and sexuality (Gamson 1999; Pascoe 2007), health care (Bosk 1979; Charmaz 1991; Timmermans 1999) and even scientific research itself (Latour and Woolgar 1979; Fujimura 1997).

We want to take a moment to place ethnography in the context of the related field of journalism. Ethnography and journalism share striking similarities, sometimes leading to confusion regarding critical differences in these practices. Both journalists and ethnographers travel to where the action is, working in the thick of ongoing human activity. Both rely on interviews, observations, and archival study as key research methods. Both produce written accounts that answer to carefully maintained professional standards of adequacy and truth (unlike novelists, who, while also keen observers of humanity, write with the freedom to fabricate and imagine).

The main differentiators between ethnography and journalism are the broader scholarly frame, the nature of the research activity, and the written product of that activity. As members of intellectual communities, ethnographers produce research that enters a stream of scholarly conversation grounded in an ongoing project of knowledge construction embedded in shared concerns and questions. The development of conceptual and theoretical understandings is central, and ethnographers situate their work within conversations often traversing decades. While good journalists also operate with a historical frame of reference, they are generally not involved in debates central to social scientific knowledge production. Ethnographers write accounts that present findings based on months or years of field research during which they track and record the cultural patterns and everyday lives of informants, including the mundane and routine. Most journalists, by contrast, generate copy on short deadlines and are tasked with producing "stories," usually brief texts that speak to the moment, that attain newsworthiness through political significance, "human interest," or sensation. While some investigative journalism may require months or years of research, it generally aims for a blockbuster result to justify its costs (and because journalists are generally not in the business of reporting the mundane). The demands forced by the written product in each case dictate divergent practices and behaviors, also highlighting the different forms of contribution the two traditions make. In addition, ethnography and journalism operate on the basis of different ethical considerations and have different legal and institutional requirements to which they must adhere (see chapters 8 and 9).

In providing this short history of ethnographic methods, we do not mean to imply that they are limited to sociology and anthropology, nor that the schools of thought and topics of interest we discuss are in any way comprehensive. Across the humanities and the social sciences the approach has been fruitfully adopted to examine diverse topics. Ethnography has also been widely adopted across technology fields such as human-computer interaction (HCI) and computer-supported collaborative work (CSCW). Within the confines of the handbook genre, our goal has been simply to trace some important themes in the history of ethnographic methods and suggest a few ways they might shape the design and implementation of research projects in virtual worlds. To make these potential linkages clearer, we now turn to an equally brief historical overview of virtual worlds themselves.

2.2 A BRIEF HISTORY OF VIRTUAL WORLDS

Notions of a "virtual" aspect to human existence can be traced back to cave painting, early Greek and Chinese thought, through the development of writing and the printing press, and among Aboriginal cultures throughout the world. In the past several decades such notions have been further shaped by the rise of electronic mass media, as well as work in cybernetics and computing. Science fiction and fantasy literature have played a key role. For instance, early online games and virtual worlds were strongly shaped by *The Hobbit* (Tolkien 1937) and its sequels, including *The Lord of the Rings* (Tolkien 1954), as well as other fantasy literature such as the Conan series (Howard 1932). Also influential was early cyberpunk literature, such as the novella *True Names* (Vinge 1981), which mentioned griefing (antisocial behavior in a virtual world context) and the participation of disabled persons in virtual worlds, as well as the novels *Neuromancer* (Gibson 1984), in which the term "cyberspace" first appeared, and *Snow Crash* (Stephenson 1992), which included an early use of the term "metaverse."

While multiplayer games may seem new, "the advent of single-player genres as the central paradigm for games is an historical aberration of digital technology. . . . Prior to the introduction of the computer as a game-playing platform, the majority of games played by hundreds of cultures for thousands of years, with few exceptions, were multiplayer" (Pearce and Artemesia 2009:9–10). While many of today's video games are single player, historically the earliest electronic games were single-screen multiplayer games, including Tennis for Two (an oscilloscope-based demo created at Brookhaven National Laboratories in 1958), MIT's Spacewar! (1961), the Magnavox Odyssey (the first television-based home video game system, created in 1972), and Pong (1972; see Poole 2000; Herman 2001; Kent 2001). Although single-player games remain popular, the rise of the internet and faster broadband networks have enabled new forms of multiplayer gaming and online interaction, a return to the earlier paradigm of social gaming.

The first rudimentary virtual world in the contemporary sense was probably Videoplace, created in 1970 by Myron Krueger after an initial experiment involving networked collaboration with a colleague that included their virtual hands touching in an early experience of avatar embodiment (Krueger 1983; Popper 1993; Pearce 1997). Beyond early investigations like Videoplace, the first virtual world to possess the characteristics of our core definition was the 1979 MUD, also known as MUD1 (Bartle 2004). Entirely text-based, inspired by the fantasy literature genre, invoking conventions reminiscent of the tabletop role-playing game Dungeons & Dragons (Gygax and Arneson 1974), and enabled by early university networks, MUD1 became something of a cult favorite and spawned an entire genre of text-based worlds, generically dubbed MUDs. MUDs originated many social and technical conventions that persist in online games and virtual worlds, such as statistics-based combat formats that emulate throwing hexagonal dice.

Though text-based worlds continue to be found online, graphical environments have risen in popularity over the years. The first graphical virtual world, Lucasfilm's Habitat, released in 1986, was created for the Quantum Link network, a precursor to America Online. While rendered in two dimensions and with graphics that seem simplistic when compared with many of today's virtual worlds, Habitat was a milestone that introduced a number of important concepts (Morningstar and Farmer 1991). Most important was the notion of an "avatar"—a Sanskrit word meaning "a god's embodiment on Earth." Additionally, while MUD and its antecedents were free, Habitat (which was later developed into WorldsAway) was among the first commercial implementations of virtual worlds and brought the genre to a broader public.

A third historical watershed, LambdaMOO, released in 1990, was a free, text-based virtual world. An experiment in online collaboration, its innovation was that the world was entirely user created. Beginning with descriptions of the founder's own home, LambdaMOO had a modular architecture that allowed players to add their own rooms and areas to the world, within the limits of allocated storage (Curtis 1992). Aided by the flexibility and creative affordances of text, players built a wide range of environments, including gardens, miniature rooms inside full-sized objects, sky structures, and treehouses. LambdaMOO set many precedents for user-created worlds like Active Worlds and Second Life.

In the early 1990s, on the heels of the World Wide Web, a generation of entrepreneurs embarked on making the "metaverse" envisioned by Neal Stephenson (1993) a reality. This was a period of great innovation and artistry in the development of online games and virtual worlds. Indeed, a handful of worlds created during this period persisted long after their release dates, such as The Palace (a series of graphical chat rooms), Active Worlds (the first contiguous graphical virtual world composed entirely of user-created content), and OnLive/Traveler (the first graphical world to use voice and lip-synching avatars).

More commercially successful were several game-based virtual worlds created in the late 1990s. The first of these, Meridian 59, released in 1996 by 3DO (Schubert 2003), was built on familiar Dungeons & Dragons conventions. Meridian 59 was quickly eclipsed by the similar but much more profitable Ultima Online, published by the game industry giant Electronic Arts (King and Borland 2003). Ultima Online had over 100,000 players at its peak and was justly regarded as a huge success at the time.

Many other fantasy-based online games have appeared since Ultima Online, including EverQuest (released in 1998) and World of Warcraft (released in 2004). Other themes for online games—including science fiction, space exploration, and superheroes—have also been successful, for instance, Anarchy Online (2001); EVE Online (2003), and City of Heroes (2004). Despite the differing themes, these online games largely preserve a basic format of advancing a character through skill levels via activities like team-based combat, exploring, crafting, and commerce. Many of the largest virtual worlds are oriented toward children and teenagers. Examples include Whyville (1999), Yohoho! Puzzle Pirates (released in 2003), and Club Penguin (released in 2005). Open-ended virtual worlds became more common by the early 2000s, with the release of virtual worlds like The Sims Online (2002), There.com (2003), and Second Life (2003). The number and range of open-ended virtual worlds continue to grow, but for the most part they are smaller than online games. Like many online games, some open-ended virtual worlds have shut down. For example, The Sims Online closed in 2008 and There.com closed in 2010, reopening again in 2012. Bridging both genres, so-called sandbox online games have built-in affordances for creativity. One influential example of these has been the independently produced Minecraft (2009), in which players build the world to their liking by removing and placing cubes within a three-dimensional grid.

While online games and virtual worlds draw participants internationally, many early commercial products were developed in the United States and presumed skills in English. Since the late 1990s, however, development and ownership of virtual worlds has globalized to a significant degree. For instance, Lineage, an online game developed in Korea, was released in 1998, the same year as EverQuest, but peaked at five million compared to EverQuest's roughly half a million players. Other examples of successful Korean-developed online games include Ragnarök Online, Guild Wars, Aion, and Maple Story; these and other games developed outside the United States (like the Finnish-based virtual world Habbo) have attracted tens of millions of players.

Despite the fact that the designers of many online games and virtual worlds have worked to include rich three-dimensional imagery, many of the most popular worlds have used simpler graphics, making them less taxing on computers and internet connections. This reflects a more complex story of engagement in these worlds, one often contrary to early notions of virtual reality driven by a technological fantasy of realism and total sensory immersion. While many early developers of virtual reality focused on individual hardware (for instance, head-mounted displays and data gloves), innovative virtual world builders were noticing the deeply compelling aspect of playing alongside other people. Morningstar and Farmer, the developers of Habitat, observed that a virtual world "is defined more by the interactions among the actors within it than by the technology with which it is implemented" (1991:274). Social interaction plays a powerful role for many (though not all) participants in virtual worlds, and so long as social interaction is robust, simpler renderings of the world are often sufficient.

2.3 A BRIEF HISTORY OF RESEARCH ON VIRTUAL WORLD CULTURES

As noted earlier, in the history of physical world ethnography some of the earliest and most influential accounts were produced by "gentleman scholars"—travelers, missionaries, and colonial officials without academic training—whose insights informed later academic research. The history of virtual world ethnography follows a similar pattern. From the beginning, designers and managers have offered significant insights regarding social aspects of virtual worlds, for example, Curtis (1992) on LambdaMOO, Damer (1998) and Book (2006) on many early graphical worlds, Appelcline (2009) on the text-based MUDs of his company Skotos, Bartle (2004) on MUD1, DiPaola and Collins (2003) on OnLive!, Koster (2004) on Ultima Online, Star Wars Galaxies, and Metaplace, Morningstar and Farmer (1991) on Habitat, Ondrejka (2004) on Second Life, and Ventrella (2011) on the design of There.com's avatars. Some of this work pioneered key insights about virtual world cultures, from Curtis's explorations of emergent social norms (like pretending to be "away from keyboard" when a sensitive issue was being discussed) and DiPaola's observations in regard to avatar embodiment (for instance, the discovery that players would sometimes back up when other avatars moved too close to them), to Ondrejka's insights regarding participant-generated content and Morningstar and Farmer's reflections on the emergent nature of culture even within designed systems.

While virtual worlds and online games are still surprisingly poorly understood and poorly represented in mainstream media, for decades non-academic writers have provided critical insights. In some cases these writers have been professional journalists, though many have published more informally (particularly since the rise of blogs). Julian Dibbell's "cyberspace memoir" *My Tiny Life: Crime and Passion in a Virtual World* (1998), based on his earlier *Village Voice* article (1993), chronicled his year as an embedded journalist in LambdaMOO. (Other examples of journalistic accounts and memoirs of virtual worlds include Dibbell 2006, Guest 2007, Ludlow and Wallace 2007, Meadows 2008, and Au 2008). These astute accounts have coexisted synergistically with ethnographic research.

A range of early research on computer-mediated communication also produced important insights. Starting in the 1990s, scholars (often graduate students) began to turn their attention to virtual worlds. Located in diverse disciplinary environments, early examples of such work include Rosenberg's ethnography of WolfMOO (1992) and Masterson's ethnography of Ancient Anguish (1994). A number of themes emerged in this early work that continue to resonate today, such as identity construction (Bruckman 1992; Turkle 1995; Suler 1996), gender (McRae 1997; Kendall 2002; Schaap 2002), ethnicity and race (McDonough 1999; Nakamura 2002), embodiment (Stone 1991; Taylor 1999; Kolko, Nakamura, and Rodman 2000; Taylor 2002; Sundén 2003), and the forging of community through narrative, speech, and social action (Kolko 1995; Markham 1998; Cherny 1999). Interestingly, some folklorists also developed an interest in these emerging cultures, such as Bruce Mason, one of the first people to use the term "virtual ethnography" in a published paper (1996), used by others and later adopted by Hine (2000). Another area of early and continuing research interest has been how the design and governance of virtual worlds inform the socialities within them (Mnookin 1996; O'Rourke 1998; Pargman 2000; Kendall 2002; Lastowka and Hunter 2004; Grimmelmann 2006; Balkin and Noveck 2006; Taylor 2006b; Duranske 2008; Burk 2010; Lastowka 2010). This theme has included organizational ethnographies of the companies that create virtual worlds (Malaby 2009).

As online virtual worlds grew in popularity and mainstream access, they prompted a second wave of ethnographic research, one inflected via considerations of these worlds as specifically spaces of play. Many earlier virtual world questions around identity (for instance, regarding role-play) and social interaction were taken up by game-world researchers (Jakobsson and Taylor 2003; Mortensen 2003; Copier 2005). Additional topics, including governance and intellectual property (Humphreys 2004; Taylor 2006a, 2006b; Kow and Nardi 2010), learning and mentorship (Kafai 1995; Squire 2005; Steinkuehler and Duncan 2008; Chen 2009), and relationships (Chee and Smith 2005; Carter 2005; Guimarães 2005; Bardzell and Bardzell 2007) were addressed as well.

2.4 THE USES OF HISTORY

All three of the brief histories we have recounted here—of ethnography, of virtual worlds, and of ethnographic research in virtual worlds—are intentionally truncated and provisional. This is a handbook of method, not a historical treatise. While we have included as many citations as possible given space limits, we make no claim to being comprehensive. If you are inspired to learn more about the history of ethnography (Stocking 1987) or the history of technology (Standage 2007), or to follow the breadcrumbs we have left to others' work, then these discussions have been successful. Their purpose has been to situate the historical contexts that shape both ethnographic methods and virtual worlds.

Our practice of ethnography in virtual worlds is informed by the twin trajectories of the development of methodological frameworks and ongoing technological change. With its development as a tool for the study of both local and distant cultures, its attention to everyday practice and meanings, and its conceptual disruption of Self and Other, ethnography represents a particularly powerful method through which to study virtual worlds.

Changes in technology have also opened up the field in interesting ways. New modalities, new actors (social and technical), and new configurations have emerged. Aside from some notable exceptions, in their formative period virtual worlds were primarily designed and used by white men located in universities and research labs. As network infrastructures shifted (including higher in-home bandwidth, affordable personal computers with improved graphics capabilities, and the advent of gaming cybercafés around the world), those involved in the design and use of these spaces have grown into a broader demographic. This expansion of design, ownership, and participation has stimulated a parallel growth of virtual world ethnography. Alongside the millions of people inhabiting virtual worlds, a new wave of researchers has arisen. From the earliest worlds that allowed us to begin co-inhabiting virtual spaces to our contemporary moment in which the notion of having an avatar is fairly mundane, as virtual world ethnographers we are interwoven with technology: knowing its history (including previous research) is crucial to understanding its present.

One final note about the making of history: as virtual world ethnographers we do not stand outside these trajectories of ethnography and technology—we inhabit and co-construct them. In the same way that ethnography has been nudged and tweaked by researchers who pushed it into new territory or challenged core conceptual frames, through our work (in a domain unfamiliar to many traditional researchers) we participate in an ongoing conversation about what ethnography is, and what it can be, as a method. And while we should always remain aware of the ways we and our field are continually shaped in relation to technology, this need not be a deterministic story. Technologies can be made and remade, and our work chronicles the lived experiences that involve these artifacts. In this regard, our ethnographies contribute to important debates that expose and frame critical cultural issues about technology and society.

CHAPTER THREE

TEN MYTHS ABOUT ETHNOGRAPHY

We hope that our discussion of the history, practice, and promise of ethnographic methods in the previous two chapters has inspired a sense of excitement about the power, even the beauty, of this approach. In this chapter we build on that sense of promise by examining common myths about ethnography that we have encountered in classroom discussions, public forums, written texts, and informal conversations, and while reviewing paper submissions and developing interdisciplinary research proposals.

Specifically, we now tackle ten myths that, in our experience, have led to misunderstandings about the role and value of ethnographic methods. If you worry that there might be something flawed about the whole idea of ethnography, this chapter is for you. For those of you already working with ethnography, this chapter may provide some ways to help clarify and frame the methodology when explaining it to others. The myths speak to confusions about ethnographic research stemming from its status as a primarily qualitative, field-based science, an approach that does not follow the standard hypothesis-driven model of science many of us were first taught in school. The myths reflect understandable confusions about an unfamiliar approach to research, and our goal here is to eliminate those confusions to the greatest degree possible. We want to dispel these myths, and in doing so clarify the valuable contributions that ethnographic research has made and continues to make to the scientific study of culture and society.

The ten myths we examine are:

1. Ethnography is unscientific.
2. Ethnography is less valid than quantitative research.
3. Ethnography is simply anecdotal.
4. Ethnography is undermined by subjectivity.
5. Ethnography is merely intuitive.
6. Ethnography is writing about your personal experience.
7. Ethnographers contaminate fieldsites by their very presence.

8. Ethnography is the same as grounded theory.
9. Ethnography is the same as ethnomethodology.
10. Ethnography will become obsolete.

Let's look at each myth in turn.

3.1 ETHNOGRAPHY IS UNSCIENTIFIC

The most fundamental myth about ethnography is that it is unscientific. Elementary and secondary school science education typically emphasizes laboratory-based experiments (often whole classrooms are themselves labs). As a result, "science" comes to be conflated with lab-based physical sciences, to the exclusion of observational field-based sciences. From early encounters, a notion of science emerges based on two inferences: that the hypothesis-driven model is central to scientific knowledge production, and that scientific knowledge should be expressed numerically.

We see the impact of these restrictively conceived characteristics of science everywhere, from the popular media to the academy. Informally many people bifurcate sciences into "hard sciences" (for instance, physics and biology) and "soft sciences" (including anthropology and sociology) and imply—or even state outright—that soft sciences are not rigorous. In academia this debate is reflected in the contrasting epistemologies of positivism and interpretivism. The former is the view that knowledge should ideally be expressed in terms of generalizable laws, irrespective of cultural context. However, all scientific knowledge is provisional (sometimes referred to via Clifford's notion of "partial truths"; 1986). Yet "interpretive" does not mean a lack of robustness. A notion of interpretivism reflects the immense complexity of what we study, and that our scientific success is partial because we cannot fully grasp the enormity of culture. This stance is an impetus to continually improve methods and theories; it is not a retreat to satisfaction with "second best" accounts.

Interpretivism, originally introduced in the social sciences (e.g., Boas 1887; Geertz 1973; Denzin 2003), is the view that people studying another culture have a situated understanding shaped by their own cultural beliefs. This view can also be found among scholars of scientific practice, who have long argued that social, cultural, and political contexts shape all scientific inquiry (Kuhn 1962; Berger and Luckmann 1966; Latour and Woolgar 1979; Haraway 1988).

Those who construe a search for generalizable laws as the only scientific approach generally advocate that scientific inquiry must reflect some or all of the following criteria:

- Science must test hypotheses.
- Science must be based on experiments.
- Science must be predictive.
- Science must be quantitative.

These four criteria for science contribute to the view that ethnographic research is unscientific. Ethnographic investigation is a flexible practice, but its practitioners strongly trend away from structuring their work around these four criteria. In other words, ethnographers generally focus on complex processes of culture that resist treatment as testable hypotheses; we rely on field observation, not experimentation; we develop explanations rather than prediction; and we use qualitative methods (though not exclusively). But these moves do not mean that ethnography is not empirical or rigorous. To better understand the myth that ethnography is unscientific, it will help to discuss the four criteria in more detail.

Science must test hypotheses

A hypothesis is a testable statement regarding the outcome of a particular research protocol. The hypothesis-driven model of science includes the assumption that scientists have an idea about the outcome of their research before they begin. However, while all scientific methods involve research questions, these questions do not necessarily take the form of hypotheses. Ethnography centers on discovery and interpretation. Its questions are formulated to address broad problems of social and cultural life. How are identity and community constituted in virtual worlds? Do people behave differently online? If so, why? Social process and culture involve symbols, narratives, language, chronicles, conversations, scripts, dramas, rituals, rumors, visions, ideologies, practices, inventions, imaginations, motivations, historical events, and countless other cultural elements. Research questions about these elements generally do not lend themselves to expression in testable hypotheses. Cultural elements, as a rule, do not yield congenial terms for hypothetical statements because such elements do not primarily concern *outcomes*. Cultural elements shape and underpin the meanings that form our conscious and unconscious lives. They emerge in relational ways as we act. They are often habitual, routine, mundane, and repeated, scaffolding the structures of everyday living. To pull these elements out as "effects" "caused" by "variables" is to kill their essence as flexible resources for living. As ethnographers we can discover and interpret cultural elements, but we lose the possibility of understanding their form and function if we insist that they submit to the Procrustean bed of testable hypotheses.

Because hypotheses are generally written with specificity and precision for statistical treatment, they may lead us to see only what we are looking for. Such a narrowing of the field of vision is antithetical to the spirit of open discovery fundamental to ethnography. Ethnographers, like historians, must be vulnerable to what is actually happening on the ground. Ethnographers arrive at their objects of study aware that they do not yet know what they do not know. Research questions can shift in light of new data. Social scientists have long noted that the potential for emergent research questions makes field-based methods more scientific, not less, because the research is directed toward understanding the fieldsite in its historical and geographic specificity.

As ethnographers, we frame our research as a mode of discovery, drawing questions from the fieldsite itself. A limitation of the hypothesis-testing paradigm is that it must work within the horizon of the known. If one has not yet conducted ethnographic research in virtual worlds and does not yet know of the existence of "alts," "lag," or "mods," it will be impossible to design a research framework examining them. As practitioners of a field-based paradigm, we must be open to what is happening in the flow of everyday life and craft research questions through our engagement with those lifeworlds. Like astronomers encountering new galaxies or zoologists studying the habits of whales, ethnographers conduct field-based research to study phenomena as they occur in context.

Science must be based on experiments

A good many sciences, including astronomy, biology, epidemiology, oceanography, geography, hydrology, botany, geology, climate science, primatology, and zoology, are often field based. As a practice that does not rely on experimentation, ethnography is thus part of a larger constellation of methodologies that advance science by studying phenomena in their natural environments—be they plants in a desert, birds in a forest, stars in the sky, or persons in a society.

If we conflate "science" with "experiments," we distort the scientific record and oversimplify scientific practice (Latour and Woolgar 1979; Hacking 1982; Knorr-Cetina 1999). Indeed, the most fundamental discovery of biological science arose from Darwin's careful observations of passerine birds in the Galápagos Islands. Reliance on field study is not a lack to be remedied: it is the strength of the field-based sciences that they encounter phenomena at scale, in their natural complexity as they occur in real contexts. It is difficult to imagine Darwin's paradigm-shifting insights issuing from controlled experiments.

While many phenomena are amenable to experimentation, best investigated in carefully controlled trials, culture is not such a phenomenon. We have noted that cultural elements do not easily translate to statements of hypothetical outcomes. In addition, controlled experiments cannot capture the scale, complexity, flexibility, and dynamism of culture. We cannot meaningfully "pin down" the vastness of culture such that it can be parsed into separable variables controlled in experimental tests. As a peculiar and powerful adaptation to the problems of living and survival, culture has evolved as the most responsive, contingent, reflexive, and generative phenomenon that scientists have attempted to study. Our methods must be accountable to these properties of culture.

Even when it is ethically and practically possible to conduct controlled experiments by placing people in different cultures or social settings, the level of complexity and indeterminacy in human culture nullifies any illusion of control one might entertain (LeCompte and Schensul 1999). As one of us has noted, "the construal of persons as bacteria in a petri dish or atoms in a supercollider masks how . . . culture is not simply the aggregate of individual personalities and dispositions that . . . 'bang together' and can be understood through 'direct observation' " (Boellstorff 2009a:6). Humans exist not as separable atomic units, but as inseparable elements of a cultural matrix.

To take Bonnie's research as an illustrative example, World of Warcraft might seem a petri dish of sorts; it is a virtual world available in nine languages, popular in dozens of national cultures. But to understand player experience it is necessary to take into account *where* it is played (internet cafés, dormitories, homes, Starbucks), *who* plays it (young people in China but a more mixed demographic in North America, for example), and *why* it is played (a variety of reasons). The human actor playing an online multiplayer game is not cut off from the influences of the space in which the game is played, or his or her experience of other games, or life interests and situation (Taylor 2008). While it is possible to conduct experiments in which people are paid or otherwise induced to participate as subjects in virtual worlds, experimental situations cannot reproduce normal experience—that which occurs when people follow their own inclinations and interests as they engage in authentic activities, sustained by their life experiences and personalities. Human activity flows and circulates in multiple locales, constantly inventing and reinventing itself. Many online multiplayer games, for example, are notable for the imaginative game-related activities that take place outside the game, such as modding and theorycrafting, and the production of machinima (Lowood 2008). These activities, which arose through interaction with the game and are derived from but not determined or predicted by it, occur on player-generated blogs, forums, websites, wikis, and download sites; they are part of the game but not contained within the bounds of the software platform (Taylor 2006a; Nardi 2010).

Science must be predictive

A third consideration is that science must be predictive. If we drop a rock today versus a hundred years into the future, the law of gravity predicts that, all other factors being equal, the rock will take the same amount of time to hit the ground. However, as ethnographers, our objects of study are not so simple. As anthropologist Gregory Bateson is purported to have remarked, "There are the hard sciences and then there are the difficult sciences." The powerful predictions that have made the hard sciences successful are not so easy for the difficult sciences. The materials ethnographers examine—human beings and their cultures—are highly provisional, variable, and mutable. Human life is subject to the instabilities of historical change. The nature of culture is to be agile and creative in meeting change; thus we have two orders of change to predict, each mutually dependent on the other. Anthropologist Franz Boas used the example of "the physicist" and "the historian" to illustrate a related point:

> The physicist compares a series of similar facts, from which he isolates the general phenomenon which is common to all of them. Henceforth the single facts become less important to him, as he lays stress on the general law alone. On the other hand, the facts are the object which is of importance and interest to the historian . . . [for such a researcher, the] mere existence [of a phenomenon] entitles it to a full share of our attention; and the knowledge of its existence and evolution in space and time fully satisfies the student, without regard to the laws which it corroborates or which may be deduced from it. (1940 [1887]:641–42).

In the 1970s scholars like Clifford Geertz worked to clarify this distinction by noting that "one cannot write a 'General Theory of Cultural Interpretation.' Or, rather, one can, but there appears to be little profit in it, because the essential task of theory building [in ethnographic research] is . . . not to generalize across cases but to generalize within them" (1973:5). However, while this notion that ethnographic research is "not an experimental science in search of law but an interpretive one in search of meaning" (Geertz 1973:5) is hardly new, the conflation of "science" with "sciences that seek prediction" continues to shape the myth that ethnographic research is unscientific. If this conflation is not addressed, ethnographic research will be misunderstood because its objects of study evade the regularities of, say, the law of gravity. People and culture are emergently, dynamically constituted, constantly shifting, alternately undergoing periods of destabilization and stabilization.

Scientific research must be quantitative

A fourth way in which science can be defined too narrowly is in terms of quantification. Scholars and practitioners trained in a range of disciplines, from experimental psychology and economics to engineering and computer science, are deeply wedded to quantitative methods, and good results have been produced using those methods. Quantification can be a powerful and effective approach depending on the research question. But to study something scientifically does not always mean representing that thing numerically. A range of scientific practices, including but not limited to ethnographic research, collect and represent data in a qualitative fashion. In addition to anthropology and sociology, which concern themselves with constructs such as beliefs and rituals, certain branches of psychology use qualitative methods to study phenomena like dreams, feelings, and identities. Political scientists use qualitative methods to study political events, ideologies, and historical trajectories, which cannot always be understood via quantitative methods alone.

Furthermore, it is important to understand that qualitative and quantitative analysis alike share the common base of human language. Although in practice we speak of qualitative and quantitative approaches, we should not separate them too dogmatically. Numbers are inescapably *about something*, and that something is necessarily expressed in language. Gottlob Frege, the German mathematician and logician, noted that all acts of quantification rest on a qualitative foundation: "The content of a statement of number is an assertion about a concept" (1959:59). But equally, every act of qualitative analysis refers to quantities. When we say "members of Culture A believe Z," we have made a quantitative determination regarding the membership of Culture A, even if indirectly.

3.2 ETHNOGRAPHY IS LESS VALID THAN QUANTITATIVE RESEARCH

At conferences and workshops, ethnographers sometimes find their work classified as "statistically insignificant" or "inconclusive," with years of rigorous investigation disregarded in comparison with short-term, sometimes superficial forms of quantitative analysis. These dismissals rest on the underlying assumption that findings based on numerical data are more valid than other forms of knowledge creation. For instance, when working on mixed-methods projects, we may find our work framed as "illustrating" a quantitative finding, even if it is central to the finding itself. One of us discovered a finding through participant observation that was later rediscovered by our collaborators through quantitative means; the initial finding was discounted and ignored, even though it had predated the quantitative validation of the same finding by several months.

The unique opportunities in virtual worlds to collect and "mine" vast amounts of quantitative data with relative ease sharpen the debate. We have some concerns about claims made for these methods, and their putative superiority to ethnographic and other qualitative methods (see boyd and Crawford 2012). Data mining is the extraction of patterns from digital data with the use of automated techniques such as clustering, neural networks, regression analysis, and special-purpose algorithms. Automated techniques search for patterns across data categories. For example, Ahmad et al.'s (2009) study of gold farmers, based on back-end anonymized data from EverQuest II archived by the parent company, Sony, examined the following data: experience logs, transaction logs, character attributes, demographic attributes, and canceled accounts. In less directed searching, data mining analyses may count keywords in texts and attempt to relate high-frequency terms to one another.

Data mining is often viewed as a uniquely comprehensive methodology, with sources such as logs, automated activity records, and repositories framed as "complete," "objective," "comprehensive," a "God's eye view" of an entire virtual world. Digital data seem not only complete but highly reliable; they are collected with machines. These sources appear to herald a new era of social scientific investigation. As one enthusiastic data miner said during a conference presentation one of us attended, "It's all there!"

But is it all there? Because of the vast amount of data, studies based on data mining often draw results from a relatively small slice of data, such as a month's worth of server information (e.g., Ahmad et al. 2009:342). When compared with long-term ethnographic fieldwork, a sample gathered over a single month seems meager. Was that particular month unusual? How does it reflect changes in activity over a longer time frame? Are there seasonal patterns or release dates to consider? One can imagine a similar "slice" being taken from an ethnography missing, for instance, the entire planting or harvesting season of an agrarian culture, or the intensity and excitement of a major game software expansion.

As easy as mined data are to capture, they may be onerous to parse and analyze. Such analysis may require elaborate and expensive software and possibly a supercomputer to process. Yet even with appropriate hardware and software, it is deeply problematic to suggest that such data convey objective mathematical truths that do not rely, to a significant extent, on human interpretation. Celia recalled a mixed-methods project in which an automated analysis of chatlogs from a virtual world identified the word "bunnies" as thematically significant, leading the quantitative researcher to wonder at this odd fixation on rabbits. Without contextual understandings afforded by direct engagement with a culture, there would be no way for her collaborator to have known that "bunnies" did not refer to rabbits but was a reference to "bunny slippers," a type of shoe that increased jump height.

Even purely quantitative studies require human intervention and interpretation; for instance, Ahmad et al.'s study deployed a manual analysis by game masters derived from their practice-based understandings of patterns of gold farming. With this emic interpretation, and the quantitative results, the findings of the study were still not entirely conclusive (2009:345). This leads us to ask, why is a month of quantitative data gathered by individuals who have not conducted systematic observation of the virtual world participants they are studying, augmented with subjective interpretation by the administrators of that world, somehow more accurate and valid than months or years of in-depth observation and participation in the field, engaging with participants over time, from a variety of viewpoints and perspectives?

This myth that ethnography is less valid than quantitative research is, of course, shaped by beliefs about validity itself. Validity denotes the extent to which a scientific explanation corresponds to the actual world. In the 1970s Ulric Neisser issued a sharply worded critique of the scientific validity of experiments. His provocative commentary, while directed at fellow psychologists, also articulated long-standing disquiet among ethnographers and others about the validity of data obtained from experiments: "The subject is isolated, cut off from ordinary environmental support, able to do nothing but initiate and terminate trials that run their magical course whatever he may do. . . . Experimental arrangements that eliminate the continuities of the ordinary environment may provide insights into certain processing mechanisms, but the relevance of these insights to normal . . . activity is far from clear" (1976:36). Neisser's problematic was termed "ecological validity." While ethnographers did not name the problem, ethnography came into being precisely to create a research paradigm in which human beings could be studied with no fear of compromising ecological validity. Ethnographic practice is, in essence, the opposite of psychological experimentation. Ethnographers observe people in interaction with other humans and their social and physical contexts, which together compose the "environmental supports" of which Neisser spoke. As people, we arrange our lives and societies such that the environment presents a constant, flexible repertoire of resources. Ethnographers address systems of support anchored in culture. We organize ethnographic investigation so that we can access the complex arrangements by which people solve problems and make meanings. Our work has a high degree of validity because we directly observe and interact with what we want to know; we do not wrench phenomena out of their contexts, thereby rendering them uninterpretable.

Ethnographers have been devoted to avoiding the problem of separating the human from his or her context. The ethnographic approach of landing smack in the middle of an ongoing culture or activity in order to study it means that we must rely on qualitative methods of observation and conversation to absorb and analyze what is taking place around us. The very immediacy of the experience of life, its patterns and rhythms, its artifacts and practices, is not easily expressed in numbers. An ethnographer thrust into a culture is invariably awed and humbled by its vitality and charisma; we express our understandings and insights in nuanced reports and narratives that attempt to recover as much as possible of the animation and interest stimulated by culture as an object of inquiry.

Validity is essential to science's most fundamental purpose—to faithfully represent the world. We are not arguing that human life defies quantitative study or experimental methods. Such a proposition is clearly untrue. We are arguing that qualitative research can yield profound insights that elude quantification. Arguments that presuppose that only quantitative data are the stuff of science lack cognizance of the complex material and immaterial elements that constitute human life, which is best understood through both qualitative and quantitative approaches.

Ethnography is a flexible methodology, and ethnographers devise and use whatever tools are needed for the job. Although ethnographers emphasize qualitative methods, we may use quantitative approaches as well. Indeed, a cliché of anthropology is an ethnographer beginning his research in a remote village by conducting a census. Malinowski recorded that when he reached the Trobriand Islands, "I took a village census, wrote down genealogies, drew up plans, and collected the terms of kinship" (Malinowski 1922:4). As a contemporary example of the use of quantitative methods, Bonnie had long noticed that World of Warcraft players often played with family and friends. To determine more precisely the extent of such practices, she analyzed survey data from North America, Europe, Hong Kong, and Taiwan in which about 75 percent of players stated that they played with at least one person they knew (Schiano et al. 2011). This finding contributed to the ongoing body of qualitative research dispelling notions of gamers as loners and social misfits (Taylor 2006a; Pearce and Artemesia 2009). The quantitative finding is a crisp number, easy to communicate to others, and a reasonably precise measure of the extent to which players play with those they already know in the physical world.

Qualitative and quantitative data can productively interact. In Celia's survey of Baby Boomer gamers, the majority of respondents considered PCs their primary gaming systems, even though many had consoles at home. Subsequent group and individual interviews revealed that consoles were viewed as being "for the kids," while adults in the household typically played on PCs. So while survey respondents might answer that they had a console in the home, it did not mean they played it, a detail pieced together with the use of qualitative methods (Pearce 2008a).

The use of quantitative methods in ethnography need not involve elaborate, advanced statistical treatments. A fundamental type of statistical data analysis is nominal classification, which can enhance understanding. For example, when Bonnie became interested in World of Warcraft players with disabilities, she and a coauthor conducted an online survey to discover which disabilities were present in the player population (Lim and Nardi 2011). Data about types of disabilities were classified into nominal categories (sight; nerve/limb; hearing), which provided an organizing scheme for documenting the range of disabilities players could have and still play World of Warcraft. The survey was constructed according to the authors' extensive prior experience with World of Warcraft; questions were worded to be meaningful to the player population. Clearly the notion that ethnography must be purely qualitative misrepresents the range of methods and techniques ethnographers can draw on in their research projects.

At the same time, it is crucial to remember that a given ethnography (or indeed any qualitative project) is not less valid, scientifically significant, or complete by not drawing in any quantitative material. Ethnography excels at rigorously capturing data in situ, and analysis is driven by a deep understanding of the object or culture under study, culminating in comprehensive and rich accounts that stand on their own.

3.3 ETHNOGRAPHY IS SIMPLY ANECDOTAL

The conflation of science with quantification regularly leads to the suggestion that qualitative results produced by ethnographers are nothing more than "anecdotes." In the context of findings expressed in other sciences as formulas, equations, statistics, graphs, charts, and tables, qualitative data can appear unconvincing and merely literary. Qualitative data are sometimes seen as issuing from the limited, biased observations of a researcher working without the power of numbers. Ethnographic data may appear, in fact, to be just a series of stories or a collection of anecdotes or impressions.

While part of this misunderstanding derives from the narrow formulation of science we discussed earlier, another rests with an incomplete view of the work of ethnographic texts. When crafting a book, article, or research report, ethnographers formulate holistic analyses from their data that explore beliefs and practices within and between cultures, linking together materials from a large corpus. The data are typically collected in the field over a prolonged period. They represent not isolated incidents but multiple instances and manifestations of phenomena involving many different individuals, observed in context. Ethnographic analysis involves a rigorous appraisal of a massive amount of data spanning participant observation, interviews, artifact collection, historical research, and content analysis.

Part of the challenge in ethnographic research is analyzing and translating rich qualitative data to the reader. In our written work we often present key critical cases, incidents, stories, or events to illustrate patterns we have observed. These draw attention to cultural practices, offering the reader concrete examples of issues under discussion. To misconstrue these moments, and such analyses, as "simply anecdotal" is to fragment them, taking a specific recounted incident or example in isolation, as if it speaks only to the single place and time the data were gathered. Yet ethnographic critical cases, incidents, stories, and events are always situated within the larger, more holistic context of cultural patterns.

It is notable that quantitative researchers sometimes use anecdotes to start a discussion or make a point. In such cases the anecdote serves an illustrative purpose, setting the stage for a quantitative analysis. The problem arises when such researchers assume that ethnographers create similar anecdotes and nothing more, rendering the depth of the work invisible. Ethnographers' scrupulous attention to nuance and detail, the consistency and validity derived from months of immersive data collection, and the rigorous contextual, historical embedding of the analysis situate our work well beyond the anecdotal.

3.4 ETHNOGRAPHY IS UNDERMINED BY SUBJECTIVITY

Another myth regarding ethnographic research is that it is compromised by the subjective viewpoint of the researcher. Ethnography is predicated on the idea that ethnographers produce work of high validity from situated engagement in the field. Such engagement is not subjective in the sense of being the opinion of one person and nothing more. Ethnography may appear merely subjective because the materials it seeks to understand do not yield to the prediction and control possible when objects of study exhibit little self-invention, are far less dynamic, or are amenable to experimental manipulation. Ethnographers are, in essence, tracking a moving target, one capable of continual acts of self-determination and creativity.

All science contains strong elements of subjectivity in the sense that science results from the work of *subjects*, that is, scientists. Subjectivity is an inescapable condition of science; no pure realm of objectivity exists in which the interests, biases, predilections, concerns, attitudes, dispositions, conceits, judgments, axioms, and presuppositions of investigators are absent and without impact. We always begin from somewhere. Rather than pretend a "God's eye view" of the world is possible, it is more scientific to realize that science generates situated knowledge (Kuhn 1962; Berger and Luckmann 1966; Haraway 1988; Latour 1993; Denzin 2001) that is a complex product of what is already known (whether what is known is accepted or challenged) and the contemporary worldview shaping interests and attitudes.

Subjectivity is actually a vital part of ethnographic rigor, not only for how it offers us a position from which to engage and interpret, but because it forms the backbone of intersubjective understanding. Intersubjectivity, the dynamic flow of communication and engagement between people, is one of the foundations of the ethnographic encounter. Through this grounded position and interactions with those in the field, we construct, as sociologist C. Wright Mills put it, "the capacity to shift from one perspective to another, and in the process to build up an adequate view of a total society and of its components" (1959:221).

It is useful to remember that even the hard sciences begin from somewhere, and that while their objects of study are steadier and more predictable, theories and scientific truths change over time as scientists' dispositions, assumptions, and so on, are more informed, developing through historical processes of discovery and reformulation (Kuhn 1962). What appears at one moment to be unproblematically "objective" is often seen later, as science shifts forward, as a subjective and situated outcome of a particular place and time. Now-refuted "scientific" approaches such as eugenics and phrenology (which used quantitative means of measuring the skull to determine mental function) seemed perfectly objective at the time they were in fashion.

3.5 ETHNOGRAPHY IS MERELY INTUITIVE

While it is true that intuition is a vital part of ethnographic research, the presumption that intuition is *all* that is required is both erroneous and dangerous: "Rather than devising research protocols that will purify the data in advance of analysis, the anthropologist embarks on a participatory exercise which yields materials for which analytical protocols are often devised after the fact" (Strathern 2004:5–6). This procedure, central to ethnographic practice, does sound like the dictionary definition of intuitive: knowlege "that consists in immediate apprehension, without the intervention of any reasoning process" (OED 2011). Dispensing with methods to structure data in advance, engaging in participation without fixing the kinds of protocols we may use, can seem an abandonment of the order and precision that characterize materials generated through hypothesis-based sciences. But to discover what is happening in the field—what people actually do as they live their lives, unmindful of the analyst's protocols—it is necessary to participate in the activities of a culture. It is out of such participatory exercises that we devise analytical protocols. The rigor that science cultivates is embodied in this approach—it is just that it arrives "after the fact."

The idea that ethnography is just intuition reflects a failure to acknowledge that intuition in *any* discipline is learned over time through experience. Ethnographic research is intuitive in the same way that flying an airplane or doing brain surgery is intuitive—once we know how to do them. Olympic divers execute complex maneuvers without thinking of every move in the moment: they have developed through practice an intuition no amateur can duplicate on a diving board. A concert pianist develops an intuition for when to crescendo to a forte without thinking of every finger's move, while an amateur picks out each note with difficulty. Similarly, ethnographers develop a set of embodied intuitions for participant observation that far exceed those of everyday interaction.

All science relies powerfully on forms of intuition. As Kuhn (1962) showed long ago in his discussion of paradigm shifts in science, scientific progress depends on the intuitive transcending of existing conceptual frameworks. Even Albert Einstein remarked that "knowledge is limited, whereas imagination embraces the entire world, stimulating progress. . . . It is, strictly speaking, a real factor in scientific research" (2009:97).

3.6 ETHNOGRAPHY IS WRITING ABOUT YOUR PERSONAL EXPERIENCE

Ethnography is an immersive, naturalistic methodology, but not all personal experience constitutes ethnography. We have occasionally heard persons say they conducted an ethnography because they advanced a character in a game or spent two weeks hanging out in Second Life. These statements equate ethnography with simple experience rather than understanding it as a systematic method.

Personal experience is part of ethnographic research. However, the converse is not true: ethnographic research is not just personal experience. Nor is it simply the recording of firsthand experience. Thus it is a myth that writing about your own experiences is the same thing as ethnography. This reduces ethnographic research to an exercise in data collection, to the consternation of many ethnographers. Anthropologist Diana Forsythe recounted:

> I remember my own chagrin shortly after joining a medical informatics project at hearing the senior physician characterize my role in observing hospital work rounds as being "a walking tape recorder." As it happened, I had tried carrying a tape recorder for several days for this project and had taped the work rounds. The resultant audio tapes contained an indecipherable babble. . . . In contrast, on the basis

> of my written fieldnotes, I consistently produced readable transcripts with additional analytical comments . . . [but the physicians] did not perceive the creativity of the work I was doing. (1999:140)

Forsythe emphasizes her analytical expertise in understanding the data, not just recording it; expertise that was invisible to other professionals in her research setting.

A small genre of ethnography involves accounts in which the ethnographer is a member of the community or a participant in an activity. The written product from such research can legitimately be termed an "autoethnography" (Reed-Danahay 1997). Like ethnographies more generally, however, autoethnographies are based on careful research design, intensive data collection, and extended data analysis. Autoethnography is not the same thing as autobiography, nor would an autoethnography be constituted by brief forays into a virtual world, or examination of related materials such as pictures of avatars. All too often the term "autoethnography" is used to mask a lack of method (or even justify deception), rather than to pursue a legitimate course of study that, when carried out with rigor, can yield new insights and discoveries.

3.7 ETHNOGRAPHERS CONTAMINATE FIELDSITES BY THEIR VERY PRESENCE

An ethnographer's arrival in the field may stir interest, attention, even excitement or trepidation. However, in maintaining a lengthy presence in the fieldsite, we normalize our presence by being on the scene, observing and participating in everyday activities. Malinowski noted: "As the natives saw me constantly every day, they ceased to be interested or alarmed, or made self-conscious by my presence, and I ceased to be a disturbing element in the tribal life which I was to study" (1944:6). In making this statement Malinowski was not so naïve as to think that the members of this community on an island in the Pacific stopped noticing the presence of a Polish-British anthropologist. What he meant was that the presence of such a person was no longer that of an "outsider" in a simple sense: the outsider had become familiar and was no longer a "disturbing element."

This does not mean that ethnographers become invisible to those they study. No culture is completely isolated; all cultural groups have a history of taking in various forms of outsiders such that their members come to take these persons for granted in the flow of life. Furthermore, it is often through interactions with outsiders that the most fruitful insights can be gleaned: what insiders think newcomers should know about their culture tells us a great deal about what is important to them. After initial interactions, study participants adjust over time once they become more comfortable with, and used to, the researcher.

Thus it is important not to overemphasize the impact of ethnographers on the cultures we study. Though we may affect a community (particularly in the case of more activist and policy-focused work), for the most part ethnographers are simply one of a multitude of actors within the space of a culture. Cultures exist in history; they are always changing. The presence of an ethnographer is rarely the driver of such change: "Every group is a collection of personalities and styles. As a consequence, the presence of an observer should not be too worrisome, as long as the impact is not excessively directive or substantive" (Fine 1993:283). Additionally, cultures always contain multiple points of view; the ethnographer can add new perspectives but does not shatter a fragile unity. Were cultures so vulnerable to change, they would not persist over time or in the face of disagreement, debate, external influence, and displacement.

3.8 ETHNOGRAPHY IS THE SAME AS GROUNDED THEORY

Perhaps because of their shared close attention to data and overlapping techniques (such as interviews or participant observation), ethnography and grounded theory are at times seen as the same thing. But this conflates a specific *analytic* technique and goal (grounded theory) with a *methodological* approach (ethnography). While grounded theory generally rests on qualitative data and methods, it is quite specifically focused on the inductive development of theory from data (Glaser and Strauss 1967). The investigator collects data and, through its coding and analysis, pulls out elements and relations to form a theory. Grounded theory contrasts, for example, with "grand theory," in which an existing comprehensive theory such as Marxism or structuralism frames and informs data analysis. Researchers using grounded theory eschew the use of working with existing theories in favor of letting new theory emerge directly from the data. Breaking data down into small analytical units in order to identify comparative or generalizable patterns becomes key: "by making frequent comparisons across the data, the researcher can develop, modify and extend theoretical propositions so they fit the data. At the actual working level, the researcher begins by coding data in close, systematic ways so that he can generate analytic categories" (Emerson, Fretz, and Shaw 1995:143). While grounded theory has branched into several different schools of thought and diversified from its early positivist roots (Clarke 2005), analysis within it centers on the systematic development of a coding scheme. This approach, in which codes are sometimes applied to data very early and then iteratively adjusted over the course of the project for the purposes of generating theory, forms its backbone.

Ethnographers can deploy a range of approaches to coding, from quite open to linguistically precise. The data being coded can also be generated in a somewhat different manner. Some grounded theory practitioners slice up their field in specific ways, where "'sampling' is driven not necessarily (or not only) by attempts to be 'representative' of some social body or population or its heterogeneities but especially and explicitly by *theoretical* concerns that have emerged in the provisional analysis to date" (Clarke 2005:xxxi, emphasis in original). Theoretical sampling is central to some grounded theory approaches, whereas ethnography allows for flexible and diverse approaches in handling the issue of representation, sampling, and data collection. Finally, ethnographic research does not demand a particular stance toward theory. Ethnographers may employ grand theories such as actor-network theory, or "mid-range" theories targeted at explaining just a specific slice of things, such as those associated with studies of computer-mediated communication (Nardi 2005), or they may provide accounts that are primarily descriptive, with minimal theorizing. Ultimately, grounded theory can be used as an analytic approach in conjunction with ethnographic methods, but it is not in and of itself ethnography.

3.9 ETHNOGRAPHY IS THE SAME AS ETHNOMETHODOLOGY

Though anthropologists and sociologists attend to the creation and maintenance of social life, researchers drawing on the framework of ethnomethodology emphasize the micropractices or "methods" that people perform to enact orderly social life. Reacting to what they viewed as an overly formal, sterile sociology in which theories had little correspondence to everyday human social activity, ethnomethodologists called for studying the "commonsense knowledge of everyday activities" of members of some natural language group (Garfinkel and Sacks 1970:341). The ethnomethodological approach is distinctively anti-theory; it "refuses the call to engage in theory building," seeking instead to "recover" practical activity "in its endless detail" (Suchman 2000:17).

Ethnomethodological accounts may recover minute details of small events, such as a phone conversation or a brief episode at a workplace, to describe the wealth of commonsense knowledge necessary for even the most apparently mundane activities. The attention to social order is understood as deeply residing in embodied actors and their interactions. As such, ethnomethodology poses powerful provocations for those researching virtual worlds. For instance, it calls us to remember not only the open or "free play" aspects of these worlds, but the role of social order. It also helps researchers explore how that order is rooted in participants' actions, not simply in computational systems.

In some fields, such as human-computer interaction, the "pairing of ethnographic fieldwork and ethnomethdological analysis has often been a source of confusion . . . sometimes [leading] people to believe that they are the same thing, or that one necessarily implies the other" (Dourish 2001:76). While some of the techniques used by researchers employing this approach are shared with ethnographic practice (see Pollner and Emerson 2001 for an extended discussion), some ethnomethodologists also use other methods that would be considered anathema to core principles of ethnography. These include experimental interventions in the social order designed to expose various aspects of commonsense practice, such as the intentional breaching of social norms, for instance standing in line at a grocery store and trying to pay more for an item than its listed price, entering an elevator and facing the rear of it instead of the door, or behaving like a lodger to your family in your own home. Interviews within this tradition may also introduce deceptive materials and scenarios (Garfinkel 1991). Such methods are not ethnographic and raise ethical issues since they often involve forms of deception that are at odds with the values of ethnographic research (we discuss deception at length in chapter 8).

Ethnomethodological approaches have also been critiqued for inattention to larger-scale power dynamics not reducible to individual action (see Schegloff 1997; Wetherell 1998). Ethnographers regularly situate their studies of specific communities in broader social, cultural, and historic patterns. In this regard ethnographers move beyond the microfocus of most ethnomethodological work.

While researchers employing both ethnomethodology and ethnographic methods share an interest in the everyday life of participants, including the mundane details of those lives, they can differ in their orientation to theory, their willingness to experimentally intervene, the level of "distance" they may assume in relation to the field, and the broader construction of a treatment that moves beyond microanalysis.

3.10 ETHNOGRAPHY WILL BECOME OBSOLETE

In discussing the nine myths above, we emphasized common and understandable misconceptions regarding ethnographic methods. Many factors shape the persistence of these myths. As noted earlier, ethnography is not a topic most people learn about in high school or even college. While ethnographers are often eloquent spokepersons for their approach and work in a range of interdisciplinary environments, we do not always succeed in conveying the value of our work to nonspecialists. However, in turning to our final myth, that ethnography will become obsolete, we address the politics of knowledge production.

In recent years there has been a trend in some schools of thought to dismiss ethnographic research as ineffective, exacerbated by a methodological partisanship asserting that only experimental or quantitative methods are valid (see Boellstorff 2009b). In this regard we have encountered scholars of virtual worlds claiming not that approaches other than ethnography are valid (a claim with which we wholeheartedly agree), but that ethnographic methods are by definition unscientific. Some have even sounded a "death knell" for ethnographic methods in virtual worlds (Bloomfield 2009) or suggested "a major realignment of social science research methods" that would involve eliminating research supposedly "based on the researcher's impression after having spent 12 months living with a small subset of one of the populations" (Castronova 2006:184). Such mischaracterizations entail a vision where only laboratory and experimental methods remain.

Some researchers subscribing to this view see virtual worlds as a dream come true, potential "laboratories" to test hypotheses about human nature (Castronova 2006). For those who consider ethnography beset by imprecision and subjectivity, the allure of laboratories holds the promise of a leap forward in social science that would render ethnographic methods irrelevant. But as we have sought to show throughout this chapter, understanding human culture is a complex endeavor. It may be tempting to temporarily create a controlled virtual world for the purposes of research, as some economists and other social scientists have done. However, we cannot overemphasize the fact that to create a virtual world in this manner is not simply a laboratory experiment. It is potentially creating a lifeworld, a place of social interaction where unexpected and emergent meanings can take form, from new friendships to works of art and social movements. The rationale of such experiments seems to be that researchers can observe as an unobtrusive "fly on the wall," collecting information in the form of pure, unbiased data. However, no virtual world is a Petri dish hermetically sealed off from outside influences. Even as virtual worlds have certain boundaries in the sense that one logs into them and leaves them, they take in and transform ideas and practices from other virtual worlds and internet social contexts, as well as physical world cultures.

For other researchers, doubts about the future of ethnographic methods originate not in the temptations of laboratory-like experimentation, but in the possibilities for using the massive body of raw data automatically gathered by virtual world software. It can seem as if such "big data" methods, deploying terabytes of data to carry out calculations, could provide a comprehensive picture of human action in virtual worlds, replete with testability and generalizablity.

Many who pursue this line of reasoning assert that one of the core foundations, and challenges, of quantitative methods—the sample—will fall away. It is as if the numbers capture everything, comprising an entire population and not just a sampled segment, and thus have the power to speak for themselves. The truth will emerge unproblematically. In our view this confidence in the sheer mass of numbers often sidelines more important considerations regarding research design, data handling (for example, during the "clean-up" process), whether the findings have anything interesting to say, and if in fact the big numbers are truly complete.

All research results, including quantitative results, require *interpretation.* Indeed some who work with these types of data concede that they are not comprehensible on their own (Williams 2010). Frege (1959) shows us that numbers rest on a qualitative foundation of language. boyd and Crawford (2012) point out that numbers alone have no philosophical basis; what Berry (2011:11, cited in boyd and Crawford 2012) calls the "regulating force of philosophy" is essential to thought. Any turn to quantitative datasets therefore "reframes key questions about the constitution of knowledge, the processes of research, how we should engage with information, and the nature and the categorization of reality" (boyd and Crawford 2012:4). Howison, Crowston, and Wiggins offer strong cautions. They examined a big data methodology used in social network analysis in which "digital traces," for example, transactions or conversations in a social network, constituted the data. The authors argued that while such methodologies can be productive, they should not be used uncritically as they often are. The authors noted that "a set of pernicious validity concerns" afflicts much current big data research (2012:52).

As increasing scholarly and corporate funding and attention turn to data-mining projects, or to designing small virtual worlds to carry out laboratory-like experiments, the value of ethnographic research has come into question. The danger is when ethnographic work is rejected outright or seen as limited to providing context or helping with illustrative stories, its ability to generate valid social scientific data is elided. The result is a privileging of quantitative and physical science approaches to knowledge production. This privileging often takes the form of inequitable access to funding, as noted, for example, in the U.S. National Science Foundation report on qualitative research (Ragin, Nagel, and White 2004). When misconceptions about the supposed limits of ethnography take hold, institutional and systemic problems arise, such as more funding opportunities for quantitative research, the emphasis of grant criteria better suited to quantitative research, and the populating of review panels primarily with quantitative experts (ibid.). As we have hoped to show throughout this chapter (and this book), the value of ethnographic techniques for understanding human culture cannot be overstated; such policy decisions have deleterious scientific consequences.

Historically, false alarms regarding the obsolescence of qualitative methods have been sounded before. We can trace a bias toward quantitative methods to Cold War funding priorities, the growth of big science, and the totalizing ideology that all phenomena can be represented through numerical models (Edwards 1997). And yet ethnography has survived. It is resilient because ethnographers offer compelling tools for understanding human action and society. Indeed, many quantitative researchers cite and collaborate productively with ethnographers, acknowledging the "peril of large datasets" and noting that on their own they are frequently opaque (Williams 2010). These scholars appreciate that ethnographic research can capture a culture in a specific time period, charting the dynamics of history in the making. Ethnographers' focus on meaning making allows them not only to describe social action but to provide interpretations that utilize both etic and emic perspectives. Huge volumes of data may be compelling at first glance, but without an interpretive structure they are meaningless, and it is in this regard that ethnographic approaches excel.

Thus in the face of this myth of obsolescence we would argue that, on the contrary, ethnographic research is a vibrant paradigm with a bright future. Ethnography has been widely and enthusiastically embraced by a range of scholars interested in online sociality because of ethnography's particular value in an age of networked cultures. In our view, a far greater concern than ethnography becoming obsolete is that it will become so broadly defined as to lose all meaning. We have reviewed papers or heard talks in which researchers claimed to have "done ethnography," "ethnographically inspired" research, or even "ethnography lite," when in reality they merely conducted interviews or made brief visits to a fieldsite, never participating in everyday life and becoming known to those they studied. Such work may be fruitful and valuable, but it is not ethnographic research. If, for instance, someone conducts a project involving interviews and a literature review, this would best be termed "qualitative research," not ethnography. Our challenge lies in making sure we continue to develop and use a sophisticated methodology in the best ways possible, upholding standards of integrity and rigor. It is for these reasons that careful research design, the topic to which we now turn, is so important.

CHAPTER FOUR

RESEARCH DESIGN AND PREPARATION

4.1 RESEARCH QUESTIONS: EMERGENCE, RELEVANCE, AND PERSONAL INTEREST

The most fundamental, consequential, and personal step in designing an ethnographic project is choosing the question we seek to answer. It is the decision from which all other choices and challenges follow, including that of selecting informants and fieldsites. Any ethnographer of virtual worlds must "ensure that that his or her research questions are both coherently addressed and adapted to the cultural landscape that emerges" (Hine 2009:2). We discuss three principal concerns regarding formulating a research question: emergence, relevance, and personal interest.

An obvious yet profound insight of ethnographic research is that in the end, everything is connected to everything else. It is the researcher's task to derive from this blooming, buzzing confusion a research question that will guide data collection, determine which literatures are most relevant, and shape the writing of the ethnography. We are in a historical moment in which the body of published research employing ethnographic methods for the study of virtual worlds is relatively small. At the same time, the number of potential research questions increases at a dizzying pace as new virtual worlds come into being and change, and as we learn more about them and appreciate their complexities.

From this abundance, the ethnographer must identify a workable line of inquiry for research. As LeCompte and Schensul note, "All good ethnographers try to create an overall design in which anticipated details and activities are spelled out as far as current information permits" (1999:98). This line of inquiry, however, can be broad and emergent—shaped by curiosity and "aha!" moments as much as a preset agenda. We can start with very little as long as we are pointed in a general direction. Bonnie began her ethnographic research in World of Warcraft armed only with an interest in how people socialize in online multiplayer games. Tom began his ethnography in Second Life with the general question, "How does 'culture' work in virtual worlds?" Celia's research on the Uru diaspora began with the question, "What is the relationship between the software affordances of virtual worlds and the emergent behavior that takes place within them?" T.L. began her work on text-based worlds with the question, "How does embodiment work in virtual environments?" We can have a broad research question at the outset of ethnographic study, but that question must be clearly articulated and carefully linked to the methodological design of the research itself.

Often the research question emerges from observations gathered during informal visits to a fieldsite, before we have even begun to think of it formally in terms of research. We may prefer to conduct research in a particular virtual world and seek a research question appropriate to study in that context. Perhaps we have ventured into an online environment as a distraction from our work in another, only to find resonant research themes there. The research question might also arise out of an observation in a given context that leads to a new area of inquiry. Ethnographers often revisit the same site with a new set of questions.

In our own ethnographic projects, we can attest to many cases in which key research questions emerged only once participant observation research was well under way. For instance, while T.L. originally entered into her EverQuest work thinking about avatars and embodiment, over time her focus shifted as she saw the formation of social life there and the often complex relationship between the emergent culture of players and the role of corporate owners. Tom found that the seemingly incidental phenomenon known as "lag" fundamentally altered his core research question regarding how human culture takes form in virtual worlds. Exploring practices around lag allowed him to address key specificities of everyday experience in Second Life and also allowed him to link his Second Life ethnography to issues of temporality that are of broad interest in studies of computer-mediated communication and beyond. Bonnie developed an interest in governance in online worlds once she discovered the existence of modding communities and their relationship to Blizzard. Before she entered World of Warcraft she had no idea that players created mods. Governance is a facet of sociality and was thus within her original purview of interest, but the topic developed into a set of specific investigations. Celia's discovery that former Uru players self-identified as "Uru refugees" led her to questions about the role of community in the construction of individual identity.

Crafting a research question is thus often linked to exploration. As Hine observed, "ethnography is thought of as one of the most open of research approaches, which adapts itself to the social situations it finds. This does not mean, however, that ethnographers just wander around aimlessly: Ethnography may be adapted, but it is still purposive" (Hine 2009:6). Ethnographers must be prepared to modify questions based on what they encounter in the field. Malinowski noted the need to both center on a question and open oneself to what he called "the pressure of evidence" as ethnographic research proceeds. In *Argonauts of the Western Pacific*, he emphasized that while "foreshadowed problems are the main endowment of a scientific thinker," it is also true that "If a [researcher] sets out on an expedition, determined to prove certain hypotheses, if he is incapable of changing his views constantly and casting them off ungrudgingly under the pressure of evidence, needless to say his work will be worthless" (1922:9).

The core method of participant observation allows the investigator to alter ethnographic research midstream in a manner difficult with many methodologies, including survey and experimental approaches. The adaptability of the method is one reason fieldwork requires a significant time investment. We might be interested in a practice such as role-playing; we may do preliminary visits to several communities and find one that approaches the practice in a particularly interesting manner. Other possibilities are that we already have strong contacts in a community or find one community receptive to our research. The research question may thus be formulated iteratively, in dialogue with the quest for an appropriate fieldsite. There is nothing remiss in such bootstrapping approaches to research design; indeed it is the most common approach employed by physical world ethnographers as well. Ethnography is an emergent process of discovery; participant observation is intended to stimulate and scaffold open discovery as much as possible.

Despite this flexibility in relation to emergent research questions, a second issue is that a good research question must, ultimately, center around issues relevant to wider research communities. Ideally ethnographers research narrowly and think broadly, in the sense that they link a delimited and thus doable research question to larger debates. These debates can be specific to the field of virtual worlds research, but they may also connect to other disciplinary and interdisciplinary discourses. Such connections are important because virtual worlds represent a new domain of study whose relevance may not be recognized in certain scholarly communities. For instance, it may not be apparent to everyone that virtual worlds can teach us valuable things about selfhood, embodiment, governance, globalization, learning, and many other topics relevant even to those without much interest in online technologies. It is easy for us to become absorbed in our own personal and sometimes obscure fascinations. Pushing ourselves to answer larger questions like "what is at stake?" and "why does this matter?" is a way of helping link a study with larger literatures, frameworks, and sets of concerns.

To arrive at a relevant research question, it is essential to read and think deeply about prior work. The broadness of the centering question may sometimes seem daunting with respect to locating suitable literatures. It is usually best to think of some general topic areas relevant to your project and then just plunge in and start reading. Part of the productive work of doing a literature review is it allows you to begin to see the contours of the research domain you are interested in, mapping what has already been said about the subject and, as a result, helping you sharpen your own interests, sense of what issues are most important, and potential research design.

This process is easier for more experienced scholars, but social networking as well as online and library searches go a long way for everyone. A good starting point is to use the online resources of a library; most university libraries provide databases of books and journal articles (such as JSTOR) that can be searched by publication, keyword, or author; much virtual world research is currently available in electronic form and, increasingly, under open-access agreements. If unsure of how to conduct a robust review of the literature, one can usually also take advantage of consulting with a reference librarian, on whose expertise we can draw in navigating and searching databases. We attend carefully to the bibliographies of interesting work we read; these often act as pointers to other relevant research. We can find authors we like and visit their websites to discover new materials and even write to them, as not all websites are updated frequently. We can talk to people with shared interests. The essence of ethnography lies in talking to people and following emergent trails; it is useful and productive to apply the technique to searching for relevant readings, much like a detective might go about solving a mystery.

It is critical that we think historically. Even in a field of study as young as virtual worlds research, we often see publications that have neglected early studies such as the extensive investigations of MUDs. If our list of references does not include anything published before 2000, we should try again! Early work on virtual worlds goes back to the 1980s, but we should not stop there when looking for theoretical and conceptual footholds. It is also useful to go beyond the research literature on virtual worlds in building generalizations. By connecting to scholarly work in other domains we can bolster our claims, helping broaden the conversations in which we are engaged.

As ethnographers refine their research topics, new literatures become relevant. Celia found particular relevance in Paul Willis's (1978) research on the customization practices of British motorcycle gang members, which related to both productive play and identity construction. She also found Erving Goffman's classic theory of frame analysis to be applicable to play, a point that Goffman himself observed in its formulation (1974). T.L. found herself engaging with the work of legal scholars and cultural critics (Coombe 1998; Lessig 1999) as she sought to understand the pivotal relationship between intellectual property and emergent player practices. The issues we engage with in virtual worlds often have important links to larger cultural conversations, and incorporating literature that goes beyond the digital can be a way of formulating stronger and more interesting arguments.

While relevance is important to arriving at a research question, we cannot overemphasize that all good science flows from a scientist's passion to learn something he or she is deeply curious about. Thus a third consideration for finding a research question is that, although it is important for the work to be broadly relevant, the question should be personally interesting and exciting to us. It is vital to underscore this point because we are best served by honoring our own passions and intellectual journey when deciding on a research question. Any ethnographic research project requires a lengthy period of engagement. The work is based on participant observation, which entails significant commitments of time, emotion, and energy. Because the socializing, interactive self is the foundation of ethnographic research, the more engaged we are in conducting research, the more patient, gregarious, and involved we will be, and the better the data will be as a result. Ethnographic work requires not just a clear head but fire in the belly—an enthusiasm for the research that can sustain us through the frustrations, wrong turns, dead ends, and conundrums that accompany long-term fieldwork.

Overall, arriving at a research question is the foundation of successful ethnographic research. It is for this reason that we speak of a research question in the singular. Of course, all research investigates multiple topics and each question has multiple facets, but simply pluralizing "question" into "questions" obscures how all successful ethnographic research begins from the conceptual work of specifying a focused objective. Crafting this intellectual point of departure can involve painful choices. Difficult decisions involve which questions to set aside because of lack of time and resources. The richness of what we will encounter during fieldwork will present new temptations for opening new avenues of exploration, risking the clarity and focus essential to a good investigation. A grounding research question, once established, asserts and protects precision and focus.

4.2 SELECTING A GROUP OR ACTIVITY TO STUDY

Historically, ethnographic studies have concerned specific people and the cultures they construct and inhabit; this is no different in virtual world ethnographic research. One of the challenges all ethnographers face is determining what constitutes the core unit of study. For example, Bonnie chose to study collaborative guild-based activity in World of Warcraft in contrast to, for example, solo questers or those who game the "Auction House" to make thousands of game gold. Celia had to constrain her study of Uru refugees to two subgroups in order to obtain meaningful data. In comparison to his Indonesia research, in which he focused on gay communities, Tom decided to explore Second Life culture in an overall sense for his book-length study; this meant, however, that he was unable to discuss issues like sexuality in an extensive manner. T.L. focused primarily on one particular world, Dreamscape, within a broader platform in her exploration of embodiment and graphical avatars. As with all decisions regarding the group to study, something was gained and something lost in this decision.

While ethnographers often say they study "communities," it bears noting that there is no agreed upon definition for "community" in the social science literature. As far back as 1955, sociologist George Hillery found nearly 100 definitions (Hillery 1955), and the situation has not improved; if anything, notions of "virtual communities" (Rheingold 2000) and "imagined communities" (Anderson 1983) continue to expand the conceptual space. If we denote our unit of study as a community, it is imperative to explain what we mean.

We do not always find precisely bounded geographies or communities in virtual worlds. Within online multiplayer games, for example, there are typically numerous servers, each of which replicates the basic game software. Within each server are various types of social groups and activities that may be configured in different ways depending on how their members define them and how the virtual world software shapes participation. Virtual world communities and activities are diverse and heterogeneous. Example group types include guilds, communities of practice (such as modders), and members of offline groups such as a professional organization, family, or workgroup that enters a virtual world together, as well as diasporic game communities who choose to play together.

Ethnographers may also choose to investigate an activity rather than a particular group. In many game worlds, a study of pick-up groups or player versus player (PvP) battlegrounds would typically involve research on a series of temporary teams (which may play together for only a few minutes) rather than following a stable group such as a guild. The study of activities such as theorycrafting, in which players analyze game mechanics through mathematical, statistical, and logical means, may focus on the analytics of statistical treatments, computation, representation, and writing (Choontanom and Nardi 2012). Similarly, activities like modding could be important. Looking in detail at the sociotechnical components of these small bits of software as they were used within the game for creating and maintaining collective action became a part of the analysis and story (see also Taylor 2006b).

Once a group or activity has been chosen, how many people should be studied? Most research communities will be skeptical of very small sample sizes in any published work. Through lengthy fieldwork we encounter numerous people in a range of social contexts. Over time and with experience, we begin to get a feel for an adequate group size, which will arise from the themes and the community or activity we wish to study. Ultimately there is no hard-and-fast answer. It is important to note that in ethnographic work we study through a variety of modalities so there is no single measure; we will have a collection of interviews, fieldnotes documenting hours and hours of participant observation, even perhaps catalogs of objects and artifacts (including virtual ones) for analysis. Different projects will have different thresholds depending on the overall size of the field, the scope of the project and its research questions, and, ultimately, its claims. Bonnie generally aims to have at least twenty participants in her studies, although she has published papers with fewer, and she interviewed hundreds of people for the World of Warcraft research. T.L. tends to let this issue be led by the natural configuration of the field, with some fieldsites lending themselves to larger numbers of participants. Celia has studied groups of as many as three hundred people.

As ethnographers we often do not know in advance what the right number will be (in terms of either interviews or hours logged in the field). The answer is often emergent: "Ethnographers begin research with a set of questions, revise them throughout the course of inquiry, and in the end emerge with different questions than they started with. One's surprise at the answer to a question, in other words, requires one to revise the question until lessening surprises or diminishing returns indicate a stopping point" (Rosaldo 1993:7). One guiding principle to help us determine when data collection is complete is that of saturation. When we start hearing the same reflections repeated in interviews, when we are no longer seeing new things or getting new insight while undertaking participant observation, when we have reached a point where we can anticipate answers, practices, and the general everyday unfolding of the field, we have likely reached the point of diminishing returns in our data collection and can consider that phase complete. It indicates that reliable patterns have been established and we have begun to grasp the culture. Once we feel we have enough data to say something interesting and meaningful, that the sample is large enough to provide a cohesive foundation for our arguments and is up to academic standards, then enough work has been accomplished to turn our attention to writing up our findings. The arrival at this point is contingent on the foundation of a strong central research question from which other questions, and cohesive findings, can emerge.

4.3 SCOPE OF THE FIELDSITE

How we conceptualize the scope of our fieldsite will shape the way we formulate our research questions. The traditional fieldsite of anthropology in the early twentieth century was often construed as geographically discrete. Typically the site was a "village"—a recognizable place with a name and clearly delineated boundaries. In the past few decades, however, ethnographers have developed techniques for "multi-sited ethnography" predicated on "multiple sites of observation and participation that cross-cut dichotomies such as the 'local' and the 'global,' the 'lifeworld' and the 'system' " (Marcus 1995:95). "Modes of construction" for engaging in such ethnographic work suggested by Marcus include "follow the people," "follow the metaphor," and "follow the artifact." In other words, sites of investigation are in dynamic dialogue as we trace linkages between them, attempting to establish and explain critical interrelations. These issues are not just present but magnified with regard to virtual worlds, where "tracing the boundaries of the chosen social groups remains a challenge for the ethnographer interested in the local cultures in cyberspace" (Guimarães 2005:148).

Selecting which virtual world or worlds to study requires critical consideration with respect to the range of options and the research question being addressed. Virtual worlds may encompass millions of people, although the way virtual world populations are counted can sometimes be misleading. For instance, Linden Lab, the company that owns Second Life, counts the Second Life population in three ways: the total number of accounts, the number of participants who logged in during the past sixty days, and the number online at any one point (concurrent users). However, since many people with Second Life accounts seldom use them, and some residents have multiple accounts, the first metric is not accurate and the company eventually began emphasizing the latter two metrics. In online games that allow multiple avatars attached to a single subscription, an individual player may have multiple characters, or multiple players may share a single account. Popular perceptions of virtual world size may be less a product of actual numbers than the result of press coverage—be that the positive coverage emanating from the public relations departments of the companies that own them, or the negative coverage of journalists seeking sensational stories of addiction, sex, and crime. For instance, based on her calculations (including verifying numbers with the developers), Celia concluded that it was likely that There.com had a larger population of regular users than Second Life during the time of her fieldwork, though it was less well-known. A large virtual world population is not a precondition for research relevance; ethnographers have produced important findings from studying communities with only a few thousand or even less than a hundred members. On the other hand, some virtual worlds with relatively large populations (for instance, Habbo and Maple Story) have been understudied.

A fieldsite may be understood as an assemblage of actors, places, practices, and artifacts that can be physical, virtual, or a combination of both (Taylor 2009). Multi-sited ethnography may thus be useful for capturing a holistic picture of the life of a community or activity, and the scope of the fieldsite may itself be emergent. Through participant observation, Celia discovered a constellation of activities when investigating how players of the game Uru: Ages Beyond Myst migrated to a different game, There.com, when Uru closed. She learned that an online forum was their primary form of communication, defining the group as transcending any one of the virtual worlds the diasporic community inhabited. As players moved around and virtual worlds came and went, the forum's "world agnostic" status became increasingly important. Although she had initially set the goal of maintaining exclusively online interactions with participants, when key group members collectively decided to attend the Real Life Gathering hosted by There.com's creators, she literally and figuratively followed her informants into the physical world. Later, in her study of the University of There, Celia decided to visit participants in their homes to see how play contexts influenced their inworld activities.

To "follow the artifact," Bonnie "followed" World of Warcraft to China to investigate play activity there. She was interested in the extent to which the software artifact itself shaped player experience. She visited internet cafés, dorms, and homes where people played World of Warcraft. During her stay, issues of censorship and national governance of video games arose, and she took advantage of being on the scene to study matters responsive to "empirical changes in the world and therefore to transformed locations [in the world system]" (Marcus 1995:97). Bonnie also followed the artifact of software mods, studying modding in China and North America (Kow and Nardi 2011), an exploration guided not by a notion of community but by the existence of a particular software artifact and its related practices.

The need to account for one's fieldsite in terms of research design pertains regardless of whether one frames the research as single-sited or multi-sited. It is often forgotten that in his influential article on multi-sited ethnography, Marcus emphasized the importance of what he termed "the strategically situated (single-site) ethnography" (1995:110). His example of such work was Paul Willis's *Learning to Labor* (1977), a "now classic study of English working-class boys at school," in which "the particular kind of interest that [Willis] develops in the boys at school, *on which he focuses solely*, is guided by his knowledge of what happens to them on the factory floor" (Marcus 1995:110; emphasis added). In other words, Willis considered how factory labor affected working-class boys, though he did no ethnographic work in the factories himself. This notion of the strategically situated single-site ethnography describes Tom's research in Second Life. Tom did all his data collection online and did not conduct participant observation or interviews in the physical world. However, he constantly considered how physical world cultures affected the virtual world culture he was exploring, from notions of visual landscape derived from nineteenth-century European painting to assumptions about creating virtual world content shaped by religion.

4.4 ATTENDING TO OFFLINE CONTEXTS

In some cases our research leads opportunistically toward offline contexts; at other times we design explicit attention to offline concerns from the outset. We may, for example, want to attend to specific infrastructure issues, or to political conditions relevant to our informants. Bringing in the offline may occur simply through the process of following the field where it leads, for example, by attending a fan convention or frequenting an internet café where our participants play. Depending on the research and its questions, we may find ourselves weaving together online and offline contexts and components in the fieldwork.

The relationships between physical world concerns and the virtual worlds we study may vary between worlds, as well as within the cultures within the worlds in question. Some of these relationships may be embedded within the software configuration itself. While some game servers segregate players by region, others operate with a more global structure, allowing everyone onto the same server. We should be aware of how this basic organizational mechanism shapes the field. In the case of Second Life and There.com, Tom and Celia could study participants from across the globe given the ways their respective virtual worlds were structured. In some cases virtual world participants do not know the physical world location of other participants. In other cases it might be common for geographical location to be divulged as part of the "getting to know you" process within a culture, or it might come up within normal conversation, such as discussions of the weather or current events.

Physical world considerations such as time zones, national identity, and language may come into play. For instance, the Uru community met regularly on their self-run servers at noon Pacific standard time to accommodate both U.S. and European members. If Celia wanted to interview someone in a different time zone, special arrangements were sometimes necessary. The significance of offline locality may, depending on the research interest, become an important analytic component of the project. Although T.L. did not encounter formal regional segregation in her EQ research, in both her and Bonnie's work in World of Warcraft they had to account for this division of the playerbase. While North Americans could, conceivably, order a copy of World of Warcraft from abroad, normally they would be confined to playing on North American servers. T.L. has written about the ways national identity is often complexly negotiated within European servers (Taylor 2006b). Issues of regionality and access highlight not only the ways we should be reflective about the scope of our field, but also the ways virtual world communities at times must negotiate their own internal regional diversity.

Infrastructural issues, such as quality of bandwidth (and resulting "ping times" and lag) can also form an important part of how a virtual world's culture is shaped. Studies of the differing physical world socialities linked to some virtual worlds can also reveal important differences, as when Bonnie found a propensity of players in China to play World of Warcraft in internet cafés in comparison to players located in the United States, as well as a comparatively smaller number of female players in China. Chinese players were also not afforded the same direct communication lines with Blizzard developers (through official forums) as North American and European players (Kow and Nardi 2009). In cases like these, we do not assume that the virtual world culture in question extends seamlessly from a design experience originating in relatively distinct locales (say, Southern California, where Blizzard Entertainment produces World of Warcraft). Important disjunctures may occur as technology traverses new geographies. While we do not want to make a reductionist move in the opposite direction and assume that World of Warcraft in China and World of Warcraft in the United States are utterly separate, our research question may concern how players in differing physical world regions engage with a virtual world. For some projects, highlighting the complex negotiation between local cultures and global software products (the virtual world) may become an important point of exploration.

We would finally note the ways physical world social relationships may also be critical. All of us have encountered physical world friends, couples, and families who play together online, including those who, like Bonnie's Chinese World of Warcraft players, play online while physically co-located, or the family members T.L. spoke with who played EverQuest together. Virtual worlds have a long history of leveraging offline social connections for inworld affiliations and activities. And in a related move, they also have a solid tradition of offering people a possibility of forming new offline connections based on ones begun inworld (Kendall 2002). Carter, for example, noted that many of her informants eventually met face to face after becoming acquainted in the virtual world she studied, and two even married each other (2005:161). Virtual and physical world sociality often intertwine in meaningful ways.

One very important caveat here. Moving across cultures to expand and deepen research is not always aimed at finding difference; commonalities and linkages are just as important (see Boellstorff 2005; Nardi, Vatrapu, and Clemmensen 2011). The pressure to provide accounts of difference is strong, and we need to be particularly diligent about resisting such attempts when they do not fit the data. Bonnie is invariably asked, in reference to her field research in China, "What are the differences between Chinese and American World of Warcraft players?" But as noted in her book on World of Warcraft, "My biggest finding in China was that, overall, Chinese players were remarkably like the North American players I studied" (Nardi 2010:179). Thus it is important to engage both difference and similarity in our analytics. A good ethnographic account weaves together difference and similarity, showing commonalities where they occur yet also documenting the variable cultural formulations that demarcate cultures and make the very notion of the word "culture" so powerful. People are fundamentally the same in many key ways, deriving from our bodies and physical evolution, as well as our common need to deploy culture as the main adaptation for survival. At the same time, cultures develop powerful differences through varied historical trajectories and contexts. It is not easy to sort all this out, but it is the special burden of ethnographers to examine and analyze similarity as well as difference. Remaining alert to both is a critical aspect of good ethnographic practice.

CHAPTER FIVE

PARTICIPANT OBSERVATION IN VIRTUAL WORLDS

5.1 PARTICIPANT OBSERVATION IN CONTEXT

Ethnographers have an extremely broad methodological palette. Our work can include everything from individual and group interviews to historical research, quantitative surveys, and analyzing mass media, to name only a few common approaches. However, one method above all others is fundamental to ethnographic research. This method is participant observation, the cornerstone of ethnography. Participant observation is the embodied emplacement of the researching self in a fieldsite as a consequential social actor. We participate in everyday life and become well-known to our informants. If a methodological toolbox does not include participant observation, the approach may be legitimate and effective for exploring any number of topics, but it is not ethnographic. Through participant observation, ethnographers step into the social frame in which activity takes place. We sing with the congregation at a church service, feel the heat of the fires as slash-and-burn farmers prepare a patch of tropical forest for planting, sit on the bus with immigrant workers heading to a factory in the morning, watch strange fish swim into view with oceanographers thousands of feet below sea level. We also slay virtual dragons in the company of guildmates, play hide-and-seek in a virtual garden, attend a steampunk dance in Victorian attire. Becoming directly involved in the activities of daily life provides an intimate view of their substance and meaning.

Such participation, however, does not necessarily mean you need to be a practitioner of the cultures you are studying. While embodied engagement forms a central strength of ethnography (Wacquant 2004), offering us grounded experience in practices and entree into shared worlds with our participants, at the same time pragmatic and conceptual concerns dictate a range of appropriate and feasible levels of participation for any given project. For instance, it is not necessary to become a brain surgeon to study brain surgeons, or a physicist to study physicists. On the other hand, it would be difficult to conduct a close study of raiding without becoming a raider because the venue is not available without full participation. Each of a small number of spots in a raid must be filled to fight a boss, and "spectator" is not an option programmed into the game. But we do not have to construct arcane mathematical models to investigate theorycrafting; websites are replete with freely available material to peruse, and interviews with theorycrafters can be arranged. We might well use the results of theorycrafting analyses to improve our character, adding an authentic element of participation. Participant observation is not unreflective engagement; it is a refined craft that entails a particular kind of joining in and a particular way of looking at things that depends on the research question, fieldsite, and practical constraints.

Embodied participant observation work (even when in avatar form) is shaped by the many aspects of our subject position, which may include gender, age, race, social class, accent, national origin, sexual orientation, language skills, religion, occupation, and political commitments. But do these specificities introduce bias that hobbles research? Certainly every ethnographer has a "view from somewhere," and potentially it can affect what the ethnographer sees. But ethnographers' "patient, careful, and imaginative life study . . . remaining in close and continuing relations with the natural social order" (Blumer 1954:10) mediates, to a large extent, the concerns of subject position. Our extended presence signals commitment and sincere interest, opening dialogue with a variety of informants whose viewpoints and insights can be analyzed and represented in the ethnography.

Subject position bears on matters such as access to certain kinds of participants and the interpretive frames with which we approach data analysis. But subject position does not paralyze the ethnographic enterprise nor render us incapable of good research. To turn this concern on its head, subject position—in its manifold dimensions—affords resources, not only constraints. Making sense of the subject positions of others is a complex task that can be at least partially informed by one's own position. Practical knowledge, such as how to behave appropriately within a particular social group or culture, or realization of some of the challenges faced by a culture or group, may arise from membership. Specialized knowledge, such as language skills or familiarity with a religious tradition, can be leveraged to move effectively in a field setting. Early feminist ethnographers found that their gender offered them access to the female aspects of culture, but as "outsiders" they could also gain entry to male-only rituals to which native women were prohibited (Powdermaker 1966; see also Visweswaran 1994).

Because ethnographers often study small groups, the question of statistical significance sometimes arises in relation to the method of participant observation. However, ethnographers are not always sampling for discrete characteristics, as they are for certain statistical analyses. We are studying cultures, communities, and activities composed of diverse participants in interaction with each other. An ethnographer successfully integrated into the fieldsite, for instance, can easily approach a "100 percent response rate" by talking to everyone (or nearly everyone) in a village, guild, team, or other social unit. Mail and online surveys have far lower response rates.

Ethnographic research is fundamentally a holistic project; we seek to understand shared practices, meanings, and social contexts, and the interrelations among them. As we use participant observation to move through different instances of the social units in the domains we study, we learn, for example, whether the first guild we were in was atypical or typical, and in what ways. We read the work of researchers seeking to understand the same social dynamics we do. For example, given what we now know from prior research, it would be a waste of effort to construct a random sample to discover whether most World of Warcraft players use Voice over IP (VoIP) programs during raiding (they do) or whether they use mods (they do). Participant observation allows us to understand the particular ways that voice communication is integral to virtual world socializing and how modifications allow players some measure of self-governance. No amount of quantification can fully illuminate these issues; nor can experiments discover authentic behaviors that arise out of the everyday experiences of interacting in a virtual world.

Since participant observation is the foundation of ethnographic research, we devote a portion of this chapter to its provenance. The history of participant observation is intertwined with the history of ethnographic research discussed in chapter 2. In anthropology, it is linked to the transition away from "armchair anthropology" where most early anthropologists, including E. B. Tylor and James Frazer (whose book *The Golden Bough* was extremely influential (see Frazer 1922)), did no research themselves. Instead, they used data gathered by travelers, merchants, missionaries, and colonial officials. Some of these data were inconsistent or judgmental but could also be of surprisingly high quality and have influenced the history of ethnographic research (e.g., Schoolcraft

1851; for examples and discussions of other historical precedents, see Spencer and Gillen 1899; Hinsley 1983; Stocking 1992; Povinelli 2002).

By the early twentieth century, the notion of "armchair anthropology" was being called into question. W.H.R. Rivers's influential "General Account of Method" drew a clear distinction between "intensive study" and "survey" research, emphasizing the need to learn local languages and the importance of "volunteered information" relative to that obtained through elicitation (Stocking 1992:37). Above all, Bronisław Malinowski helped establish the centrality of participant observation to ethnographic research (Pelto and Pelto 1973; Salamone 1979; Kuper 1996). He not only trained influential early cohorts of anthropologists but wrote extensively about methods. These discussions appear throughout Malinowski's oeuvre, but the best-known appears in the opening pages of *Argonauts of the Western Pacific* (1922). Not long after the famous passage in which Malinowski asked the reader to "imagine yourself suddenly set down surrounded by all your gear, alone on a tropical beach close to a native village, while the launch or dinghy which has brought you sails away out of sight" (1922:4), he identified as "the most elementary . . . principle of method" that an ethnographer "ought to put himself in good conditions of work" (1922:6), which he recounted as follows: "Soon after I had established myself in Omarakana (Trobriand Islands), I began to take part, in a way, in the village life, to look forward to the important or festive events, to take personal interest in the gossip and the developments of the small village occurrences; to wake up every morning to a day, presenting itself to me more or less as it does to the native" (1922:7). By the 1930s, discussions of method valorized "the fieldworker" as "justly recognized to be the most important person in the sphere of social anthropology" (Westermarck 1936:241; see Wolcott 2005 for further discussion).

Participant observation has a dual origin, since its history in sociology is as lengthy as in anthropology. Sociological writers of the late nineteenth and early twentieth centuries were already thinking about questions of method along the lines of participant observation, as in Simmel's notion (1908) of the "the stranger," or in the work of Durkheim. Layton observes that Durkheim "anticipated the value of participant observation" when emphasizing that "the social scientist must go into the field to discover how a society conceives of its own institutions" (1997:20). Early on, these concerns were put into practice within sociology itself: "the method has very, very deep roots in sociology. Beatrice Webb was doing participant observation—complete with note taking and informant interviewing—in the 1880s and she wrote trenchantly about the method in her 1926 memoir" (Bernard 2006:346). Debates over participant observation have continued throughout the history of sociology, including its role in community studies (Lohman 1937), its relation to issues of empiricism (Bruyn 1966), the emergent character of research questions (McCall and Simmons 1969), and the use of participant observation to address questions of power (Burawoy 1991; see also Jacobs 1970; Pelto and Pelto 1973). These debates have in turn informed discussions of participant observation in anthropology (DeWalt and DeWalt 2002).

5.2 PARTICIPANT OBSERVATION IN PRACTICE

We have taken the time to revisit this history not just because we believe that practitioners of participant observation should be cognizant of it, but because we see these fieldworkers as providing vital tools for research. Like physical world ethnographers, virtual world ethnographers should take advantage of extended fieldwork to study cultures through participation that is authentic in that culture's own terms. This can sometimes entail acquiring new skills at a very high level. Bonnie and T.L., for instance, learned to perform as raiders to study raiding activity in World of Warcraft. They had to show up on time for raids, pull their weight, and act as a full member of the raiding team (see also Steinkuehler 2006; Chen 2009; Golub 2010). In many cases virtual worlds allow ethnographers fuller participation than in physical world contexts and can be more demanding from a skills acquisition perspective. For instance, when observing slash-and-burn agriculture in Papua New Guinea, Bonnie lit no fires and felled no trees. Yet in Second Life, Tom learned how to build things, including Ethnographia, his home and office in Second Life, just as his participants had.

Participant observation is built on the alignments between engaging in everyday activities, on one hand, and recording and analyzing those activities, on the other. The trickiness of this alignment often leads to the question, "Are you playing or researching?" The either/or nature of this question misses that participant observation means that participating—including playing—is absolutely essential. We cannot pick one or the other. Good participant observation means play and research in parallel, as the same engaged activity.

Owing to practical and cognitive limitations, however, one activity often takes precedence over another at a given moment. For example, if conducting an online interview, it is difficult to simultaneously play a game. Still, sometimes, engaging in both modalities more or less concurrently can entail juggling multiple tasks at once. For example, at one point in her research, Bonnie had missed several raids during which raid leaders established a requirement to use a player-created modification called AVR. Upon realizing she needed this modification, Bonnie scrambled to log out, download and customize the modification, and try to understand how it worked. While doing this, through the group's voice chat channel she heard players discussing the modification's features, as well as rumors that Blizzard disliked AVR and would soon disable it. Since Bonnie had been tracking player-corporate relations around the issue of modifications as a key part of her research, this conversation caught her attention. She realized that even as she was struggling to get the modification working, she needed to immediately begin noting the conversation in as much detail as possible, as well as players' jokes about misuses of AVR. Issues of governance, community, skill, and creativity emerged in the conversations simultaneously with the demands of the performance of play.

One day in April 2006, Tom was doing fieldwork in Second Life when he received an invitation to participate in a "wings dance party." Tom teleported to the dance, only to realize that he did not yet have any wings for his avatar. He asked the host "know a good place where I can buy a pair real quick?" and the host replied "no, but I probably have a pair I can send you." After searching his inventory, the host offered Tom some wings. Even as he started dancing, Tom was thus already thinking about avatar embodiment, commodities, and gifts. After about an hour of dancing, Tom left to play a game of Tringo (a combination of Tetris and Bingo) with several other residents. As the game started up, one resident talked about how "I'm happy-go-lucky tonight—glad to have the day off from rl [real life, the physical world]." Another resident said "I'm ill in rl, yet somehow this helps take the pain away." The ensuing discussion between residents—a kind of discussion that would never happen in an interview—helped Tom think about questions of the body and relationships between the physical and virtual, particularly when linked to his earlier experiences at the dance. The juxtaposition of different kinds of participation helped Tom formulate key questions about virtual embodiment.

Sometimes our informants actively shape our level of involvement (Behar 1993). Early in her research with Uru refugees in There.com, Celia took a fairly passive approach, trying to minimize her impact. But the players, who were proactive and emotionally invested in the success of her research, confronted her with the criticism that she was too detached—that in order to understand their culture she needed to engage in activities with them, rather than simply watching from the sidelines. Shortly after this discussion, an opportunity arose to do just that. Uru refugees had invented a new sport called "Buggy Polo," using the dune buggy vehicles found throughout There.com. The "ball" was a translucent, spherical hover vehicle that behaved like a large beach ball. Although the ball did not have to be driven, someone had to control it in case it went out-of-bounds, since it was otherwise irretrievable. One of the group leaders, who was disabled, had been manning the ball and decided to dismount from it to take a break to rest her hands. Celia was flying about in the trees taking screenshots when the ball got stuck in one of the tree branches. The other players called to her to bring it down, but the only way to do this was to actually board the vehicle. She did so, steered the ball back into the middle of the field, and stayed at the center of the action for the remainder of the game, taking the role of the ball that had previously been held by the other player. This marked a turning point in her level of engagement, increasing both her trust and her esteem with the group. Greater involvement in play activities gave her a deeper understanding of the group's signature play styles, which were a major component of her findings. The players gained greater respect for her and were more willing to share their culture and stories as a result of this increased engagement in their activities.

T.L. once found herself back in a virtual world she was studying after having attended a physical world event where about thirty people from the virtual world had gathered for a weekend of socializing offline, many of them meeting each other for the first time. At the physical world event, several people remarked that they were glad to finally learn T.L.'s gender. She was both amused and surprised to learn she had picked an avatar that confused many people (though to her it seemed perfectly fine at the time—a standard female head paired with a relatively generic male body that read a bit androgynous to her). That first evening back inworld, T.L. wandered into a virtual room where a number of people were hanging out. The fact that she was still using a "confusing" avatar triggered a playful round of discussion and experimentation that began with persons who had attended the physical world event but then grew to include others. People (including herself) would wander off, use the virtual world's "body change" machine to put on a new avatar body, and then return, all the while joking and chatting about the meaning of avatar bodies. In a very concrete way, the avatars became "objects to think with" (Turkle 2007). An initial stumble on T.L.'s part (embodying herself in an apparently confusing way) proved to be a productive prompt for a fascinating discussion about embodiment, identity, and playful performance, all of which were core themes for her research project.

As these examples demonstrate, participant observation is built on a number of general principles that persist across all contexts, while at the same time remaining flexible enough to be responsive to practices unique to the culture being studied. To support this foundation of flexibility and variability, we now discuss five suggestions for effective participant observation tailored to virtual worlds research. Note that while we have no choice but to present these suggestions sequentially, they will often take place concurrently as we prepare for and enter into fieldwork.

5.3 PREPARING THE RESEARCHING SELF

A first issue is to consider how the physical work environment hinders or helps our researching selves. We can set up our workspace to minimize fatigue, bleary eyes, and even things like carpal tunnel syndrome. For instance, Tom often works while walking on a special treadmill, and T.L. has a desk that can adjust to standing mode, a welcome option after years hunched at a keyboard took its toll on her neck. Some of us may prefer to work in our conventional lab or office setting, but just as often we may want to set up a home office to create a private, discrete work space. Even if we work primarily from a lab, a home office may also be useful since much virtual world activity takes place outside regular work hours. On the other hand, some may find the noisy bustle of the dining room table, enabling interaction with our families, more conducive to productivity. If we travel or have busy schedules, as many of us do, we may find ways to pitch our tent in a coffee shop or hotel room.

Second, technological issues are paramount in terms of setting up optimal conditions for entering the fieldsite. Our home space (and work office, if we have one and use it for ethnographic research) should have a reliable internet connection. The lag created by poor connectivity can make interaction frustrating and even cause programs to crash. Most virtual worlds have minimum system requirements involving everything from graphics cards to hard drive space, and it is important to consider these when choosing the computer on which to work. We should also think about how, if our computer is significantly worse (or better) than the norm among our informants, we will in some sense potentially be out of step with them experientially; we might see a lower-resolution version of the virtual world or not be able to see far into the distance. Given that our fieldsite is constructed in part through technology, it is important to attend to both software system requirements and the configurations our informants typically use. This is particularly the case in game settings where synchronized activity is critical to the outcome of group maneuvers. We should strive be in step with our participants, including technologically. We may even be conducting research in venues such as internet cafés and not be using our own dedicated machines. In such cases we will, by default, experience the same problems and opportunities as our informants.

Third, preparation for fieldwork involves not just one's workspace, but one's ethnographic self. Such preparation might not include language training but will always involve technical proficiency. It is our responsibility to get up to speed regarding the basics of everyday life in the virtual world we wish to study. This includes keyboard and mouse control, navigating menus and commands, customizing the look of our avatar, learning technical and linguistic conventions for text chat and voice communication, and learning how to engage in typical activities, from basic avatar movement to building or wielding weapons and spells. It is important that we do our homework (any available tutorial, for example) so as not to overly burden our informants with our own inexperience. While our informants may teach us advanced combat tactics or navigation techniques, we should begin with at least the basic facility to walk and adjust our voice volume before entering fully into the field. T.L. spent hours looking through various object codes in text-based worlds, including that of her own character, so as to better understand what actions could be performed. She then often practiced commands while alone to get a feel for inhabiting that space. When beginning his fieldwork in Second Life, Tom spent a week flying over every parcel of the entire virtual world (which was possible at the time because Second Life had only about five thousand residents). This allowed him to get a feel for common types of buildings and activities.

Later on in fieldwork we will often want to gain additional technical skills, including adapting to new features and learning to use modifications and plug-ins created by participants themselves. One of Celia's early stumbles was an initial failure to develop aptitude with settings for voice, which had been added as a feature to There.com and was quickly adopted as a social convention. Later Thereians widely adopted a plug-in that changed the appearance of the different standard hairstyles. In debating the pros and cons of using the plug-in, several players encouraged Celia's students to use it: many were selecting the standard hairstyles based on their appearance while using the plug-in, rather than the original unmodified hairstyle. This meant seeing avatars as the players meant for them to be seen.

Overall, then, conducting research in virtual worlds requires acquiring considerable expertise, not only in the culture being studied but in the mechanics of the software itself. The ethnographer must know how to navigate the world, play the game, construct the items—whatever is needed to participate. This necessity for expertise is less pronounced in traditional physical world contexts. Bonnie has studied, among others, brain surgeons, geneticists, reference librarians, accountants, and slash-and-burn farmers. In no case did she acquire expertise in these endeavors. But in a game-oriented virtual world with eighty-five levels, the researcher must have a level 85 character to study level 85 players, since parity will typically be the only way the researcher can meaningfully participate alongside his or her higher-level informants. It is not possible to ethnographically investigate virtual world cultures without dedicated participation.

While preparation is critical, it is also true that all fieldsites have their own logics into which we are immediately drawn, ready or not. T.L., Bonnie, and Tom knew nothing whatsoever about virtual worlds when commencing their research. Even without asking, each was helped by friendly participants, a first indication of the sociality of the spaces. These early encountered players were not informants per se. Neither T.L. nor Bonnie nor Tom approached them for research input, but their gifts of advice and instruction informed the researchers about important aspects of the virtual world's cultures. Participant observation, then, may move ahead almost under its own power the moment we step into the field. It is part of the method to be receptive to unexpected experiences.

We thus do not need to have total facility in the world's activities at the outset; asking questions of other participants can be a useful way to learn about cultural norms. In classic ethnographic parlance, we must "acculturate" ourselves to the virtual world we study. An important component in becoming familiar with a world is documenting and reflecting on our own process of socialization into it. The "newbie" experience is pivotal for ethnographers, and we should not sidestep the value we gain from watching ourselves go through that process. We need to balance acquiring skills in ways that are not overly disruptive, yet allowing our novice status to work as a productive point of entry for conversation and exploration. Showing some preparation is helpful (and necessary in, for example, hard-core game cultures where entrée is impossible without it), but a willingness to learn is important as well. As we become more expert, we may at times even be asked to teach relative newcomers about the virtual world we are studying. In such circumstances learning both what people find easy to grasp and what they find difficult to master can help us better understand the virtual world culture.

Fourth, preparing ourselves for virtual world fieldwork also includes creating our embodiment as an avatar, which shapes not only our identity but our social life inworld. In most virtual worlds, some degree of avatar customization is possible. In more gaming-oriented virtual worlds, this may be limited within the boundaries of a particular race or class, decisions that may be dictated in part by the players we seek to study. Our informants will often see our choices in customizing our avatars as saying something about how we wish to be understood as a participating observer. In many virtual worlds it is also possible to change avatar embodiment as often as we like: in such cases how often and in what way we alter our avatars will shape how informants understand our presence inworld. For example, T.L.'s choice of a gnome character in EverQuest shaped her fieldwork experience. Though originally selected simply because she preferred the way gnomes looked, she discovered that their small size and stereotype as a "playful" race facilitated interactions with strangers. When she later used a female barbarian avatar, its hulking, sexualized form elicited a quite different set of initial reactions from people. Celia once gave a tour of Second Life to a researcher who randomly selected a furry avatar from the default choices, thereby unwittingly establishing himself as part of a particular culture.

As these examples indicate, we may not always have enough information in advance of entering a new world to select the optimal embodiment for our goals, and we will always reckon with the ways our avatar bodies, not unlike our corporeal bodies, carry with them various social meanings. In virtual worlds where avatar embodiment is somewhat malleable, this is less of an issue as we can adapt flexibly. But in games and worlds with fixed races and classes that cannot be changed once selected, it may be useful to do additional research before selecting a character, trying out a few different variations to find one that suits the goals of the research, and seeking counsel from prospective informants as to appropriate avatar embodiment choices for the culture being studied. On the other hand, the ethnographer must start somewhere. It is often easy to begin a new character or even alter the race and gender of a current character, so there is no need to be overly concerned as long as we find an avatar with which we are happy.

The fifth and final aspect of preparing the researching self is establishing the type of presence we wish to have within the worlds we are studying. This will vary based on the context. In some virtual worlds selecting a particular faction or server (role-playing or non-role-playing) or joining a specific group, guild, or forum will establish a certain type of presence. Bonnie, Celia, and T.L. have all joined guilds of various types in the game worlds they have studied. In virtual worlds that feature affordances for dwellings, this may entail creating a field station, which both Celia and Tom have done. A dwelling can be a component in establishing identity, as well as providing a facility in which to conduct interviews. While having a dwelling is not a requirement, it may also have the social function of sending a signal that we are there for the long term.

A final consideration is to prepare to devote substantial amounts of time to the ethnographic endeavor. Physical world ethnographers often (though not always) travel to remote locations; they are typically removed from everyday tasks and responsibilities that would otherwise compete for their time. By contrast, in studying virtual worlds, we can sit right down at a computer anywhere and engage the research. It is tempting to try to slot data collection between other obligations and activities. However, that is not how ethnography is done. We must be on the scene, immersed in local activity, if we are to understand it. We cannot miss key events (such as a guild meeting or special lecture in an educational world) just because there is something we might want to do more in the physical world. We do not know in advance when interesting things will occur inworld, and we must be present to experience them. We are trying to apprehend complex cultures, and time is required to grasp complexity. Ethnography is in some ways a brute force method in which sheer massive exposure to the culture produces the insights ethnographers seek. Simply put, ethnography demands commitment. If studying a virtual world, we must clarify with family and friends in advance that the ethnography may supersede regularly scheduled activities, or opportunities for, say, enjoyable last-minute excursions that normally we would embrace. Ethnography cannot be done on the side, nor is it an enterprise to undertake lightly.

5.4 TAKING CARE IN INITIATING RELATIONSHIPS WITH INFORMANTS

One of the most important steps in the participant observation process is to take care in initiating relationships with informants. Success in establishing rapport and trust can shape an entire research project. One common practice is to begin by reaching out to influential members of a group. For virtual worlds, this can be done via forums, by email (or private messages), or inworld. We should be upfront from the outset, explaining in clear language the goals of the research, what we want to do and for how long. We should not assume that informants understand terms like "ethnography" or "participant observation" and so should specifically describe what we plan to do. If possible, providing a link to a webpage with a description of the work can be helpful. When studying some groups we may also need to rely on group leaders to guide us as to the best way to reach out to the community, based on their own communication customs. Negotiating entrée via group gatekeepers is something that often has to be done when working with more formal organizations or groups that keep tighter boundaries around themselves. Depending on the group, we might be invited to attend a meeting or event where we can be introduced to members. We might ask the group leaders to post about our research on the group's forum, or seek permission to post ourselves. In that case we want to address issues of consent and consider the research procedures of our institution (see chapters 8 and 9 for more information on research ethics and institutional review requirements).

Some communities may not have a clear leadership structure. For instance, at the time of Tom's Second Life research, the virtual world did not have well-defined community leaders. Tom thus began by purchasing land in Second Life, learning how to use the platform to build a house, participating in as many events as possible, and building a network of acquaintances. T.L. similarly undertook her work in EverQuest by learning to become a player like any other, building up networks and eventually guild relations over time. Celia had been a beta tester in There.com before embarking on research, and she met with another game refugee community before settling on the Uru refugee group. In cases where we make entrée more informally, it is important to clearly and consistently let people know we are researchers whenever possible.

In our experience, and in the experience of many other ethnographers, it is surprising how responsive people can be to the request to be studied. It is easy to underestimate the effectiveness of showing interest in people's lives as a social scientific method. All ethnographers can testify to the raw power that accrues through authentic interest, communicated to study participants tactfully and respectfully. People often find their own lives fascinating; even when they do not, they can become interested and intrigued when a researcher expresses interest. If we explain our research clearly, participants can share in our enthusiasm to better understand their culture, becoming supportive partners in inquiry.

However, it is also possible to encounter resistance from individuals or even the majority of potential informants. Such resistance can be obvious, as when members of a community flatly refuse to be studied. But it can also be more subtle. Celia eventually gave up studying a group because they would often neglect to tell her when they were getting together to play. Although they had formally agreed to be studied, their actions demonstrated that they were not as open to being the topic of a research project as they had originally indicated. If members of a community say explicitly that they do not want to be studied, or indicate this implicitly through their behavior, it is best to back down and find another group. Additionally, even if members of a community do, on the whole, welcome us as researchers, we should respect the decisions of individuals of the community who do not want to participate. One of the many differences between ethnographers and journalists is that ethnographers do not conduct research on people who do not wish to be studied. A journalist might write an exposé on a corrupt official—and this certainly can serve a needed purpose—but for good data collection and for the ethics of the research itself, ethnographers work with informant consent (see chapters 8 and 9 for details). This means we do not study people who decline participation, and we do not report on their individual activities even when encountered through more informal participant observation techniques.

In some cases our work is enriched through interactions with "key informants," that is, individuals who prove particularly benevolent and helpful as we navigate an unfamiliar culture. In one project T.L. was fortunate to have a longtime community member who was very involved in grassroots documentation and archiving the history of the world enthusiastically embrace the research and introduce her to other key participants, as well as provide backstories about various relationships and subcultures. In the beginning this was especially helpful in getting a handle on the social terrain. When Celia experienced a crisis with her Uru participants, one of the players intervened, helping her to acclimate to the community and better understand its history. This initial encounter developed into a deeply collaborative relationship, with the informant becoming an invaluable resource throughout the remainder of the process, as well as a supportive friend. Key informants can be especially valuable when we are working in a different national culture. Kow described how a key informant guided him through the Chinese modding community, especially a chat room he was studying: "Xiao Bao, a very warm hearted Chinese modder, was chatty, fun loving, and had a way with words. He was also often present in the chatroom and talked to everyone. He turned out to be my most important guide to Chinese modding early in the research. He updated me on the latest developments in Chinese World of Warcraft, and at times encouraged others to help me" (Kow 2011).

Key informants are often socially adept, kind, and alert to the predicaments of the ethnographer. They constitute a special resource and have been a vital part of ethnography since its inception. Key informants seem to materialize on their own; it is not possible to seek them out, and not every investigation is fortunate enough to acquire such guides. When they are present they become an invaluable asset in opening up new vistas of understanding, regularly leading the ethnographer to other informants. Key informants should never be our sole data source and are no substitute for getting to know a range of people. However, they can often enhance and deepen the ethnographer's knowledge of the culture, serve as researcher advocates, and provide entrée to other informants within the community.

Finally, as we become more experienced and known within the worlds we study, we will sometimes find that we have established contacts and goodwill in communities that can also provide access to other groups and new fieldsites. Celia took advantage of her established relationships with Uru refugees in There.com to develop a new study of the University of There. Her connections with both Uru and There.com refugees in Second Life have also opened new avenues of inquiry. Developing trusting relationships with informants over time may expand the possibilities for future research.

5.5 MAKING MISTAKES

Participant observation research is not for the shy or faint of heart. It requires plunging into activities that may be unfamiliar or strange. It is essential to go with the flow and be flexible; therefore do not be afraid to participate and make mistakes. In a virtual world context we might be asked to suddenly take part in a group quest, sit in the pews at a virtual wedding, or don an outfit for a fashion show or a themed event. Through such engaged participation we learn things that could never be learned otherwise. We gather materials to shape and enrich interviews, and suggest other data collection methods that may be needed.

When engaging in such a broad range of activities, it is normal that we will make mistakes. It is important to be gentle on ourselves and pay attention: we are not the first people to whom this has happened! Indeed Malinowski himself noted how "over and over again, I committed breaches of etiquette, which the natives, familiar enough with me, were not slow in pointing out" (1922:8). Even if embarrassing at the moment they occur, such blunders can be useful. When someone shows us how we have done something wrong and how to do it correctly, we often obtain succinct explanations of some aspect of the culture we are studying.

Although it is gratifying and helpful to be invited into the life of a community, it can sometimes happen that we will be asked to participate in activities that make us uncomfortable or even raise ethical questions. How does the level of "participation" in "participant observation" vary, and with what consequences? This is a difficult issue. In principle we recommend the greatest degree of engagement possible. It is important as ethnographers to be pushed out of our comfort zones and exposed to beliefs and practices that challenge preexisting assumptions. However, total participation is not a requirement of an ethnographic approach: "immersion is not merging" (Emerson, Fretz, and Shaw 1995:35), and there may be activities in which researchers choose not to engage. Ethnographers studying marriage (in a virtual world or the physical world) need not get married themselves. We should not do something that violates our core beliefs or, in our assessment, constitutes a breach of ethical principles. There may thus be times when we will decide to politely decline to participate in an activity. In such cases informant reactions to our refusal to participate can constitute useful data.

There may also be the rare instance where our participants suggest something that may be dangerous or risky to them. Hortense Powdermaker tells the story of a black male informant in a segregated town offering her a ride in his car, a gesture that would most certainly have put him at risk of violence by the white townsfolk (1966). In this study, Powdermaker encountered another challenge, which involved her decision to address the black members of the town with the respectful "Mr." and "Mrs.," a choice that caused consternation among the white citizens. There may be times when, like Powdermaker, we are thrust into situations in which we have to consider our position with regard to a controversial issue. We want to use our best judgment and avoid, when possible, taking sides in a conflict—even if we have an ethical disagreement with some aspect of the culture. We cannot, of course, always live up to this aspiration; we kid ourselves if we think we will not prefer some individuals and groups over others, or that we will not have a personal opinion about some practice or action. Rather than deny such preferences, it is important to acknowledge them. We should be aware that favoritism may carry social consequences that can affect our position among our informants. In addition, as mentioned earlier, participants can often construe our attention as flattering and affirming, so we may want to be cautious not to create the impression that we favor certain members or subgroups over others.

While active engagement can be one of the most exciting and fulfilling aspects of ethnographic research, participant observation often involves a lot of what may seem to be "dead time." In some cases we will find ourselves hanging out with people for hours on end; the conversation might seem tedious, mundane, and uninformative. One of the most important skills ethnographers can develop is the ability to pay attention even during long stretches of apparently boring interaction. This is because at any moment the conversation could take a new turn, or some interaction or incident might occur that could provide valuable insights. Culture is not simply a series of memorable events; it exists above all in the minutiae of everyday life. What might at first seem banal could turn out to be pivotal.

Indeed, activities that take place outside the focal point of our research may provide us with a wealth of knowledge. In attending classes at the University of There, Celia instructed her research assistants to stay after class as long as students and instructors were present, as seemingly unimportant informal, post-classroom discussion often revealed interesting details about group members, teaching, or learning practices. Bonnie picked up on the texture of life in World of Warcraft by hanging around the capital cities of Orgrimmar and Ironforge. She often ran into players she knew and carried on informal conversations that revealed what players were thinking about when they played World of Warcraft. In Second Life Tom learned vital information about differing uses of "local chat" (which was public) versus "instant messages" (person-to-person private communication) by examining many examples of chat in everyday socializing whose content was not itself particularly interesting. And though situated in the offline world, T.L. learned that hanging out all day at fan gatherings, even through the lulls, proved valuable both in being seen as a real participant by others and in actually being present when unpredictable, interesting things happened. We should never use participant observation solely for the purpose of learning official accounts or formalized beliefs. While sometimes trivialized, seemingly minor chitchat such as logistics or gossip can suggest topics for later interviewing and new avenues of inquiry. Much of this informal talk happens during all that apparent downtime that constitutes an important part of participant observation.

5.6 TAKING EXTENSIVE FIELDNOTES

While it is important to prioritize participation, the "observation" aspect of participant-observation is no less important, so it is critical to take extensive fieldnotes. If we fail to write it down, it might as well not have happened! While we are sometimes fortunate to remember details and incidents after the fact, much can be lost in memory over the course of months or years. Everything is important and worthy of being documented until proven otherwise. Indeed we may not know what is important while it is happening; thus we should err on the side of over-notating.

There is a growing body of scholarship discussing the practicalities and theoretical implications of writing fieldnotes, as distinct from writing ethnographies as final products (e.g., Sanjek 1990; Emerson, Fretz, and Shaw 1995). Nonetheless, writing fieldnotes is something of a black art. In a study of ethnographers, Jackson found that most would "complain in some manner, saying they received no formal instruction in fieldnote-taking," but that they also felt that given the range of "different styles, research focuses, and fieldwork situations . . . designing a course on fieldwork and fieldnotes that will be useful for all . . . appears to be a challenge few instructors meet successfully" (1990:8). With few exceptions (Wolf 1992), ethnographers rarely include raw fieldnotes in their published work, and for good reason: it is the job of researchers during analysis and writing to select and contextualize data that will support their arguments, so that readers are not overwhelmed by a flood of detail. But if there is no one way to take fieldnotes, some general issues are certainly worthy of discussion.

When and where to actually write fieldnotes will be determined by the type of research we are doing and the activities in which we engage. In physical world ethnography, it is sometimes (though certainly not always) difficult to write fieldnotes while directly with informants, because it is disruptive or may keep the ethnographer from full participation. For ethnographers who do not take fieldnotes in front of their informants in the physical world, memory and skill with rapid note taking thus become important (see Emerson, Fretz, and Shaw 1995). A similar skill can be called on when we are absorbed in intense activity. For instance, while raiding Bonnie had to remember interesting things that occurred and jot them down during a lull in the action, typing up more extensive notes following the raid or in the morning. During very active group activities in virtual worlds (such as inworld quizzes or parties) T.L. has regularly found it most productive to make small notes during the session (often taking screenshots) and then flesh them out later. Such "scratch notes" (Ottenberg 1990:148) can be helpful in capturing key data points soon after they occur. Expanding and refining fieldnotes in this way is best done within twenty-four hours. The short-term memory is fresh; details can be recovered. After a day or so memory fades. This reality imposes a strict discipline on ethnographers in recording observations in a timely fashion.

In virtual worlds it is sometimes possible to write brief or rough fieldnotes during participant observation, to be augmented soon thereafter when offline. One approach is "two-boxing," a gaming term used to describe controlling two avatars on two computers concurrently. In terms of data collection, this entails taking fieldnotes on one computer while immersing oneself in the virtual world being studied on another. Tom used a similar technique on a single computer with two screens. While having two screens allows for real-time note taking, it becomes challenging when participating in more intensive activities (even walking across a landscape with several other people). This is a particular issue in gaming contexts: we may be engaged in a demanding activity for which removing one's hands from the keyboard could lead to disaster not only for ourselves, but for our group. In such cases it is preferable to write fieldnotes after the fact.

Unlike researchers in hypothesis-driven sciences, ethnographers collect data without always knowing its meaning or significance in advance. It can be helpful to begin by writing about recently encountered individuals and social groups, noting surroundings, interesting events, and important resources in use. We should strive to record informant statements as accurately as possible because ethnographies are more convincing if they include quotations taken from everyday interaction, in addition to those from interviews. Cultural details with a visual component—for example, architectural aesthetics, visual references to pop culture, or spatial relationships between artifacts—can provide useful insights. Such information can also appear in the form of audio or video, such as a song or the recurring use of a video clip. Streaming video may be part of a social event, or players may engage in a group dance to a particular song that is played through an avatar via the voice feature. We should document these uses of audio in our fieldnotes and note their context.

While having some priorities to guide the production of fieldnotes is important, is it also important to be as open-ended as possible. A common mistake of new ethnographers is pre-editing data as they capture it; such ethnographers might feel that an interaction is unworthy of note and thus omit vital details. It is particularly easy to fall into this habit when we are familiar with the virtual world being studied; we may be tempted to ignore or gloss over results that seem irrelevant. In Celia's research on the University of There, the frequent absenteeism of instructors at their own classes turned out to be a relevant finding, even though it seemed tangential at first.

Some ethnographers keep observational notes and their own interpretations distinct. For instance, we might not want to label an action "griefing" unless at least some participants designate it as such; however, we might note to ourselves "this seemed like griefing to me." For his Second Life research, Tom often kept observations and interpretations distinct by pasting text chat into one database field and his own commentary and reactions in another field. An example was when Tom was invited to participate in a rowdy bachelor party for a man who was to be married in Second Life the following day. Linked to the text chat from the party, Tom noted to himself "this makes me think about gender in Second Life; this is a bachelor party, but no one ever asks if the people attending are 'really' men." All of us would often commingle interpretation and basic observations, separating them with marginal notes, with typographical markers such as italics, or simply by the content of the text.

In addition to fieldnotes, virtual worlds provide unique data collection possibilities based on the software that underpins them. As discussed in chapter 7, these include chatlogs, screenshots, and audio and video recording. None of these data sources should be construed as a substitute for fieldnotes, but fieldnotes need to take them into account. For instance, if participants are communicating across several modalities concurrently, such as text, inworld voice, and external voice over IP (such as Ventrilo or Skype), it may be necessary to develop a notation system to accommodate the different streams of communication. In her study of the University of There, Celia noted that a social convention was for instructors to use voice during classes, while students would use text chat. In fieldnotes her team transcribed instructor speech and referenced or cut-and-pasted chatlogs where appropriate. Similarly, if capturing screenshots we may want to notate within our fieldnotes the set of screenshots that pertain to a particular participant observation session.

To augment fieldnotes, as well as assist in participation itself, many virtual world ethnographers also use other forms of notation. We may draw a diagram of social relations or a timeline of important events. While playing a game we might make sketches, maps, or diagrams pertaining to the completion of a quest or raid, or the solving of a puzzle. Scrapbooks of artifacts associated with the virtual world can be useful in the same way physical world ethnographers might use sketchbooks or collect small objects. These materials can become a way of helping assist and account for the journey our own inworld character takes, a crucial component of our data as we become socialized into spaces and participate in them. T.L.'s and Celia's notes are filled with Post-it notes, printouts, and scribblings associated with various aspects of character development and gameplay (things like items left to get, puzzle solutions, shortcuts, important spells and tactics, and who to contact for help making items like potions), all of which help them not only play the game, but also situate and recall details or events as they move into later stages of analysis and writing.

5.7 KEEPING DATA ORGANIZED

It is easy to become daunted by the sheer quantity of ethnographic data. If we leave organizing the data to the analysis phase, we will have a difficult time figuring out where to start and what is most important. This problem is magnified by the ease of data collection in virtual world fieldwork. We suggest that researchers begin managing and organizing data during the data collection phase, including not just participant observation data but data collected from interviews and other methods.

What we choose to record, and how, shapes our ethnographic writing. Fieldnotes can appear as "jottings" (Emerson, Fretz, and Shaw 1995:31) with short phrases and abbreviations to be elaborated later. T.L. regularly did a first pass at notes right after a session, an incident, or an event and would soon thereafter go over them to clarify, fix wording, and annotate. Tom set aside time to write fairly polished narratives if a significant event took place the previous day; at other points his notes were in a more jotting style.

Regardless of our fieldnote style, we need a consistent and recognizable convention for keeping data organized. Fieldnotes should be dated and time-stamped, with a title or short description summarizing the contents. Annotating fieldnotes is important so as not to lose track of contextual information—the setting where a conversation took place, the background leading up to a particular incident, the people on the scene, details of seasonal or temporal interest. In his fieldnotes Tom left notes to himself; for instance, "ME: notice how money is being discussed here." A later text search for "ME:" would bring up these reminders, facilitating data analysis. This kind of "in-process analytic writing" can gently initiate the stage of interpreting our data (Emerson, Fretz, and Shaw 1995:100).

Depending on note-taking style, there may also be a phase that involves writing up or compiling fieldnotes; there are a variety of possible approaches (Emerson, Fretz, and Shaw 1995). While it may not always matter if our notes are incomprehensible to others, if working on collaborative projects or with research assistants it can be important to generate fieldnotes that are legible to the group. In a team setting, going through several rounds of practice notes under the supervision of an experienced ethnographer can be used to develop a consistent note-taking style. Writing up fieldnotes can often take as much time or more, hour for hour, as conducting participant observation itself, so if using this technique it is important to factor this into the labor estimation.

Many ethnographers, going back to the classics of anthropology and sociology (Malinowski 1922; Mills 1959), have kept a separate ethnographic journal for more personal impressions and insights. Often the point is to keep these journals private, but some ethnographers include excerpts from such journals in their published work. Celia, for example, did this to give readers a personal, behind-the-scenes view of challenges, emotional responses to events, and interpersonal interactions that might be too sensitive for more general research notes (Pearce and Artemesia 2009).

One way to organize data is to use database and word-processing software packages. Such programs (like all programs) have limitations but can be helpful for integrating material into a single record. Tom would make such records for a day of fieldwork, an individual interview, or a group interview but would also make records for individual informants. He would then categorize fields, allowing him, for instance, to later search for all records annotated "economic issues" for which the world "shirt" also appeared. Celia also included chatlogs, screenshot numbers, and external links that University of There instructors used in teaching. Placing fieldnotes in a database allows for a search by various words to look for patterns, types of activity, or even an individual person's attendance at an event.

No matter how we organize our fieldnotes—using database, word processing, or qualitative analysis software, or even paper notebooks and file folders—it is important to duplicate and back up the data, storing it in more than one location. This should always include an unaltered master copy of any fieldnotes. Whether using a photocopy machine, hard drive, or online storage service, we never want to lose one word of the data we have worked so hard to acquire.

5.8 PARTICIPANT OBSERVATION AND ETHNOGRAPHIC KNOWLEDGE

Our discussion of participant observation has illustrated both the flexibility and the rigor that emerge from the apparent paradox of combining "participation" with "observation." In this context, "flexibility" refers to the ways in which ethnographers calibrate the practice of participant observation to encounters in the field, and "rigor" refers to the ways that robust ethnographic insights are confirmed by participant observation in a range of social encounters with different informants and in different contexts over time. These qualities of flexibility and rigor contribute to the central role of participant observation in ethnographic methods. However, another reason for the importance of participant observation is that, unlike other methods, participant observation is not predicated solely on elicitation; the researcher engaging in participant observation works within the everyday social context at hand. This point is missed by those who claim to do ethnographic research in virtual worlds but use only interviews; many cultural norms and beliefs are not immediately present to consciousness. This concern harks back to Malinowski's famous distinction between what people do and what they say they do, and his insistence that interviews alone are insufficient. The ethnographer needs to "put aside camera, note book and pencil, and to join in himself in what is going on" (Malinowski 1922:21). Culture is not always completely conscious, nor are all aspects of culture easily verbalized by informants; therefore, we cannot study it through elicitation alone. Malinowski observed that "the Ethnographer has . . . the duty before him of drawing up all the rules and regularities . . . of giving an anatomy of their culture, of depicting the constitution of their society. But these things, though crystallized and set, are nowhere *formulated*" (1922:11; emphasis in original). We wish to emphasize that attention to non-elicited cultural understandings does not imply ignoring subjective accounts of activities, nor does it imply that people's words are not to be trusted. Asking informants why they decided to join a guild in an interview or as part of participant observation produces important data, as does learning about their subjective understandings of what play means to them, how they think a virtual world romance shapes their sexuality in the physical world, or any other topic. Interviews are valuable—indeed indispensable—opportunities for exploring and probing meaning making, a core aspect of all cultural activity. The point is to avoid neglecting the critical parts of culture that are so taken-for-granted and habitual that informants do not reflect on them or bring them to present awareness (Bourdieu 1998). Participant observation plays a crucial role in forging a methodological practice in which we can learn about both explicit and implicit understandings of culture.

5.9 THE TIMING AND DURATION OF PARTICIPANT OBSERVATION

It should now be clear that participant observation can take an incredible range of forms and demands a generous investment of time and energy. Against the view that cultural differences are unbridgeable, participant observation allows for an exchange of perspectives; through this method, researchers can become fluent in another culture. We emphasize that "not unlike learning another language, such inquiry requires time and patience. There are no shortcuts" (Rosaldo 1993:25).

It is for this reason that we are concerned about pressures to radically shorten the time allotted for fieldwork, sometimes accompanied by phrases like "rapid ethnography" (Millen 2000) or "quick and dirty ethnography." These approaches involve marginalizing or even eliminating the participant observation component of the research. In the case of online research, they usually involve interviews paired with the analysis of websites or blogs. Such methods might be termed "rapid qualitative research," but they are not ethnographic; there is no shortcut to the investments of time and immersion required for effective participant observation research. First and foremost, ethnographers are long-distance runners; our research depends on "patient, careful, and imaginative life study, not quick short cuts or technical instruments" (Blumer 1954:10). Marcus echoes Blumer's comment, noting that "even as ethnography changes its modus operandi and its identity, there is nothing that suggests that the valuing of a patient, deliberate norm of temporality will not continue to be necessary" (2003:16–17).

Researchers often ask us, "How long should someone spend in the field?" Historically ethnographers typically considered one year the norm, or even longer. In contemporary research the amount of time can vary. If we have conducted preliminary fieldwork, or do not need to learn a new language, or are returning to a well-known fieldsite, the time necessary for participant observation may be considerably less than a year. In other circumstances—for example, some multi-sited projects—more than a year may be needed. Just as physical world fieldwork has traditionally been tied to the seasonal cycles of a given culture, we should fit our timeline to the temporal structures of those we are studying and their activities. For instance, Bonnie observed important World of Warcraft activities during holiday periods when the game included special quests and items themed to international physical world holidays (for example, Hallows End, Lunar Festival, Brewfest). Celia's work with the University of There would have been futile had she insisted on conducting the research exclusively in the summer, when most classes were not in session. While we do not want to give a strict overall time recommendation, in general we cannot imagine effective ethnographic fieldwork taking less than six months if research has not yet been conducted at the fieldsite in question. If an ethnographer has already engaged in research, follow-up studies of one to three months may be possible if the research question is sufficiently focused. For students contending with the constraints of quarters or semesters (which can be as short as ten weeks), we recommend regarding classwork as the *initiation* of an ethnographic study, a time devoted to learning the methodology and preparing for a lengthier effort. In practice, many students successfully begin ethnographic research in class that eventually results in publication, but unless one undertakes a very focused project in a familiar setting, the effort will extend well beyond an academic term.

Aside from the question of the total length of fieldwork, there is the issue of how much time to spend inworld per day. We have found it important to routinely spend several continuous hours inworld for purposes of immersion. Sometimes this is because of an event in which we wish to participate—for instance, a raid, a dance party, or a festival—but more often we simply need to be there to see what is happening in the world. It takes time to encounter things of interest. In other cases—to conduct an interview, for instance, or to catch up with a particular group of persons—a one- or two-hour chunk of time may suffice. Logging into a virtual world for a few minutes can be useful on occasion for brief activities such as checking auctions, responding to instant messages, catching up with other announcements, or learning when informants typically log in.

The times we choose to log in should reflect the patterns of our participants. If they spend time online at night or on weekends, that is when we need to log in. Groups with international members may have several gathering times based on different time zones. Overall, however, it is ideal to spend at least twenty hours a week inworld during a phase of intensive participant observation research, so that we become known to the groups and persons we are studying and can follow the nuances of the activities we observe as well as changes and critical developments. It is important to clear our schedules during this time. Because virtual world ethnography requires many hours of sustained attention, often at times that are not ideal for a balanced life, we may be required to make some personal sacrifices or compromises, just as physical world ethnographers must when spending multiple months apart from their friends and families to study faraway cultures.

5.10 THE EXPERIMENTING ATTITUDE

It is common to speak of a methodological divide between quantitative and qualitative research. In our view, however, the distinction between experimental and field research is more central to understanding the nature and value of participant observation. Participant observation can take almost any form, but the one thing it cannot be is "experimental" in the sense of hypothesis-driven controlled experiments. Nor can we endorse the idea that an ethnographer would concoct field "experiments," for instance, putting on a female avatar and seeing how people react. This would in fact be a faux experimental ploy, with neither the rigor of genuine controlled experimentation nor the contextualized knowledge of ethnographic study. It also violates the principle of avoiding deception. We thus find it ethically and methodologically disturbing that some researchers claiming to be ethnographers use deception in the name of "experimentation." In such cases, inexperienced researchers are adopting a form of what Nakamura (2002) calls "identity tourism" (sometimes seen among players), which is deeply problematic.

While ethnographic research differs fundamentally from experimental research, participant observation is predicated on an awareness that researchers engage in a kind of "experimenting engagement"—through the everyday consequences of social interaction as well as more deliberate events. For instance, the history of Bonnie's guild changed, in a minor way, because of the jokes members of the guild told while she was fumbling with the AVR modification. The incident where T.L. (and the participants) playfully put on different avatar bodies speaks to a kind of experimenting engagement as she responded to the situation with creative, interactive explorations.

For researchers using formal experimental methods, such influences might be construed as contamination. The ethnographic methodology does not, however, view the researcher this way, but instead as a valuable actor in the research process. The method allows us to learn about a culture through participation, including making mistakes. Ethnographers thus consider the engaged, embodied researcher a methodological virtue. An experimenting attitude—a sensibility of being open to, and willing to act within, the unforeseen, emergent, and contingent—is central to participant observation. Such engagement does not contaminate the research; it allows the research to go forward in deeper and more meaningful ways. Researchers are humans in authentic interaction with other humans. We must act within informants' social contexts as true selves; we are not automatons. Indeed, an experimenting attitude can often be fostered by the sense of playful possibilities many virtual worlds provide. This is not a notion of "experiment" as used in a laboratory paradigm and predicated on the controlled manipulation of variables; instead, it speaks to a phenomenological stance. We often have to experiment with forms of self-representation, entrée, and "skilling up" in a fieldsite, testing and trying out ideas in conversation with informants. In gaming settings, the notion of experimenting is central, and, as play researchers, we may find ourselves regularly inhabiting that stance.

We have dedicated this key chapter to participant observation because we cannot overemphasize that it is the central method of ethnographic research. It is the heart and soul of our work; the approach upon which all other methods, and our core analyses, depend. Effective participant observation is the path to ethnographic rigor.

CHAPTER SIX

INTERVIEWS AND VIRTUAL WORLDS RESEARCH

6.1 THE VALUE OF INTERVIEWS IN ETHNOGRAPHIC RESEARCH

Interviewing occupies an important but frequently misunderstood place in the palette of ethnographic methods. On one hand, interviews are so central to effective ethnographic research that we cannot imagine a project that did not include them, nor can we recall any published ethnographic research that did not include interviews. On the other hand, interviews in isolation are insufficient to constitute ethnographic research. While interviews are a legitimate, useful, time-tested method in the social sciences, by themselves they do not yield a corpus of ethnographic data.

We will speak of "ethnographic interviews" (or just "interviews" for short) to refer to the central kind of interviewing that takes place as part of an ethnographic research project. The term "semistructured" interview is also common and reflects the mix of preparation and flexibility that, as we discuss below, is important to effective interviewing. In some contexts more structured interviews are used—for instance, when ethnographers work as part of a team and need consistency in their interviewing.

It will be helpful to clarify the value interviews bring to an ethnographic project. In our earlier discussion of participant observation, we noted that the method allows researchers to grasp the relationship between what people "say they do" and "what they do." It is for this reason that interviewing in isolation does not constitute ethnographic research. However, we can think of three key ways in which interviewing does provide valuable data for any ethnographic project. First, while there is an important difference between people's speech and action, this does not mean that what people say they do is insignificant. The meanings people give to their actions and the world around them form an essential component of understanding. Interviews provide opportunities to learn about people's elicited narratives and representations of their social worlds, including beliefs, ideologies, justifications, motivations, and aspirations. These are part of any culture. They are emphatically not epiphenomenonal or second-order artifacts of an underlying social order; they are part and parcel of that social order and thus have causal power. For instance, official dogma and the stated views of believers are not identical with everyday religious experience but certainly influence such religious experience.

Second, while culture is not always completely conscious to its members (which is why participant observation, not predicated on elicitation, is a pivotal ethnographic method), people are aware of many aspects of their own cultures. As a result, informants can sometimes be eloquent commentators about their cultures, as ethnographers have long noted (e.g., Mead 1928; Tsing 1993). Through interviews we learn about secret histories, internal power struggles, and unofficial customs. Interviews allow researchers to study social dynamics and cultural conventions from a range of perspectives that may not always see the light of day in group interactions. Even Malinowski, the figure so identified with participant observation, "also insisted that the adequate investigation of a culture demanded . . . the natives' commentaries on action, their beliefs and ideas" (Kaberry 1957:79).

Third, while participant observation involves spending time with persons in contexts that are not always fully public (for instance, dinner at a family home or an intimate conversation among a small group of friends), interviews provide an opportunity for truly private discussions that can reveal beliefs and opinions difficult to access otherwise. People often hold views or engage in activities that they will discuss only in a one-on-one interview. T.L. found, for example, that one-on-one conversations (sometimes in participants' virtual homes, which added another layer of privacy and intimacy) allowed her to explore nuanced issues regarding how interviewees were constructing identity or sexuality through avatars, or to follow up on incidents she had seen in a public setting but was unable to explore in depth in that setting. For instance, interviews allowed her to untangle the often secret dual identities some players held through the use of "alts." The interview format offered informants a safe way of sharing behind-the-scenes understandings of identity while maintaining anonymity with regard to the community. Because Second Life residents often did not know (or even care to know) about each others' physical world identities, Tom found interviews helpful for exploring how virtual selfhood could shape physical world selfhood, including issues of gender, romance, and disability.

In regard to interviewing, we emphasize that interviews can be fruitful online or offline: people can lie or tell the truth in either context. This is one way in which "virtual methods could act as interrogators of traditional method. . . . [I]n pondering on whether a virtual interview qualifies as a real interview, we can also think more deeply about what it is that we valued about interviews as a methodological stance" (Hine 2005:10). We must take seriously the social reality of virtual environments and not treat avatar interaction as inauthentic, valid only if always corroborated with interaction in the physical world. While physical world friends and family make up a portion of an informant's virtual world interlocutors, many informants also have rich, meaningful, and enduring social interactions with people they never meet offline.

6.2 EFFECTIVE INTERVIEWING

Like participant observation, the practice of interviewing depends a good deal on the fieldsite context. However, we see some common patterns across our research projects, and those of our colleagues, that support effective interviewing. Listening is perhaps the ethnographer's single most critical skill, so for that reason we begin with seven general suggestions that also apply to physical world interviewing and then discuss five issues specific to virtual world contexts.

Articulating the relationship between interviews and participant observation

Our first general suggestion is that we should always articulate in our research design how interviews will link up to other methods, particularly participant observation. In some cases, interviews can be a good way to enter a fieldsite, gain trust, and gather basic information. In other cases, we will want to spend weeks or even a couple months conducting participant observation before beginning to interview. The two methods complement each other: interviews help identify topics to prioritize during participant observation, and participant observation helps frame questions for interviews. For instance, during interviews Tom would usually ask, "Do you have any alts?"; if the answer was affirmative, he would then ask, "What do you use alts for?" Before beginning participant observation work, however, Tom did not know that it was possible to have more than one avatar in Second Life, nor did he know that such additional avatars were commonly known as "alts" (derived from "alternates"). Alts turned out to be an important way to learn about embodiment and identity.

Developing trust and rapport

One of the key skills of an ethnographer is developing trust and rapport with our informants. This forms the basis for frank, open conversations. Our participant observation work should have already set the stage for such rapport once we begin to conduct interviews. However, even with strong rapport in place, interviews represent an opportunity to build still deeper connections. We can cover topics in more depth and draw out new insights and reflections from our informants. Spradley speaks, for example, about the ways ethnographic interviews can be thought of as "conversations into which the researcher slowly introduces new elements to assist informants to respond as informants" (1979:58). The intimacy of one-on-one interviews can also provide informants permission to speak about subjects they may not feel comfortable discussing with other group members.

A starting point for building trust in interviews is a non-judgmental attitude, reassuring informants that our aim is to gain a fuller understanding of their lifeworlds and experiences. Some participants may be suspicious because of bad press that has been propagated about their world or negative prior experiences with inexpert researchers. Make sure to let them know—through your words and behavior—that you are there undertaking a serious study to help others better understand their perspectives. Encouraging open conversation, reassuring them that there is no right answer, and providing positive feedback will all help to build the special rapport so crucial to a successful interview.

Even with informants we have not yet met, rapport can be built by association. A referral from a well-respected community member or friend of the informant can help provide a foundation for trust. Awareness and acknowledgment of the person's role in the community, whether it be as a respected creator, a forum administrator, or a guild member, will provide a basis for interview questions. Celia once interviewed an Uru community member in There.com who rarely came online when others were present, but who was the most prolific producer of Uru-themed artifacts in the community. Prior to conducting an inworld interview, Celia studied his artifacts in detail and was therefore able to ask salient, meaningful questions about the significance of his work. She also met with him in his studio/showroom where he provided a tour of his various projects, providing him with a comfort level and using his own work as a jumping-off point for discussion. Such awareness helps to validate informants and motivate them to be forthcoming and generous in sharing perspectives and knowledge. The use of objects or environments as conversation pieces can thus be useful, especially in cases where artifacts or creative practice are connected to the research. As noted above, a tour of a player-created space, for instance, can be a productive way of structuring an interview.

Prompting in-depth responses

A key aim of ethnographic interviewing is to generate in-depth responses from informants. Ethnographic interviews are sometimes termed "semi-structured" because ethnographers encourage informants to delve into the nuances and particulars of topics of interest as they arise in the conversation. To keep the informant talking, simple questions like "What else?" or "Can you tell me a bit more?" are often all that is required. When informants are interviewed for the first time, they may not understand our desire to get to the bottom of things, and that we are prepared to listen patiently for as long as needed. These open-ended prompts productively slow the conversation, allowing pauses in which informants can reflect and deliberate, bringing to mind further thoughts. In our fast-paced world we are accustomed to the simplicity of forced-answer choices in surveys, and communicating within the brevity of tweets and text messages. More than ever, informants need to know that ethnographers seek depth and nuance in answers to complex questions, and even ambiguity, as we probe for deeper insights.

The list of questions

Interviews are a flexible tool, ranging from very structured to impromptu. Many ethnographers have a short list of questions—between about three and ten—with which they carry out lengthy interviews. While it might seem one would want a longer set of questions, our experience (and that of many ethnographers) is that because we want to provide sufficient time for responses, and since one question often leads to several additional issues, a longer list is not needed. In fact, a long list of questions can have negative consequences, making researchers feel they must pressure informants into providing rushed answers.

Thus, as a guide, we might wish to develop a list of preliminary questions, arranged in a rough order, clearly marking which ones are follow-up questions to be used only if a certain answer is provided. For instance, the question "What prompted you to start creating mods?" makes sense only following a question like "Have you ever created any game mods?" Within ethnographic interviewing there are many types of questions, from those that seek descriptions or biographical data to those that prompt the participant to compare and contrast (see Spradley 1979 and Agar 2008 for extensive discussions of query approaches). Ultimately interview questions should be open-ended so as to elicit rich data, rather than "yes/no" questions that might result in a short or binary response. Often we will ask questions in a different order from how they appear on our list, to move with the informant's train of thought, following up on useful points. Or we may find that we can check questions off our list as informants answer them in the course of the conversation. Some questions may be about specific topics. The most important thing is to listen to what the informant says. We cannot know in advance the interesting things that may arise in conversation, and we have to catch the ball when it is thrown. Flexibility and responsiveness are key.

Asking about others

Another suggestion is that interviews do not have to seek information only about the person being interviewed. Many interviews include some kind of life history narrative, but members of a culture can often provide valuable insights about others. Individual claims may or may not be verifiable; however, the value of interview data is derived not from their truth narrowly conceived but from the cultural logics they reveal (which may provide ideas for further participant observation research). For instance, if in an interview someone says, "All people in Second Life care about is shopping," this obviously does not prove that every resident in Second Life cares only about shopping, but it may reveal a broader cultural assumption that shopping is common, and that the activity is stigmatized in some fashion. Furthermore, conflicting reports reveal how different people ascribe meaning to events, or how conflicts are resolved. Different versions of the same story can be highly informative, illustrating the many facets of how individuals view a collective phenomenon. At the same time we may be surprised to find how consistent our informants' opinions are on some topic. Without exception all Uru refugees that Celia interviewed for her research described being "explorers" as the hallmark of their play culture.

Asking about others can also be a way to learn about topics for which the informant may not want to reveal personal information. For example, we noted above that Tom often asked informants, "Do you have any alts?" and "What do you use alts for?" However, sometimes he asked "What do people use alts for?" This allowed people to safely talk about others when in reality they were describing their own beliefs and practices.

Impromptu interviewing

We should be prepared for the possibility of impromptu interviews that grow organically out of participant observation. For instance, we may be hanging out with a small group of people who leave one by one until we are left talking to a single person in a manner that approximates an interview. This is a reason to keep our list of interview questions handy during participant observation. Or we may work completely on the fly in this situation, generating questions that have arisen out of the context of the shared activity. Impromptu interviews may be relatively short, but we should embrace opportunities to delve into pertinent topics if they come up in informal conversations.

When an interview emerges in this fashion, stopping the flow of conversation to expedite consent procedures may be impractical; in our view the standard ethical and institutional procedures used in participant observation are sufficient (see chapter 9 for further discussion). In other words, if after an informal group discussion we are left talking to one person for an additional twenty minutes and end up asking that person two or three interview questions, it is okay to treat this as part of the participant observation encounter and not ask the person to sign a consent form. Other options are to inform the person of applicable consent procedures (particularly if the discussion becomes more involved and interview-like) or to schedule a future stand-alone interview.

Informants asking questions

Ethnographic interviews can be two-way affairs. They may present opportunities for the informant to ask questions as well as answer them; in formulating such questions, informants often reveal fundamental insights about their cultures. It is for this reason that it can be useful to ask toward the end of an interview, "Do you have any questions for me?"

Examples of responses to this question by Tom's Second Life informants show how perceptive informants can be in their engagements with ethnographic researchers:

> Well, basically just one. . . . I have read your bio. . . . I saw a bit what your line of research is and I was wondering why you suddenly started to research things like SL. For someone completely outside the field isn't it a major change? Or do you think it can be an "extension" on your line of research [in Indonesia] as well?

> Wow, I'm terrible at asking questions, but here goes. Okay, you're mixing up two agendas in SL. The research and presumably, just fun and games too. Don't you find that one affects your perceptions of the other? Since you're going at this from a research point of view, doesn't it shatter the illusion?

T.L. does something similar by asking informants about other angles she should be taking into consideration. A useful question Bonnie often asks toward the end of an interview is "What else should I know?" This question may yield surprising data, including topics that have been in the back of the informant's mind, suggesting issues to address in future interviews. For example, Bonnie was asked by players whether she thought World of Warcraft was "addictive." This question indicated that informants had concerns about spending too much time in the game, and that they had picked up certain normative notions of addiction. One group Celia was researching turned the tables by requesting an interview for their newsletter. This allowed one of the group members to represent the collective questions of the community, revealing their interests and concerns.

Allowing informants to question the ethnographer need not be left to the end of the conversation; in our experience such a sensibility can inform interviews as a whole. This is particularly the case when interviewing someone with well-developed and explicit positions regarding topics in which we are interested. T.L. often encourages informants to "push back" on her underlying framework as a way of offering them the chance to query her assumptions. She will regularly set her own position up as distanced from herself and try to allow interviewees to respond to it abstractly, for example, by saying something like "What do you think of the argument that . . . ?" One of our goals as interviewers should be to help people feel authorized to speak freely, to honor their expertise and encourage them to convey their insights to us.

These suggestions for effective interviewing are valid for all fieldsite contexts, online and offline. However, some specific issues arise with respect to interviewing in virtual worlds. We have suggestions for dealing with five of these issues, all of which are relevant to participant observation research as well.

The "person" we are interviewing

The first regards the issue of the "person" we are interviewing. The concern is not who they are in the physical world or how we can validate what they are saying. As noted earlier, questions of truth and veracity show up online and offline; it is often not possible to verify informant claims, nor is it typically necessary to do so, since we are interested in cultural meanings and practices and can usually confirm broad patterns through participant observation and interviews with other informants.

The relationship between a physical world person and an online avatar can be complex. T.L. has pointed out that residents of virtual worlds have multiple bodies and plural existences (Taylor 1999). Because virtual worlds often allow several avatars to be attached to the same account (or allow persons to have more than one account), players and residents may frequently switch avatars, for example, to gain a desired raid configuration, or to engage in activities they do not want associated with their primary avatar identity. Conversely, a single avatar may be shared by several physical world individuals. Celia once encountered a teenage boy in Lineage who shared his (female) avatar with his stepmother. Because the boy had confided in Celia about his home life, she was always careful to double-check which physical world person was inhabiting the avatar. In another case a married couple in There.com initially presented as opposite genders but eventually switched avatars to match their offline genders when voice was introduced to the world. Subsequently they would occasionally appear in their original cross-gender avatars. Gender swapping is not uncommon in virtual worlds, and disclosure may vary depending on the context. Worlds in which participants use voice can complicate gender swapping.

How should we approach these multiplicities of identity? The best policy is to follow the social conventions set down by participants. If two avatars of the same person are treated as a single person, we should follow suit; likewise if they are treated as different people. If a female avatar we know to be inhabited by a male person is treated as a woman and addressed as a female, then we should do the same. If in interviews the topic of physical world versus virtual world identities should arise, we may naturally pose some questions to clarify the relationship between the two. Physical world and virtual world identities may intertwine in various complex ways. How we address these issues depends on our research questions.

Textual listening

Another issue regarding interviewing that is more specific to virtual worlds regards becoming a more astute "textual listener." While most virtual worlds now have the option of voice, many participants continue to use text chat in many social contexts, and text chat is useful for interviews. Some virtual world participants may be more comfortable being interviewed in text for various reasons. They may feel it allows them to speak more freely or provide more reflective answers than would be the case in a physical world interview, or even a virtual world interview using voice. They may prefer to maintain anonymity in terms of gender, nationality, or age. If they are not native speakers of the language we are using for research, they may be more comfortable typing; additionally, some players may prefer typing because of a disability. In any case, textual communication remains common. Textual listening is a skill that is unique to online research and requires an understanding of the nuance and conventions of online communication.

When text is involved there are fewer conventional cues, such as volume, tone and inflection of voice, or gaze. Such diminishing cues can make it harder to determine who is speaking to whom, on what topic, and with what degree of emotion. However, virtual world participants often develop rich textual communication practices to which we should be attuned. Most persons using text chat rapidly become conversant in a wide range of typographical conventions, such as the use of emoticons and emotes to express emotions (e.g., :) , lol), names to direct a comment (e.g., "lol @ Tom"), symbols to indicate misspellings (e.g., nice mouse/*house), or capital letters to indicate shouting, to name only a few. It is also a common convention to use slash commands to express actions, such as "/me rolls eyes." In most virtual worlds such an entry will show up as an action in the text chat along with spoken utterances. Additionally players in some worlds have elaborate mechanisms for drawing pictures using text characters, recalling "ASCII art" that was prevalent in non-voice online contexts. Attention to these various social conventions should also be considered forms of textual listening.

Conversations between two people can contain multiple threads where various topics are being woven together. Sometimes typists will use ". . ."

at the end of a long line to signal a thought is not finished. But just as often multi-threading occurs. This common practice requires a slight shift in how we think of standard turn-taking. Though generally both parties are adept at cycling through various parts of the conversation, we may at times want to slow down the pace to make sure we do not breeze past a particularly interesting comment too quickly.

The pace of real-time text communication is, indeed, very different from oral communication. Typing cadence can be an issue. We may be faster typists than some of our informants, so it is important to pause when necessary to allow those with whom we are conversing sufficient time to reply. We should be alert to typing patterns; for example, T.L. once noticed an increase in typographical errors during an interview that turned out to reveal that the informant was getting excited about a topic and typing more quickly. Some virtual worlds visually indicate when a participant is typing (for instance, the default setting in Second Life is that an avatar's hands mime a typing motion). During an interview Tom once noticed that the typing animation was appearing for an extended period, followed by only the short statement "yes, that's true." It turned out that the informant had typed out a partial answer to a question but then deleted it to write something else. A follow-up question revealed what the informant was about to state before the hesitation.

Some of these conventions are common across a wide range of virtual worlds (and beyond, into social networks, blogs, and even email); others can be specific to a virtual world or even a small group within a virtual world. Learning these conventions is important to effective interviewing when using text.

Multiple conversations during an interview

A third issue is that in many cases, informants are carrying on other conversations during the interview. This is a significant difference from most physical world interviewing. In most virtual worlds it is possible to have textual (and sometimes voice) chat with individuals or groups that is not visible to those around us. We could be interviewing someone in what appears to be the calm quiet of a virtual world house, with no avatars nearby, but the informant is engaging in text chat with other persons or groups without our knowledge. In some cases they might just be saying "please don't bug me right now, I'm being interviewed!" In other instances they might be involved in a more substantive discussion. Regardless, this means that we should be prepared for pauses and lapses when an informant might not seem to be responding to our questions.

We must be patient, not least because we as interviewers will also often be receiving messages from others while we are interviewing, and we may feel compelled to respond to those messages, even briefly, so as not to cause confusion or offense. To help address these issues we may choose to use some form of closed group chat or instant messaging, so at the very least other avatars nearby cannot overhear the interview, but issues of side conversations during an interview may well persist.

The relative lack of facial expressions and gestures

While text chat in virtual worlds creates new possibilities and challenges for interviewing, the relative lack of facial expressions and gestures constitutes an issue of which we should be aware. Some virtual worlds continue to become more lifelike, with ever-increasing graphical realism. Others have become more simplified so that they are easy to use and can be accessed without a dedicated client program (or even be embedded in a social network site like Facebook). Even in the case of more photorealistic virtual worlds, however, facial expressions and gestures remain rudimentary. In some cases they are automated so that avatars will laugh when the word "funny" appears in their chat bubbles or will shift their arms and legs at random intervals. Though sometimes customizable, such gestures can be misleading since they do not represent individually user-controlled actions but are instead automated animations. There are usually ways to control avatar gestures, but they remain basic and typically require extra keystrokes or commands that most virtual world residents forgo unless there is a specific reason to use them. As a result, when interviewing we often lack the kinds of nonverbal cues that can be extremely useful in physical world interviewing. The location of a virtual world interview can carry meaning, as can basic proxemics—are we sitting next to our informant across a table, or side by side on the ground? Overall, however, we may have to rely more on linguistic cues (be they voice or textual). Additionally, in many virtual worlds gestures or animations that are user controlled look different from those that are automated, and we should learn to recognize the difference.

Lag and interviewing

Finally, when interviewing in virtual worlds we must be prepared to deal with lag (when things slow down or freeze up because of problems with internet connectivity or computer processing). In some forms of online research (for instance, when using email) interviewing is asynchronic, based on the exchange of messages that can be separated by hours or even days (Kivits 2005). When conducting interviews in a virtual world context, we have the advantage of synchronic interaction, but this makes lag a new concern. If severe, it may take a while for an informant's typed answers to be visible to us, and informants might experience a similar delay in seeing our questions. If using voice, we might have to switch to a third-party program like Skype or continue the interview using only text. Lag can be mitigated by adjusting settings such as graphical quality or going to a location with fewer avatars or complex structures. However, it can happen that the problems become so severe that we, our informant, or both crash out of the virtual world entirely. When this happens the avatar can sometimes remain in a "ghosted" fashion, seemingly present, but unresponsive since the person is no longer inworld.

When loss of connectivity occurs, it is always best to log back into the virtual world as soon as possible to let the informant know we are okay and check on them, then either complete or reschedule the interview. If we have the email addresses or other contact information of our informants, when appropriate we can of course contact them in another fashion to touch base. In some cases informants have dedicated email accounts for their avatars, so communicating via email poses no specific concerns in regard to confidentiality. Others may use group forums with messaging capabilities that also do not reveal physical-world identities. If informants are already accustomed to such forms of communication, we can employ them to touch base after an interview is interrupted, or even to ask a follow-up question: "the ability to read, reread, and then respond to someone line by line via e-mail can be very productive . . . [but] it is important to be receptive early on to the medium any particular respondent will be most comfortable with" (Taylor 1999:444). In some cases it may be possible to conduct an interview using only email or some other asynchronic mode of communication, if we already have a strong relationship with the informant through participant observation in the virtual world context.

6.3 THE VALUE OF GROUP INTERVIEWS IN ETHNOGRAPHIC RESEARCH

In the previous chapter we discussed the central methodology of ethnographic research—participant observation—and in this chapter we have examined the important method of interviewing. We cannot imagine legitimate ethnographic fieldwork that does not include both of these methods. Group interviews (also known as "focus groups") are less central to the ethnographic repertoire. While some researchers have expressed concern about their being less "naturalistic" than other methods (Morgan 2001), they can be a useful form of data gathering to complement other methods in a virtual world ethnographic study, prompting conversations often not found in one-on-one interviews.

Group interviews originated in the business world for market testing and research in the 1950s (Krueger 1994), particularly from the work of Robert Merton (Kratz 2010). Beginning in the 1980s group interviews moved into the social sciences, including in human-computer interaction (HCI) research, as a method for testing new products and interfaces. For instance, Celia was first exposed to group interviews through her work in the museum and attractions field. In that context they were used to explore the interests and tastes of target markets, get feedback from prospective customers regarding sample branding and content, and discuss results of game prototype playtests.

To better identify the methodological niche group interviews occupy, we can briefly review the strengths of participant observation and individual interviews. Participant observation is vital to ethnographic research because it provides non-elicited data about social and cultural lifeworlds in the moments of their enacting. It allows the researcher to see how practices and beliefs shape each other in contexts of everyday interaction. In contrast, individual interviews are important for ethnographic research because they allow us to ask specific questions of individuals that may not come up in everyday interaction. They allow the researcher to learn about shared history and consciously held ideologies and beliefs, so as to better understand these continuities and divergences.

In a sense group interviews lie between these two methodologies. Like individual interviews, group interviews create new social situations and can be used to ask specific questions but do not reveal much in the way of cultural practices (though when carried out in virtual worlds, there may be interesting opportunities for embodied demonstration and play). Like participant observation, group interviews allow for comparison within a culture, eliciting diverse opinions. As discussed earlier, debate and multiple viewpoints are aspects of all cultures, and we should attend to the range of these differences.

Group interviews allow informants to engage with each other, not just the researcher, and can thereby foreground both common and divergent beliefs (Schensul 1999). T.L. had several very productive group interviews—both online and at a fan convention—in which the interplay and conversation between participants provided lively data given their history and relationships with each other (many of which predated T.L.'s arrival inworld). Celia complemented her Baby Boomer gamer survey with online group interviews. This allowed players to compare their first experiences with video games, which turned out to vary significantly by generational cohort. Tom used group discussions in Second Life; among their many benefits, they revealed how residents understood aspects of Second Life culture. In short, group interviews "seek both to capitalize on the ways that cultural categories, values, and social relations become apparent through conversation and interaction and to control that knowledge production by maintaining a central topical focus and defining a foreshortened period for discussion" (Kratz 2010:806).

Group interviews can also be employed to learn important history about a culture, not least because members of the group interview can correct each other's memories or collectively produce a history. In one virtual world T.L. studied, it was not unusual in group situations for people to also use digital artifacts in the world, pulled out of their "virtual pockets" on the spot, to help move a story or critical point forward. It is important to remember that the social production of knowledge can take place across a range of cultural contexts; group interviews allow us to tap into those interconnections in a very immediate way. They can additionally help unpack community practices and conventions. For instance, in her Uru research Celia was particularly interested in collaboration. Online group interviews with Uru community leaders helped her better understand their management style, both by observing their interactions and by noting the content of their conversations.

6.4 SIZE, STRUCTURE, AND LOCATION FOR GROUP INTERVIEWS

Like individual interviews, group interviews can vary in the degree to which they are structured, including their size. Classic group interviews typically have around ten participants. We have conducted effective group interviews with as many as forty participants, but issues arise when a focus group gets larger than around twenty. This is because group interviews function best when participants can identify each other. Collections of five hundred or even fifty persons thus constitute group interviews in only a limited sense. Indeed, it is sometimes most useful to have group interviews with less than ten participants—even as few as the definitional limit of two participants. In her University of There research, for instance, Celia conducted an offline interview of a mother and daughter at the mother's home, where they frequently collaborated on virtual world projects.

In the physical world researchers have historically conducted group interviews as single or multiple sessions in which participants meet either in an informal location like a community center or home or in a more formal laboratory, office, or researcher's field station. In some cases it can be useful when some or all the participants in a group interview already know each other, but group interviews in which participants are meeting for the first time can also yield useful data (though usually more about more public issues than intimate concerns). In its least structured form, something like a group interview can emerge spontaneously from participant observation work: "like participant-observation and life-history interviews, group discussions can resemble and be part of more natural daily settings and interactions" (Kratz 2010:806). For example, Celia once stumbled into a spontaneous discussion among Uru refugees in There.com about the existential relationship between There.com and Uru. This discussion eventually took on the characteristics of a loosely organized group interview. Group interviews that are part of an ethnographic study are less likely to take place in formal settings. Some of Celia's group interviews, for instance, took place at one of her field stations within the Uru communities in There.com. Online group interviews were conducted in private chat so that participant responses could not be overheard by avatars in the surrounding area. T.L. had one of her most useful group interviews in someone's physical world hotel room where a handful of people had gathered after the evening's formal program was over. With participants seated on the floor and bed, the informality of the space brought out an open, conversational tone in which they were just as engaged with talking with each other as with directing their attention to T.L. as a formal interviewer.

From his participant observation work, Tom learned that "events" were a common feature of Second Life culture during the time of his research, and that one form of event was a weekly discussion group. Tom then created the group "Digital Cultures" and held weekly meetings at his home in Second Life, Ethnographia. When announcing each upcoming meeting, Tom would post a theme (for instance, "trust," "disability," or "love"), as well as a prompt. For example, for the April 23, 2007, meeting, entitled "SL/RL," Tom provided the following prompt:

> As its very name suggests, Second Life is related to what we usually call real life or first life. . . . What are the relationships between Second Life and the physical world? What about relationships between Second Life and other aspects of online life: other virtual worlds, online games, and things like blogs and websites? When we move back and forth, in and out of Second Life, what changes? What does not?

User forums, email lists, and other forms of online interaction can sometimes act as venues for a group interview. For example, for her Baby Boomer gamer study Celia conducted a group interview via a forum in which she asked participants to reflect on the reasons certain play preferences were emerging. A lively conversation ensued, which included participant theories about relationships to historical events like wars, as well as media consumption habits.

Because forum-based group interviews do not take place within a virtual world, data gathered from them must be extrapolated to their associated virtual worlds with caution. Not all residents of any virtual world will participate in such forums "beyond the platform"; on occasion participants in such forums may not even be active residents. With these caveats in mind, however, a group interview taking place though a user forum can be valuable in many ways. They can be used to coordinate an inworld group interview and can also allow group interview discussions to take place in an asynchronic manner, with members posting contributions over a period of time. This mitigates the problems of coordinating schedules and accounting for differing time zones.

Because group interviews can foreground so clearly the social interactions and shared meanings of a culture, we should pay particular attention to how the deeply social context of the group interview shapes our data. Morgan (2001) for example, cites a study by Wight (1994) in which teenage boys in individual interviews indicated high sensitivity to girls' expectations in relationships. The same boys in a group setting with the same interviewer, however, exhibited a much more macho attitude, bragging about their ability to manipulate girls. Celia recounts a similar story told to her by two separate game company executives in which adolescent boys in group interviews initially denied playing The Sims, later reluctantly admitting that they had played (and liked!) the game, which has often been compared to a "dollhouse." While such examples may seem to question the validity of data from group interviews, we would reframe the issue. If one was, for example, particularly interested in public versus private configurations of gender identity and performance, the comparison of data from these two different modes would be quite beneficial, although both modes of interviewing would be required to elicit the nuances.

Owing to the deeply social nature of group interviews, we should keep in mind issues of power inequality between participants. While in many instances the interviewer may decide that conversation among a heterogeneous group will be feasible and valuable and thus seek a mixed selection of participants, there will be times in which a more homogeneous group makes sense. For instance, depending on the topic, some researchers prefer to segregate group interviews by gender, age, class, or other relevant factors. In terms of virtual world research, Tom found that "newbies" in Second Life, even if they were older adults in the physical world, tended to defer to those with more inworld experience. To ensure that the experience is as productive for everyone as possible, before setting up group interviews we should therefore give careful thought to how the various internal dynamics we have observed in the field are likely to influence the group interview dynamic.

For all these reasons, we cannot overemphasize the importance of good moderation of group interviews. It is the ethnographer's job as facilitator to ensure that different opinions get expressed and everyone has the opportunity to contribute. This is particularly the case with more open group interviews where anyone can show up and attend. In such cases the moderator must stay attuned to the conversational dynamic as participants come and go. Being prepared to handle a dominant personality who can easily overtake the conversation is also key. To manage the conversation, it can help to use techniques like (gently) inquiring if a quiet participant would like to respond to a specific point, or taking a more vocal member's statement and using it as a jumping off point for others to consider (versus allowing the vocal member to continue to dominate). Good group interviewing involves a delicate balance of providing enough guidance to keep a productive conversation going among *all* members while staying out of the way enough to let the participants meaningfully shape the group interview itself.

These examples illustrate the important point that, like all the methods we discuss in this handbook, group interviews should not be taken in isolation but be used in combination with other methods, depending on the context. As part of an ethnographic palette, they should be used in concert with participant observation.

6.5 TRANSCRIPTION

When audio interviews are part of the corpus, a key issue is transcription. For some researchers transcription is solidly located in the data collection phase of a project; for others it resides in a later period of full-fledged data analysis. In this section we discuss the mechanics of transcription—how to get it done and done right—but important issues of analysis may also arise during transcription, which we discuss in section 10.6.

Some researchers advocate full, word-for-word transcription of every interview. Such a complete record is of immense value to them. Extensive transcription requires careful planning; it is time consuming and/or expensive. In our experience at least four hours of transcription are required for each hour of conversation, and double that time if translating from another language. While undertaking transcription requires a significant time investment, we particularly encourage new researchers to do this work themselves. It is important, especially as we develop skills as ethnographers, to cultivate a feel for the special qualities of an interview conversation (watching cross-talk, leaving enough silent spaces for an interviewee to fill, asking good follow-up questions). The hard work of transcription not only brings us close to the material we need to analyze, it offers an opportunity to reflect on our own technique by paying careful attention to it after we have a bit of distance.

Once we have become adept at interviewing and transcribing, we may find it beneficial to hire a professional or student to transcribe some or all of the interviews. This can obviously save an enormous amount of time during the data analysis phase and, in the case of bringing students onto a project, offers aspiring researchers the chance to see what ethnographic work entails. However, several issues must be considered.

A core ethical value underpinning our work is ensuring the anonymity of participants. If outsourcing our material for transcription, we must do so in a way that ensures confidentiality. If we are working with students or others in the university, there is likely a much stronger shared framework, grounded in accepted institutional norms of confidentiality. We can also retain more control of the original tapes or audio files by requiring the work be done on-site. If, however, we decide to use an outside professional service, we should consider developing a clear legal document (via something like a nondisclosure agreement) that our transcriber can sign. It should specify the deletion of any audio files and associated materials after the work is completed.

If we use transcribers, they must be instructed in the lingo and jargon they will hear in the interviews, which can be considerable in virtual worlds research. Online colloquialisms and slang can confound an outsider and should be carefully explained to transcribers. Both T.L. and Bonnie provide a list of all the terms they can think of before the transcriber begins, and they discuss words the transcriber does not understand as they arise on a case-by-case basis. Depending on the situation, providing a list of words may not be sufficient, and the researcher should be attentive to the level of cultural insight required to transcribe. Transcribers may need to be trained to the nuances of a given subculture. In some cases this may not be possible. This is a common problem in physical world ethnography as well. For instance, the interviews of gay Indonesians collected by Tom made use of specific slang terms that even most Indonesian speakers outside the gay community could not transcribe, and thus Tom had to do all transcriptions himself.

Given issues of funding, language, and time, the general principle is that the researcher should listen to all audio-recorded interview data and obtain full transcripts. When full transcription is impractical, partial transcription—transcribing only key passages—can produce good results. Of course, knowing what counts as "key" is part of the art of data analysis. In this sense full transcription is easier because decisions do not have to be made while transcribing. It is important during partial transcription to take notes linked to time-points in the interview, for example, "identity is discussed at [5'33"]" (five minutes and thirty-three seconds into the interview), to facilitate retracing potentially useful passages not transcribed at the outset. Such time markers are useful in full transcriptions as well.

Whether undertaking partial or full transcription, some basic procedures will make transcribing easier if we are doing it ourselves. A foot pedal allows us to start, stop, speed up, and slow down the audio without removing our hands from the keyboard. A good pair of headphones can also be helpful, as interviews are not always recorded in perfect conditions—even virtual world interviews sometimes take place in contexts where there is background noise. If such noise is significant enough to make understanding the audio difficult, we can often mitigate the problem by changing our equalization settings or, if a digital audio file, running the file through the noise reduction filters included in many audio software packages. There are also transcription programs that automatically turn voice into text; we have never used such programs. They should, however, be used with caution and their output double-checked by hand because they are often idiosyncratic to specific voices and are not good at handling puns or double entendres, unconventional words, different languages, or slang.

A key issue is consistent transcription procedure. This includes deciding how to handle hesitations in voice interviews (like "umm"), as well as pauses, laughter, and unintelligible words. It is best to stick to a single convention; sociolinguists have detailed and useful protocols for transcription (e.g., Milroy and Gordon 2003). Whether we record each pause and hesitation depends on our research objectives; most researchers do so only for specific passages, as transcribing every detail in this fashion is unnecessary for most analyses. If one is trying to get a feel for emotional topics, pauses and hesitations may be revealing. If one is just gathering data on when a player started to play and how many avatars they have, such detail is likely to be irrelevant and will clutter the transcript.

One challenge in transcribing with regard to contemporary online communities is multi-modal communication. While interviews may be conducted in voice or text chat, there are many circumstances in which participants use multiple forms of communication concurrently. Because some members were unable to type owing to disabilities, for instance, some of Celia's informants used text chat in group interviews while others used voice. When text and voice communication are taking place simultaneously in an interview, a helpful practice is to take notes on what is being said verbally as the interview progresses with chatlog notations, and then later integrate the saved chatlog into the interview transcript.

A few additional notes are in order about some specific issues in dealing with group interviews. While those conducted only in text chat offer ready-made transcription because virtual world platforms list the speakers before each line of text they type, they can be made more complex by conversational "threading," where multiple discussions overlap. When the group interview is in audio form, it can pose some unique challenges, particularly if there are more than two or three participants. It may be hard to tell who is speaking at any given point; when participants get excited and drawn into debates, they may interrupt or speak over each other. When conducting audio interviews, it is often helpful to take notes in real time, to capture the nuance of interaction and to disambiguate between speakers. Used on their own or in conjunction with transcriptions, such notes can help resolve confusions that arise in audio-only recordings. While video recording can help untangle these issues of multiple voices, it requires more data storage and may raise ethical issues (see chapter 8).

CHAPTER SEVEN

OTHER DATA COLLECTION METHODS FOR VIRTUAL WORLDS RESEARCH

While we have emphasized participant observation and interviews as central to ethnographic research, ethnographers frequently augment these methods with other forms of data collection. Virtual worlds provide special affordances for certain types of data capture (some of which are shared with other online contexts). This ease of data capture can sometimes create the false impression that the methods enumerated earlier, such as taking fieldnotes based on participant observation, are unnecessary. Why go to all that trouble when we can just capture the data digitally? This temptation is false: we cannot stress enough that as useful as digital records are, they cannot stand alone without the rigor of a detailed accounting of interactions in the field.

When automatically capturing data such as chatlogs, screenshots, video, or audio, data should be labeled, date- and time-stamped, and stored in the appropriate file. Many of the data collection tools discussed in this chapter will automatically label digitally captured data, but some will not. At the very least we need to specify a file destination; in some cases, we may also need to specify file names so that we do not find ourselves sifting through an endless set of documents entitled "screenshot" or "chatlog" to find the material we seek. We also highly recommend the important precaution of backing up data, on either an external server or a hard drive. A personal computer hard-drive failure can mean the instant evaporation of numerous hours of hard work.

7.1 CAPTURING CHATLOGS

One of greatest boons to the online ethnographer is chatlogs. Chatlogs can easily be saved and parsed in a variety of analytically useful ways. Chatlogs usually include time stamps, so the time of every chat comment is known, allowing for fine-grained analysis. Some virtual world software automatically saves chatlogs or can be adjusted in settings to do so. Some programs use a key command, while others require cutting and pasting into a word processing or text file. In the first years of Second Life's existence, the software would automatically record and save everything typed within thirty virtual meters of an avatar, but these chatlogs had to be cut and pasted into an external world processing program. In World of Warcraft complete logs of chats could be recorded simply by typing "/chatlog." Uru used a similar command. There.com chatlogs were automatically saved to a file within the client folder. It is important to ensure that chatlog files are accurately labeled with date and time so they can be connected to fieldnotes and other related data during analysis. While some of the virtual worlds we studied labeled the chatlogs in this manner, others saved them simply as "log1, log2," so we should not assume that the software will automatically do this work for us. (In some cases automatically saved chatlogs overwrite each other.) We also suggest directing saved chatlogs to a specific folder so they can easily be found when needed.

Chatlogs may end up containing a wide range of intermingled ethnographic data—from formal interviews to informal conversations and environmental data generated by the virtual world software (e.g., "Wizard casts firebolt"). The danger is that this blessing of automated data collection becomes the curse of data burdened with so much tangential information that key points or vignettes are difficult to retrieve. In some virtual worlds this process can be managed by selecting only those features of chats we wish to see in a chat window.

At the moment of data collection, it is not always clear what will be done with chatlogs, but eventually such data will likely prove useful. For example, in Bonnie's research on World of Warcraft, chatlogs piled up for months before she began to focus on topics of collaboration, learning, and player-generated culture. The chatlogs contained a wealth of data on these topics. She was able to document many things, including the average amount of time that elapsed before a question in chat was answered (Nardi, Ly, and Harris 2007). In Celia's study of the University of There, chatlogs helped her understand how social conventions emerged within the classroom, as well as the discursive dynamics of collaboration in staff meetings.

7.2 CAPTURING SCREENSHOTS

Screenshots can be an important aspect of data collection. Visual ethnography has a long history, and the context of working within an environment constructed entirely of software opens up new opportunities for the use of visuals. We should keep in mind the same cautions for screenshots as photographs—that they "are most usefully treated as representations of aspects of culture; not recordings of whole cultures or of symbols that will have complete or fixed meanings" (Pink 2007:75). Capturing images is not a shortcut for interpretive or analytic work. Photos or screenshots are never simply representations of objective social facts. That said, they can be incredibly rich data points as a source of in-depth analysis when used in the context of other materials.

Screenshots can be particularly useful if our work concerns visual culture, such as artifacts or aspects of movement in space. They can help illustrate an observation or show the appearance of the virtual world we are studying. They can jog our memories, reminding us about a significant event or issue. A screenshot, for instance, can provide an instant summary of who was present at an event or help us recall patterns of movement and visual details. We can also use screenshot analysis to provide a visual explanation of cultural phenomena. One of Celia's students used annotated screenshots extensively in a master's thesis about the appropriation of space by role-players in World of Warcraft; the screenshots were color coded to show the function of different areas (Chan 2010). T.L. has made extensive use of screenshots in documenting fieldwork over the years and branched out in one project to include asking participants to take screenshots of their own user interfaces to give to her when she began exploring modding in World of Warcraft.

Because they are easy to capture unobtrusively and can be used for a range of analytical purposes, screenshots can quickly become daunting in terms of sheer numbers. Many virtual world platforms allow users to take screenshots, and there are external programs for this purpose as well. Some programs stamp each image with the date and time, which makes it easier to correlate the screenshots with fieldnotes and chatlogs. Other software may require manual labeling. If we take screenshots to accompany particular sets of chatlogs or interviews, we should collate and organize them with descriptive file names.

An additional practical consideration regarding screenshots is protecting the privacy, confidentiality, or anonymity of those in them. (See chapters 8 and 9 for more in-depth definitions of these terms.) Avatar names can be hidden in most virtual worlds through settings by turning off nametags, or after the fact with the use of an image-alteration software program. Depending on how much customizability there is in the world, we may also need to consider how distinctive and recognizable people are (as avatars) and filter this into our consideration of confidentiality.

Even if avatars are not completely distinguishable, we will also want to consider the type of activity and how the person might feel to see his or her avatar publicly shown in the act being depicted.

7.3 CAPTURING VIDEO

Depending on research goals, we may want to use video recording as part of our data collection strategy. In some cases a virtual world will have video capability built into the software; in others an external program may be either necessary or preferred (because, for example, it allows for more control over the details of the video capture or causes less lag). Video enables us to create a record of participant observation for later coding or presentation purposes. Video capture can have many benefits, especially if we are observing activities in which the timing of events is important. For example, Bonnie was interested in how text moved across the screen during raiding in World of Warcraft, something most easily analyzed with a video record. She created a ten-minute clip out of which she typically uses one or two minutes for analysis and presentation.

Physical world video is subject to ethical and practical problems not unlike those faced by still photography (Mackay 1995; Pink 2007). The camera, much like the ethnographer at the outset of fieldwork, is not a natural object in the field; we must remain alert to the possibility that participants may overact or feel self-conscious in the camera's presence. We must also take care when considering the anonymity of participants, especially when recording in public spaces.

Video recording in the virtual world space does not bypass ethical issues. We can consider, for example, how issues of capturing natural behavior are shaped when the camera moves to the virtual world. Because there is no visible video camera (unless the act is graphically symbolized, as Jakobsson (2006) did by adding a camera to his avatar when he recorded), virtual world informants do not have the sensation of being "on camera," with all its cultural implications and scenarios. Physical world ethnographers who use recording equipment face a careful process of naturalizing the camera among subjects, as it transitions from an artifact that may be played to or hidden from to an ambient part of the environment. Virtual world ethnographers who are recording inworld generally do not face the same challenge because of the de facto invisibility of the process.

Ethically the obligation remains that the ethnographer explain that video is being recorded. The anonymity of participants should be considered if the video will be used in public lectures or disseminated in other ways. If labels such as avatar names are removed (as for screenshots) and the distinctiveness of the individual avatar is minimal, the identity of the person behind the avatar can remain anonymous. On the other hand, there may be situations where the avatar's appearance is quite easily identifiable as an individual. As with screenshots, we cannot presume that just because we are recording avatars there are no issues with protecting confidentiality. Very often the links between offline identities and inworld avatars either have been made explicit by community members or could be pieced together with some simple sleuthing. As with all potentially identifying material, we should take special care in considering the anonymity of participants.

A few practical caveats regarding video are in order. Proper equipment is needed. Video recording slows graphics processing and may hobble the ethnographer's experience to such an extent that it impedes data collection. Video requires a large amount of data storage, and an additional hard drive will probably be needed. Video may be time-consuming to analyze in comparison to other data sources, depending on what is being analyzed. For Celia's study of the University of There, the original intent was to video record all participant observation sessions; however, this idea was scrapped after testing revealed that it would be untenable with the human resources available. Data transfer alone would have taken hundreds of hours and would have detracted from activities more central to the analysis, such as participant observation and fieldnote transcription. Thus video may best be used selectively.

7.4 CAPTURING AUDIO

As noted in chapter 2, early virtual worlds (MUDs) were composed entirely of text; historically many graphical worlds, from Habitat to Second Life (2003–2007), had only the possibility of text chat. However, while there is no reason why virtual worlds in which communication takes place only via text could not persist into the future, a trend is for virtual worlds to have the capability for voice chat built into them. In addition, many participants use third-party VoIP software. As a result, audio capture can be an important aspect of virtual world ethnographic data collection.

If participants use voice, we should be ready to do so ourselves in our participant observation and interviews. In many cases voice may be used only in certain situations (for example, specialized activities such as raiding) or when the persons involved are already familiar with each other.

Sometimes the ethnographer may be listening concurrently to inworld voice and external VoIP communication.

In addition to voice, ambient virtual world sounds, from footsteps to wind, can play an important role in social interactions within a virtual world (for instance, letting people know of the presence of an avatar behind them). Music is common in virtual worlds, from soundtracks in games to internet radio streamed into clubs in virtual worlds such as Second Life. Live music performances may occur. Capturing these forms of audio can be useful in developing a robust ethnographic archive.

Without the benefit of visual cues, a purely audio file can be confusing to analyze after some time has passed and the researcher no longer recalls the details of what was taking place during the recording. This is especially the case when what was recorded was not an interview but a stretch of participant observation during which persons may have arrived and left, the researcher may have moved to different areas of the virtual world in question, and so on. For this reason it is essential to note when and where the audio was recorded. It is usually better to keep a separate file noting additional details including the names of persons present, events that took place during the recording, and so on.

7.5 DATA COLLECTION IN OTHER ONLINE CONTEXTS

Although virtual world participants may interact exclusively through the virtual worlds they jointly inhabit, many extend their engagement to other sites, including forums, FAQ repositories, blogs, wikis, guides, videos, email, Facebook, Twitter, instant messaging, podcasts, other virtual worlds, and gaming databases. Even if being "in" World of Warcraft or Second Life is the fundamental relation to the virtual world, participants often spend time on associated websites or follow friends to other virtual worlds. For the diasporic cultures studied in Celia's work, where a play community was distributed across multiple games and virtual worlds, player-created forums became a home base that transcended the presence or absence of any given game or world. T.L.'s work on EverQuest showed a rich construction of player life across many websites and venues well outside the game itself. Bonnie studied websites such as those devoted to modding and theorycrafting, as well as studying the production of machinima (Lowood 2008) and the vibrant player forums World of Warcraft has spawned (Paul 2010).

A basic principle of ethnographic research is that we should take our lead from our informants, following them to wherever they engage in relevant activity. As part of this process, we need to archive data about places beyond the platform. It is important to remember that anything on the internet is transient. It is unwise to simply preserve a link and assume the material will be online indefinitely. This is why we recommend capturing all such data, rather than trusting it to still be there when we return to a forum or website many months later. Including URLs in our data will be necessary; however, any salient data should also be copied into fieldnotes for long-term preservation. Data from such sources can be collected in screenshots, by cutting and pasting text into a document, or by saving the website as a PDF. Fieldnotes regarding these sources are useful, to document why we turned to them in the first place and how informants use and understand them. For instance, Celia wrote fieldnotes summarizing the contents and approaches used by University of There instructors who produced video tutorials and web-based course materials.

Searching forums for specific information can sometimes feel like looking for a needle in a haystack, as they are not always organized in a way that makes searching for a particular point easy. To use forums efficiently for this purpose, we should not hesitate to seek guidance from group members as to where the salient historical details are buried. Groups engaged in some type of collaborative activity often use wikis. Employing their function that documents changes over time can also provide useful data. Noting who is adding new materials versus editing, as well as periods of high versus low activity, can reveal a group's collaboration patterns.

When ethnographers study forums and wikis, it is in the context of participant observation research. In other words, while humanities scholars study texts in and of themselves, ethnographers study texts as they link up to people in a community or activity. Texts may be part of that study, but in the case of virtual world ethnography, texts alone are not sufficient. We study forms of interaction, meaning making, and cultural production through text. It can be tempting to take conversations that take place in online forums as indicative of larger patterns within a culture; however, this is not always the case. For instance, there can be active participants in a Second Life forum who spend little time in Second Life itself and may not even have a clear understanding of the cultures within it. Forums run by game companies often attract particular players who may not accurately reflect the community at large and, if studied out of context, misrepresent player perspectives. By the same token, players who are very actively engaged inworld may not even read forums, let alone post to them. While forums, wikis, and other such texts are important, they need to be looked at in a larger context. The holistic perspective of ethnographic research, which captures a variety of facets of lived experience, is key to our consideration of these data sources. They should be taken as part of a larger corpus that factors in a variety of other materials.

7.6 HISTORICAL AND ARCHIVAL RESEARCH

Culture always has a history. Even virtual worlds, which can seem unprecedented, have histories that should be a priority for data collection. Archival work is, in our view, essential to any ethnographic project. Historical and archival research can include reading previously published material on the virtual world we are studying, and on earlier virtual worlds as well. To some extent this kind of data collection may shade into data analysis, as it entails engaging with literatures relevant to our research. It is desirable to read published work specifically for what it tells us about past ways of thinking and acting in virtual world contexts that may be shaping our fieldsites.

Online sources such as forums and wikis (and the range of materials discussed above, as well as journalistic accounts) can be vital sources of archival knowledge, particularly for learning about the origins and early history of a virtual world. For instance, both T.L. and Bonnie have tracked changes in modifications to World of Warcraft through official Blizzard forums as well as user forums. The mods themselves have changed, as have Blizzard policies regarding how they are used and distributed. Both consulted detailed archives that record guild rankings, player histories, and even combat logs from specific fights. Tom learned from historical sources that there had been important shifts in the user-generated content paradigm undergirding Linden Lab's business model for Second Life, from a "prim tax" on the number of objects one created to a land-based system in which residents had a maximum number of objects allowed on land for which they paid a monthly fee after initial purchase. Celia found fan sites demonstrating that the "productive play" pattern identified in her research was a pervasive characteristic of Uru fandom across all groups, not just players who had migrated into other virtual worlds. She also used forums to learn about events of the Uru migration that had taken place before she began her research.

It is also often possible to engage in historical research inworld. T.L. drew on inworld community-maintained museums (in-game housing spaces that collected and displayed world artifacts) not only to track changes in artifacts (including avatar bodies), but also to tap into the ways players creatively sought to tell their own stories. Celia charted one Uru refugee group's history of migration by visiting earlier inworld settlements and museums. Tom found locations in Second Life that had been unchanged since the early days of the virtual world, and these provided information about norms for building and the construction of social space. Interviews with "elders" in a virtual world can represent another important source of archival data. Such persons may have detailed knowledge of the early history of the fieldsite that is not recorded elsewhere, and they may even have virtual artifacts they are willing to share (early designs for building or clothing, or early texts). Bonnie interviewed players involved in the earliest World of Warcraft modding community. There may also be cases where interviews with employees of virtual worlds may be a useful source of archival data; for instance, Celia interviewed There.com staff about the original impetus for the founding of the University of There, and T.L. conducted interviews with the developers and community managers of Dreamscape to get a better understanding of the developmental history, and choices, for the world.

The use of Wikipedia as an archival tool remains controversial but is common in online research. In some cases Wikipedia can provide a detailed account of a virtual world's history, depending on the culture. Celia discovered that Myst and Uru players were avid contributors to Wikipedia, where the most complete, accurate, and up-to-date information about the game could often be found. In fact when she helped set up a new secret test server to consider the feasibility of re-releasing the game, players figured out overnight who owned the server and posted it on Wikipedia. Tom found Wikipedia to be useful for learning about early video games that influenced the history of virtual worlds but were otherwise poorly documented. In other instances Wikipedia entries can be sparse or incorrect. For this reason Wikipedia is best used in tandem with other research materials rather than as an authoritative source.

7.7 VIRTUAL ARTIFACTS

When ethnographers conduct research in the physical world, artifacts play an important role in understanding culture (Appadurai 1988; Spyer 1997; Hoskins 1998; Miller 2005). The artifacts of a community—how they circulate, are incorporated into everyday life, and are given meaning—help illuminate culturally specific meanings and practices. When we speak of "virtual worlds," the term "world" is not just a metaphor. One way in which virtual worlds resemble physical world fieldsites more than other online contexts (like blogs or social networking websites) is that they have place and space, embodiment, and objects.

Ethnographic data collection should thus take virtual artifacts into account. The range of these objects is near limitless and includes clothing and armor, furniture, weapons, accessories, toys, functional objects, knickknacks, body parts, and architecture. Some of these objects will be manufactured by the company or organization that governs the virtual world; others may be user-generated or modified; some may even be self-replicating. Going back to the earliest days of virtual worlds, virtual objects (even those composed solely of text) were key to social life and profoundly shaped personal identity. For example, inhabitants of a space may use an avatar accessory to tie them to group membership. In Celia's study of Uru refugees, virtual artifacts, from clothing to vehicles to buildings to ornamentation and landscaping, including flags, were vital markers of group identity (Pearce and Artemesia 2008). Tom discovered that virtual objects were central to a common valuation of "crafting" in Second Life, which influenced beliefs regarding commodities and capitalism online. Bonnie found that World of Warcraft players were deeply engaged with the weapons and armor they accumulated, developing strong interests in the artifacts' functional and aesthetic properties. T.L. found that in Dreamscape the artifacts of the world (especially particular avatar heads) often signaled group affiliation. Virtual objects can shape senses of both community belonging and individual distinctiveness.

During fieldwork ethnographers can often obtain examples of virtual objects for later analysis and study. In some cases (like Second Life), objects contain data revealing who made and owns them, as well as whether the object is free to be given away or can be modified. Such information can reveal norms for commodification and sharing. We can also attend to how virtual objects are used. Do certain objects have a special status or act as social capital inworld? Do communities use particular objects to signal membership? How are objects used to structure and perform personal identity? How do the affordances of virtual objects, such as interactions with virtual gravity or an ability to be scripted, affect their use and meaning? In some virtual worlds ethnographers can learn about cultural norms by observing how participants creatively repurpose preexisting items. In Dreamscape T.L. examined how players used various boxes and knickknacks to create everything from living rooms to hot tubs. Celia's informants in Uru and There.com reappropriated items to create their own sporting events, using traffic cones as bowling pins and tent tethers as tightropes.

Using objects to stimulate conversations with our informants can be a powerful tool for exploring aspects of a culture that might otherwise go unspoken. In Dreamscape a group of participants created an inworld museum (complete with official visiting hours) to chronicle important virtual objects, many of which were rare and demonstrated changes to the world over time. When T.L. visited the museum, talking about the objects stimulated insightful conversations with the curators, who had extensive knowledge about the virtual world's history. Celia spent many hours with Uru refugees in Second Life and There.com discussing the various Uru-inspired artifacts they created, including their own virtual museum that charted the group's history.

Virtual objects are not limited to things avatars can hold in their virtual hands: they also include less portable objects like buildings and trees, as well as landscape elements like rivers and mountains. Understanding this aspect of the world may even extend to exploring underlying code, as when T.L. analyzed the way player bodies were actually constructed, via the software, in early MUDs (Taylor 2004). Collecting data about such objects and code can be valuable in crafting ethnographic accounts. For instance, informants may express important things about themselves through the ways they construct and customize their virtual houses, stores, and landscapes. The creation of spaces and objects for others to use or duplicate was a prime social activity T.L. saw in early MUDs. Celia found that members of the Uru community in There.com frequently used player-created, Uru-themed dwellings as their homes, shaping a sense of group association. When Uru refugees opened the University of There campus, these structures became a prevalent feature, even though the campus was not Uru themed. We can use participant observation to learn how informants move through virtual buildings, which can reveal norms for embodiment and group dynamics. For example, Tom learned that a norm in Second Life was that a resident should stand up and actually walk out of a home before teleporting away. If an avatar vanished from a home or other published location without the proper salutation (referred to as "poofing"), other residents would often worry the person's computer had crashed or might conclude the person was impolite for teleporting out of the social setting without saying goodbye. Interactions with virtual artifacts and spaces are regularly an important aspect to be attended to within our ethnographic practice.

7.8 OFFLINE INTERVIEWS AND PARTICIPANT OBSERVATION

For some ethnographic studies of virtual worlds there is no need for offline interviews or participant observation, given the research question (though of course the physical world always affects any virtual world, even when research is conducted solely online). However, many researchers (including several of us) find physical world interviews rich and rewarding and turn to them as a prime source of data. We might also be researching a topic with a locatable physical world dimension; for instance, a virtual world educational community based around a specific university in the physical world. In still other cases we might wish to research the physical world locations from which informants log into a virtual world, such as an internet café (see Orgad 2009).

The location of offline interviews should be carefully considered to provide a comfortable context. A location related to the fieldsite is one possible locale for interviews. Bonnie conducted interviews in internet cafés in China as part of her fieldwork there, although she sometimes moved informants to a neighboring establishment if the internet café was busy and noisy. Celia requested interviews with University of There staff in their homes where they typically logged onto There.com, so she could see their work environments. In some cases informants opted to meet her in a restaurant near where they lived. However, restaurants can be noisy. Bonnie once lost an entire audio-recorded interview that took place in a crowded restaurant. We do not recommend conducting interviews in a laboratory setting because this sets up an artificial scenario (although there may be some circumstances in which this is the appropriate context for an interview). Interviews conducted in places where informants spend time provide the added bonus of seeing the informant's space and the opportunity to ask questions that arise in response to the environs ("You play World of Warcraft with your brother! Tell me about that.").

Physical world interviews can be leisurely and lengthy and can span a wide variety of contexts in comparison to what may be possible in some virtual world contexts, such as games. Bonnie learned about alcohol and marijuana use during World of Warcraft play from leisurely explorations of a variety of topics in physical world interviews. She expanded this knowledge inworld through chat texts in which mentions of bongs, mixed drinks, and so on augmented the interview comments with vivid online examples. However, she might have missed the significance and prevalence of players' altered states without prior physical world interviews.

For her study of creative collaboration in University of There, Celia interviewed staff of the virtual university in their physical world homes to see the contexts from which they conducted their creative collaboration practices. Through this she found that one staff member got ideas for educational installations from the Discovery Channel, which she left playing on a television in an adjacent room while logged into There.com.

Some virtual worlds develop in such a way that parts of the community meet offline. This can take the form of small group gatherings or, as in the case of big commercial environments, large gatherings such as fan conventions. T.L. has, from her earliest days doing research on text-based worlds, found herself invited to small gatherings (often at a community member's house) where participants wanted to get together to meet each other for a weekend and hang out. She has also attended several much larger fan conventions (both for EverQuest and for World of Warcraft), which provided an opportunity not only to interact with players, but to hear from developers themselves. Tom attended a Second Life Community Convention during his fieldwork, where, even though it did not figure directly in his research, he was able to meet a few of his informants and also hear discussions between residents and Linden Lab staff regarding the norms and future direction of the virtual world. Bonnie has attended several BlizzCons, Blizzard's annual convention in Anaheim. In addition to hearing from Blizzard developers and seeing plans for future releases, she had the opportunity to meet and interact with some of the modders she had been studying.

Events such as offline gatherings can be valuable sites for data collection. They are generally activity filled and socially intense. As in any fieldwork, we cannot predict when the most interesting things will happen, so we should be present for as much of the event as possible, even when things seem to be at a lull. Very often it is in such moments that interesting conversations strike up. Offline gatherings can provide a great place to meet new people. Individual interviews can sometimes be snuck in between activities, and group interviews can work well in these settings. There may be opportunities to make connections with group members who were previously unavailable. While attending an EverQuest fan convention, T.L. met a number of people from her online server she was then able to socialize with inworld. Offline gatherings can also allow for comparisons in play styles and other types of behavior. When Celia followed Uru refugees to There.com's Real Life Gathering, she was able to participate with them in a number of offline activities, such as exploring and playing card games. This aspect of the field research provided unique insight into the ways that play patterns spill over into physical world behaviors.

These events can also be great places to collect small artifacts or photos that provide additional anchors or insight into the community. T.L., for example, found it particularly interesting that at one small community-led convention she attended, a number of people had crafted stuffed-animal versions of a popular inworld pet to use as prizes for a quiz. They reminded her of the ways she had seen virtual objects act as core artifacts of the world's social life. At the There.com Real Life Gathering, players donned physical versions of There.com's signature nametags and some wore bunny slippers, used in the virtual world to amplify jumping height. Photos taken at such events can help document activities, people, and interactions that will later be useful in analysis. While these events can present wonderful opportunities, we should not underestimate how tiring they can be and should carve out a few moments for reflective note taking, a quiet cup of coffee, or just a small walk and breath of fresh air to keep us going.

Through interviews and physical world events, we travel "out from" the virtual world, but we may also journey in the opposite direction. We may, for example, meet players of an online game we are studying in the physical world and decide to check out their servers or even other games they play, or meet and talk to physical world friends and family with whom they play. Or we could attend a physical world event and be introduced to game designers or purveyors of third-party software used by participants in our virtual world, and decide to conduct research related to their pursuits. Such physical world activity may lead to fresh lines of investigation, opening new research questions. For example, both Bonnie and T.L. have met gamers in their apartments. T.L. found that being in the physical space, talking about the game and being shown things on-screen, opened up new understandings about play styles. Bonnie, by being invited to observe roommates playing together, found new vistas of interest in relations between physical and virtual worlds, which she followed at various points in her study.

7.9 USING QUANTITATIVE DATA

Ethnographic research is usually associated with qualitative methods, and our discussion of participant observation, interviewing, and archival research reflects ethnography's emphasis on qualitative methods. However, ethnographers may draw on quantitative data as well (see Murnane and Willett 2011 for an overview of quantitative methods for social scientists). Some ethnographers collect quantitative data themselves, such as administering a survey or census at the outset of a research project. They may also use quantitative data collected by other researchers, either in the form of previously published data or from quantitative scholars with whom they are collaborating.

Though participant observation is the core method of ethnography, ethnographers craft diverse assemblages of data to satisfy the unique needs of a given project. We may draw maps and diagrams, count things, conduct surveys, or develop structured questionnaires to collect information about topics for which we want precise information from a given sample. We may use specialized techniques like triads tests (in which participants decide which two of three things are most similar) or pile sorts (in which participants place like items in groups) (de Munck and Sobo 1998).

Ethnographers may generate statistics, especially descriptive statistics. In her study of World of Warcraft modders, Bonnie counted the number of mods available to World of Warcraft players at download sites in the United States and China. These data were used to analyze differential rates of mod production in the two countries, and the cultural and historical reasons for the differences. Celia used demographic information from the community forums in her Uru research. In her study of the University of There, she discovered through participant observation and interviews that many of the staff and students were disabled. A follow-up survey showed a high percentage of disabled players. Further interviews revealed that some of the disabled students were using the University of There for rehabilitation or to develop new job skills while on disability insurance (Pearce 2009). In an early ethnographic study of a virtual world, Cherny (1999) analyzed whether online conversations in the LambaMOO MUD were dominated by a few individuals or more evenly spread among participants. Based on careful quantitative data, she found that a few participants indeed dominated. This conversational pattern was a surprising finding in a medium in which people did not have to worry about how they looked or whether they had a loud voice, and in which status hierarchies were ostensibly unimportant.

We recognize the potential for collaboration between quantitative and qualitative researchers to bring about research breakthroughs. Quantitative data can tell us about widespread trends, but such data, on their own, are less effective at explaining what such trends might mean. For instance, data collected from a server back-end database might indicate a spike in play sessions at ten o'clock in the morning Pacific standard time in a certain game, but will not reveal why the spike is occurring. Participant observation and interview data make quantitative data more useful by making it more meaningful.

In this chapter we have discussed methods beyond participant observation and interviewing that may be useful to ethnographers of virtual worlds. The remarkably wide range of such methods reflects the open-ended and flexible character of ethnographic research. It indicates the importance of organizing a range of data collection strategies, carefully linked to our research questions and analytical goals. Including such a broad set of methods in a research project need not compromise its ethnographic character, so long as such approaches do not overwhelm or delegitimize the central methods of participant observation and interviewing.

This is even the case with regard to the quantitative methods we have just discussed. We noted in chapter 3 that when quantitative approaches are seen as more scientific, ethnographers may find others attempting to subordinate their research to such work, to the degree that ethnographies are sometimes seen to merely "confirm" what quantitative researchers discover. It is absolutely not the case that ethnographic research would be better in every case if it included a quantitative component. However, when not placed on a pedestal above participant observation and other qualitative approaches, quantitative methods can play a valuable role in some ethnographic research projects.

CHAPTER EIGHT

ETHICS

8.1 THE PRINCIPLE OF CARE

Ethnographic inquiry is as varied as human activity itself. No set of a priori rules of ethics can predict the range of situations to which ethnographers must be prepared to respond with tact, sensitivity, and caution. Ethnographic research may lead us to private, sensitive aspects of social life, as well as the routine activities we normally study. Whatever situations we encounter in ethnographic research, we approach them with the guiding principle of *care*. Care is a core value to be internalized and acted on through the vigilance and commitment of the researcher. Any sets of research ethics guidelines and dicta will be ineffective if researchers do not have embedded into their practice strong values establishing ethical behavior built on the principle of care.

While ethical considerations should be designed into an ethnographic study from the outset and have long been a concern for internet researchers (AoIR 2002; Buchanan 2004; Buchanan and Ess 2009), we chose to begin our discussion of ethics in chapter 8 of this handbook because ethical principles for any research arise directly from the specific practices and contingencies of that research. In other words, we realized that readers needed to understand what it is that ethnographers do before rationales for ethical practice would make sense. This chapter is perhaps one of the most important in the handbook. Its placement after discussion of other matters does not mean we consider ethics an afterthought; rather, it is an indispensable set of concerns issuing directly from the aims and activities of ethnographic investigation.

The principle of care arises in part from asymmetrical power relations and imbalance of benefit between investigator and investigated. The investigator generally gains far more than the informant, garnering benefits that translate to jobs, money, and professional recognition. While informants may enjoy talking about their lives and culture to a researcher, they are unlikely to attain benefits at the scale ethnographers do. A key consequence of this asymmetry is the imperative that the ethnographer "take good care" of informants. This notion goes beyond simply doing no harm; it means ensuring, to the greatest extent possible, that informants gain some reward from participating in research. There are many opportunities for doing good, and each fieldsite offers up unique possibilities to which we should remain alert.

Taking care is, of course, an ideal. In practice whatever good we do is inevitably spread unequally throughout the groups we study. Still, it has been our observation that the relations of trust and mutual respect that characterize sound ethnographic research generally leave a substantial positive residue of good feeling and the satisfaction of genuine human exchange.

While the principle of care applies to all ethnographic research, ethical practice within virtual worlds comes with its own nuances (McKee and Porter 2009). The ease with which inexperienced researchers can enter virtual worlds without having thought through ethical concerns (indeed, in some cases without even being aware of what the concerns are) makes ethics a particularly critical topic for virtual worlds research. It is quite possible to overlook the fact that avatars are under the agency of real people with feelings and rights. We have seen inexperienced researchers conducting research in virtual worlds without the permission of participants, publicly blogging research results using real avatar names, and conducting "experiments" through deceptive practices.

We want to note that while at least two virtual worlds, LambdaMOO and Second Life, have formally addressed the issue of research and provided guidelines for appropriate behavior, we believe frank conversations about these issues need to take place within the research community itself. We may not always agree with guidelines established by corporations and user communities—guidelines that might impose what we consider undue restrictions on our ability to investigate this important arena of human activity. For instance, corporations have in the past created guidelines that researchers may not conduct research without written permission, or that all data collected during fieldwork are the company's property. Whether or not we adhere to these guidelines represents an ethical (and perhaps legal) judgment to be decided by the individual researcher.

To place the principle of care in the context of specific issues that arise during ethnographic research, we identify eight fundamental areas in which ethnographers should consider the ethics of the impacts of their research on informants. These areas—informed consent, mitigation of institutional risk, anonymity, deception, sex and intimacy, compensation, taking leave, and accurate portrayal—are also pertinent to physical world ethnographic research. In the discussion that follows, we emphasize their application to fieldwork in virtual worlds.

8.2 INFORMED CONSENT

The notion of informed consent originated in the world of biomedical research in the context of laboratory- and clinic-based studies. The earliest concerns arose after World War II in outrage at Nazi medical experimentation (see Office of Human Subjects Research n.d.). The Nuremberg Code, pursuant to these concerns, specified that "voluntary consent" is "absolutely essential" in biomedical research, and that experimentation should yield results "for the good of society" (ibid.).

Despite the Nuremberg Code, the infamous Tuskegee experiments, which began in 1932 in Alabama, were carried out until 1973 when a class-action lawsuit was filed against the perpetrator, the U.S. Public Health Service. The Tuskegee Syphilis Study followed 399 low-income African American men with syphilis to determine how the disease spreads and affects the body. Even when penicillin became the standard cure for syphilis (in 1947), the men were not treated so the researchers could continue data collection. Finally public health workers leaked the story to the media and the lawsuit ensued (Reverby 2009). Unbelievably, it was not until 1997 that the government apologized and President Clinton declared the study "shameful"—as it most certainly was.

In addition to risky biomedical research, psychological experiments have also been the site of arguably unethical behavior. Experiments that involve deception (and thus lack informed consent) may leave subjects feeling angry, betrayed, foolish, or even traumatized. Milgram (1974), for example, asked subjects to administer electric shocks to others and urged the subjects to continue the shocks even when those being shocked cried out. The shocks were in fact a ruse, but the subjects did not know that during the experiment. Milgram's experimental design appears highly dubious to many, yet psychologists still debate its ethical implications. Some psychologists argue that deceptive practice is acceptable if it does not cause "significant harm," and that the Milgram experiments are morally justifiable because of the scientific knowledge gained (Bortolotti and Mameli 2006:263). Bortolotti and Mameli note that assessing the harm from any particular experiment requires post hoc empirical research. We question, however, whether we have the means by which to assess what will cause "significant harm" in experiments that stretch the bounds of what would appear, prima facie, to hold potential for harm. If we cannot know in advance if harm will occur because determination of harm is "an empirical question" (ibid. 264), then acceptability is unknown. How can informed consent be "informed" when the nature of potential harm is not assessed until after the fact? For experiments as questionable as those conducted by Milgram, many researchers (including us) find deceptive practice unacceptable.

In response to the Tuskegee experiments and other violations, protocols were established to ensure, to the greatest degree possible, that human subjects are aware of the risks they take by participating in an experiment (Schrag 2009a). Such awareness remains a major concern of administrators, supervisors, and funding agencies. The notion of informed consent follows directly from the Nuremberg Code in which "voluntary consent" prescribes that a subject "should have sufficient knowledge and comprehension of the elements of the subject matter involved as to enable him to make an . . . enlightened decision" regarding whether to participate (Nuremberg 1949). Participation in biomedical research is now attained when subjects read and sign consent forms demonstrating that they have received pertinent information about the research.

However, translating notions of informed consent derived from biomedical research to the very different arena of ethnographic research presents difficulties. We cannot straightforwardly map the notion of being informed about the nature of a biomedical experiment to being informed about an ethnographic study—the two are very different.

A key consideration when evaluating differences is that we must be honest with ourselves that informants are less likely to understand the nature of ethnographic research than to understand a biomedical experiment. Typically, informants (even educated ones) do not apprehend the broader outcomes of social scientific work—especially at the beginning of a study—and know little about ethnography. People often agree to participate in ethnographic research because it seems harmless, and because they like the ethnographer and want to be helpful. They may also be curious. By contrast, in biomedical research, while participants generally do not meet the researchers carrying out the study (i.e., the principal investigators), they typically do grasp that a new treatment is under investigation and sign consent forms showing they understand that their participation can yield valuable (even lifesaving) information about how and whether a treatment works. It is unclear if informed consent—in the Nuremberg Code sense—is generally achieved in the context of ethnographic research. The filling out of forms demanding consent and the obtaining of signatures may merely be ritualized activity that mimics biomedical practice but does not end in subject comprehension.

This situation may at first appear alarming. But returning to the fundamental principles of the Nuremberg Code, we perceive that its raison d'être lies in the existence of the very real risks to subjects of biomedical experimentation. Ethnographic research almost never carries such risks. Ethnography results in neither bodily harm nor psychological distress: it typically carries what is termed "informational risk," the risk that private information could be made public. Ethnographers' objects of study are human culture and society; we need not tinker with the human body to learn what we want to know. Ethnographic research is centered on long-term field study in which trust and rapport with informants are essential; psychological distress is not part of this scenario. We do not, for example, deliberately make informants feel uncomfortable to see what happens, as may occur in psychological experiments—such an act would obviate the very possibility of ethnographic study.

Having said this, it is important to emphasize that as ethnographers we are obligated to do as much as possible to reveal to our informants the nature and purpose of our studies. Providing information regarding aims and methods is necessary to establish and sustain good relations. It is up to the ethnographer to explain the research to informants, and, at the inception of a study, to clearly identify oneself as an ethnographer. In one of T.L.'s studies she used, for example, the ability to attach the phrase "Avatar Research" and a URL to her avatar so that when people in the world clicked on her (as everyone did to see each other's details), they could then visit the website for the project to read additional information about it, as well as see the consent form. Similarly, the first sentence of Tom's Second Life avatar profile stated he was an anthropologist conducting research. Bonnie placed a halo over her avatar head (chosen by study participants!) for research she conducted on business uses of Second Life to mark her role as ethnographer. It is not of course always necessary to change one's avatar, but this may be convenient and useful in some settings.

Keeping participants informed about the research is an ongoing imperative. This obligation does not end with a signed consent form. As the American Anthropological Association's Statement on Ethics indicates: "The informed consent process is necessarily dynamic and continuous; the process should be initiated as part of project design and continue through implementation as an ongoing dialogue and negotiation with those studied" (AAA 1986). During the lengthy life cycle of an ethnographic study, we have many opportunities to converse with informants about why we are conducting the research. Some informants may, over time, develop broader interests in the ethnographer's goals, and we can nurture dialogue about these topics.

Depending on the group structure, obtaining initial informed consent can be accomplished in a variety of ways. It is a benefit that online communities usually provide a variety of channels of communication. In her University of There research, for instance, Celia first approached university staff inworld seeking their "blessing" for the project. The consent form was then posted on the group's forum and to their email list. The posts described the research and linked to the online consent form. At the start of each university class, the instructor would give the researcher the opportunity to verify that those in attendance were consenting to participate and had signed the form. In only two cases did participants opt out of signing the form, and in each case the research team avoided collecting their data.

While we encourage finding creative ways to obtain consent forms from all participants, not all situations provide a structured setting in which to do so. In many contexts it can be impractical or disruptive to ask informants to sign consent forms. As a result, awareness of a researcher's identity in the online fieldsite will vary—from those who know us well, to those who only occasionally interact with us and thus regard us as just another online participant, to those with whom we have only the most fleeting of encounters. In some settings, such as battlegrounds or arenas in World of Warcraft, Bonnie could not explain that she was an ethnographer because the interactions were short and composed of players randomly teamed together across servers only for the short duration of a match. Most people in Second Life who knew Tom during his research were aware that he was an ethnographer, but if he was visiting a place for the first time not everyone would know this right away, and indeed many people never learned this information.

In such contexts researchers must consider possible risks to those observed. Bonnie felt there was no risk in reporting anonymous comments she recorded from battlegrounds and arenas, and she has done so in her publications. T.L. has also used material from hubs in game worlds, such as the main area outside the bank in Orgrimmar (a major city), in World of Warcraft. Similarly, Tom has reported anonymous comments overheard in Second Life shopping malls. In our view it is legitimate to see subscription-based virtual worlds as having public areas where it is not necessary to have every person in an interaction sign an informed consent form—just as there is nothing inherently unethical about taking a picture of a tourist in an open, general area at an amusement park, which is a public place although an admission fee is charged.

At the same time, virtual world ethnographers have long noted that we must be diligent about how the people we study define the distinction between "private" and "public" with reference to particular communities and activities (Reid 1996; Waskul and Douglass 1996; Elm 2009). For instance, in Second Life it is possible to overhear text chat conversations meant as private through a wall, or to use visual controls to peer into a space that could not otherwise be seen. In World of Warcraft, players in less-used voice chat channels may be carrying on "private" conversations and, depending on their software settings, may not immediately notice when someone new joins the channel. There may also be times when we can ascertain that the participants speaking have a certain expectation of privacy, or a notion that it would be inappropriate to record their words for publication. We must use our best judgment, operating from the core principle of care, as to not only what is public versus private from an etic perspective, but also what the people we study emically perceive as public or private. Such notions will vary from one culture to the next.

In summary, then, informed consent in ethnographic research is constituted differently from how it is managed in biomedical research. Informed consent predicated on the kinds of risks present in biomedical or psychological research is not ethically consonant with ethnographic research, since those risks are not present. We may be required for bureaucratic reasons to obtain signed consent forms (as discussed in the next chapter), but they are not our principal means of ensuring informed consent. What is necessary is that we make clear our presence as ethnographers and maintain ongoing dialogue about our purposes.

8.3 MITIGATING INSTITUTIONAL AND LEGAL RISK

Occasionally ethnographers become involved in legal and contractual matters. We must be aware of relevant laws that govern judicial access to fieldnotes, and cognizant of the possibility that we may be obligated to provide testimony in a deposition or court of law concerning what we have observed or heard in the field. We must also understand the nature of contracts such as Terms of Service (ToS) and End User Licensing Agreements (EULAs) that govern commercial virtual worlds.

Although the legal landscape is complicated, ethnographers should recognize that in the United States (and possibly other countries), it is possible to subpoena an ethnographer's fieldnotes in a process of legal discovery, and to subpoena an ethnographer to testify in a deposition or court of law (Monette, Sullivan, and DeJong 2010). Such events occur rarely, but ethnographers should assess how to mitigate risks to informants when studying legally sensitive areas that might eventuate in a subpoena. In the United States informants accused of legal impropriety cannot be fully protected by ethnographers unless the researchers are willing to go to jail to protect fieldnotes (ibid.). While the probability of being served a subpoena is low, the potential risk to informants is high. If we have collected data that we believe may incriminate an informant, we may want to destroy fieldnotes as soon as it is reasonable to do so. We may still, however, be required to testify truthfully on informants' activities in court (or accept jail time).

On a lesser scale, ethnographers may encounter informants in virtual worlds who violate ToS or EULAs. While it is unlikely we would become entangled in account closure or suspension, caring for informants means developing a sound understanding of the nature of pertinent contracts. Informants might ask ethnographers about the possible penalties for violations of ToS or EULAs, and we should do our best to help them think about any critical issues if asked.

8.4 ANONYMITY

A key potential risk of ethnographic research is inappropriately revealing informant identities or confidential information. A properly administered study avoids this risk; in practice, ethnographers are typically remarkably diligent in this regard. As ethnographers, we must learn how to provide these protections while conducting fieldwork and within our publications. Sensitive information must be recognized as such and treated with utmost care. An informant might, for example, utter disparaging comments about a community leader, spouse, or boss. Attributing such a comment to the informant could lead to social awkwardness or loss of social status, or even endanger a job or marriage. Ethnographers may find themselves participating in secret ceremonies, observing illegal or questionable activity, or learning of politically sensitive or even perilous issues. Within a given informant's social group, it is also important to remember that disclosure of questionable activities such as hacking or gold buying might embarrass an informant or even result in community rejection. Each bit of data must be carefully examined and handled appropriately according to circumstances. Ethnographers strive to avoid negative outcomes by paying special attention to the potential consequences and risks of what we see and hear, and remembering that not everything is grist for the data mill, no matter how interesting it may be.

A simple, long-standing principle is to refrain from revealing informant identities in published work. This act of restraint removes a good deal of risk to informants because if they cannot be identified, actions for which they might be held accountable become irrelevant. As ethnographers, one way we avoid revealing informant identities is by using pseudonyms. Coming up with appropriate names may take a little planning. For instance, in his Indonesia research Tom had to come up with different pseudonyms for Muslim and Hindu informants; to refer to a Hindu Balinese informant as "Muhammad" would have been jarring. In virtual worlds, residents often have strikingly creative names, and it is useful (though sometimes surprisingly time-consuming) to come up with roughly equivalent pseudonyms that capture this creativity while protecting identities. In some cases we will want to anonymize collective identities (for instance, groups, guilds, and community organizations). Particularly if leaders of these organizations seek publicity, this decision can be difficult. In general we recommend anonymizing collective identities since being able to identify a group often makes it easy to identify individuals in the group (and leaders may overestimate the publicity our published work would provide).

While altering informant names is not particularly difficult, it is less easy to consistently maintain anonymity *within* a particular group with whom we interact. We must tread with care in discussing sensitive events or harsh comments in the community contexts in which they occurred. It is generally best to avoid taking sides in local disputes, and to stay out of conflicts. Doing so will enable us to continue the work without burning bridges. After all, we want to talk to both sides, or all sides. If we have acquired privileged information in interviews or conversations, it should not be discussed as the conflict unfolds, or even in its aftermath, unless we are certain it will not cause harm.

The reach of what is "local" expands to a wide purview among literate informants who might read our publications. Even when informant names are anonymized in written work, those who were on the scene may readily decode the cast of characters in activities in which they participated or that they observed, resulting in "deductive disclosure" beyond the control of the ethnographer. It is normal for informants, if they read our publications, to make guesses about the identities of those being discussed. As Kendall recounts regarding her use of pseudonyms in her work on a MUD:

> One difficulty that arose with the pseudonyms involved respondents themselves defeating the protections I extended to them. . . . For instance, on several occasions Jet issued roll calls on the topic of "your name in Copperhead's [Kendall's] thesis." As soon as they received copies of the dissertation, Jet and Carets created an object on BlueSky that provided a key to almost all the pseudonyms I used. (I objected to this, pointing out that it could potentially reveal identities to outsiders as well as regulars, and after much discussion, the object was removed.) (2002:243)

T.L. actually recalls encountering this deciphered pseudonym list recreated on a subsequent MUD a number of the participants came to inhabit, highlighting the ways ethnographic accounts, and participant investment in them, can have real longevity and even travel across worlds. In Celia's Uru research, because of the social structure of the community and its tie to the original game, pseudonyms were relatively transparent within the community itself. This means that we need to think about internal anonymity *between members* as well, keeping in mind that they continue to be in relation with each other long after we have left the field. The specific, identity-revealing details of a spousal conflict, a guild dispute, or a breakdown between collaborators, as well as personal information not relevant to the study, may best be concealed or altered to avoid repercussions within the group.

Sometimes the guarantee of full anonymity is impossible. It falls to us to render careful judgments to avoid causing risk to informants, up to and including forgoing the publication of potentially harmful materials. How long should we maintain informants' anonymity? The answer is forever. Even if we chose to write a memoir of our work (e.g., Powdermaker 1966; Rabinow 1977; Behar 1996), we should maintain pseudonyms to protect the identity of our informants. While we hesitate to argue that some events and revelations should never be discussed or published, we do strongly encourage that the fundamental values of care and prevention of harm guide our choices. Upholding the confidentiality and anonymity of our participants is central. Keeping in mind the unanticipated consequences if people's identities and activities were revealed should promote reflectivity on our part when deciding what is important to include in the written work.

We can, of course, never prevent astute readers from trying to piece together data. We should thus be reflective about how we use our material, carefully weighing the principle of care with the overall arguments and story we are trying to tell. We may want to avoid specific quotes in particularly loaded scenarios, pulling back to a more abstract or observational level of analysis. Sometimes informant activity may additionally carry criminal implications or be punishable by corporate purveyors of virtual worlds (such as gold farming or hacking); here a high level of informant protection is required. We may want to take extra steps to obscure the identity of people in these situations. Our ethnography may at times deal with quite difficult domains (socially stigmatized activities, internal disputes within the community, perhaps even rule or lawbreaking). We have to carefully manage our raw data and reportage in these moments.

Details for publication can be carefully selected without compromising a rich ethnography. For example, Bonnie once studied a conflict in a small working group in a hospital where everyone knew everyone else. She had to be extremely careful how she reported the data, but she was still able to present a robust account of the working group. During her study of the University of There, Celia encountered a rift between two instructors, resulting in the formation of a second university. After consulting with the dean, she determined that it was permissible to include in published reports the fact of the rift, which was well-known within the community. But she omitted details to protect all involved (Pearce 2009b).

Ethnographers accord informants anonymity by changing not only individual and group names, but also altering details in regard to the place and time of events. For instance, if during participant observation in New York City an ethnographer witnessed a heated discussion between John and Sam at the Red Dog Bar on 17th Street, he could describe how he witnessed the discussion between Steven and George at the White Lightning Bar on 19th Street without compromising vivid local flavor. Anonymizing does not require sucking the life out of an evocative vignette; the changes need not sacrifice ethnographic richness or research validity.

When virtual worlds are studied, anonymizing extends to screen names and online locations since these can be important aspects of identity and social life (Paccagnella 1997). For instance, Bonnie did not reveal the server she played on when conducting her World of Warcraft research, nor the names of her character or those in her guild. When the research was complete she changed her character's name and moved to another server. This was probably overkill, but she felt more secure using the capacities of the gaming system to obscure traces of the research. Tom changed the names and details of all persons and places he encountered in Second Life, and he paraphrased quotations from informants to make them difficult to identify using a search engine. A key point here is that in many cases persons may be pseudonymous in an online context (because they are known by a screen name), but not anonymous, because "even if other users may not know much about the offline identities of other users, they recognize their online names" (Sveningsson 2004:52).

There are two potential scenarios where the principle of anonymity may involve exceptions. One standard exception involves individuals who are historical or public figures. Both T.L. and Bonnie have interviewed founders of early World of Warcraft modding groups. Neither anonymized them in publications because they would be recognizable to many modders, who would consider them, in essence, historical figures. We would not anonymize a U.S. president, or Mother Teresa, or a movie star (nor could we, even if we tried) because their contributions to culture are so distinctive. Bonnie's modding research uncovered Chinese developers whose efforts provided leadership in establishing modding in China, as well as a Blizzard employee who single-handedly forged connections between modders and Blizzard in the early days of World of Warcraft. These individuals were named with either real or screen names. Ethnography is also history, and cultural logics emerge from the activities of people who imagine and enact new futures. It is, of course, critical to ensure that such informants give permission for the ethnographer to use an identifying name, or that they are a public figure whose name is known in public forums (as in the case of the Blizzard employee).

The second scenario in which anonymity may need to be reconsidered involves creative production. When Celia asked informants to annotate her research results, for instance, one of her informants failed to read the introduction specifying that pseudonyms were used throughout and was upset when he thought she had misattributed a poem he had written. The mistake was clarified in the commenting section of the research blog by another study participant, and the participant agreed that the pseudonym was preferable. On the other hand, in cases where designers or content creators have achieved a certain measure of fame or perhaps have a stake (professional or otherwise) in having their work attributed, participants may wish to have their names revealed. T.L., for example, made a point of clearly citing work created by a participant which was published in a web-based newspaper that covered the particular virtual world. She has also retained participants' proper names in several cases (such as with Brad McQuaid, producer and lead designer for EverQuest) where, given their singular role or status as a public figure, anonymizing would have been quite difficult. To address issues of credit and attribution, Bruckman (2002) suggested a tiered approach with various levels of anonymity depending on the situation. In most cases, however, informants' physical world identities or screen names should remain anonymous. Any deviation from this policy should be rigorously thought through.

Sometimes anonymity should be maintained even when informants request to be identified. There are two reasons for this. First, we never fully know who will see the outcome of our work, and there may be unforeseen consequences (LeCompte and Schensul 1999). For example, if we describe a player conducting an activity that is explicitly against a virtual world's terms of service, and an employee of that company happens to read our work, we could risk termination of the player's account. Second, individuals do not exist in isolation—we are all members of various communities. In ethnographic research, identifying a person potentially identifies their social networks. As a result, it is unethical to indirectly compromise the anonymity of an informant's friends, relatives, groups, fellow guild members, or colleagues since some of them may not wish to be identified. In rare cases informants may not be aware of the risk to themselves of revealing their identities. Celia experienced a case where a player self-identified as being transgender in the physical world and wished to be identified in a study by her real avatar name. While the transgender status was general knowledge among the informant's inner circle, Celia felt the social consequences to the player within the larger community were too risky to divulge this information.

The collection of visual material like screenshots and video is often a vital part of ethnographic research, but such materials can easily reveal identities. While some virtual worlds provide a minimal range of customization, and thus limited possibilities for the avatar being uniquely identifiable, others allow for rich and distinct forms of avatar design. When we plan on using video or screenshots in publications or presentations, issues around anonymity may arise that are not dissimilar to those faced by visual anthropologists in the physical world. The researcher can seek written permission from everyone who appears in the video. But it can be difficult in practice to track down every last signature, and it does not resolve the issue of indirectly violating anonymity for those in the informants' social networks.

If we receive permission we can obscure faces or other identifying parts of avatar bodies, but these techniques reduce the impact of the video or images and are aesthetically unsatisfactory. Many virtual worlds allow participants to change settings to hide names and other identifying information in the user interface. Hiding names is a simple, effective solution to ensure anonymity in visual materials, or nametags can be obscured when images are prepared for publication or presentation. However, we should be sure to look around—names may still be visible in chat windows or elsewhere and need to be blurred or moved out of view. In some virtual worlds we must anonymize not just faces and screen names, but places. Allowing the name of a well-known dance club in a virtual world to appear in an image, for instance, would identify the owners and managers of the club, and even possibly persons known to frequent the club.

8.5 DECEPTION

Historically ethnographers have rejected deceptive practice as a basis on which to construct an ethnographic study. Deceiving informants remains firmly outside the bounds of ethical ethnographic research. Often fledgling ethnographers imagine that deception is a good idea, or at least a possibility, and virtual worlds might seem to offer a particularly tempting set of possibilities for deception without harm. This appearance is false, and it is important to know that deception, while practiced in other scientific disciplines, is not ethical within ethnographic investigation.

To which deceptive practices should ethnographers be alert? Deception in field research takes two forms: "undercover" observation in which the researcher attempts to blend in to observe surreptitiously, or assuming a false identity in which some characteristic such as gender or disabled status is of interest. We occasionally receive inquiries from researchers just learning about ethnography asking whether it is acceptable to conduct ethnographic research in a virtual world as a "fly on the wall," or to pose as, say, a disabled person in Second Life to find out how disabled people experience the virtual world.

Such subterfuge runs counter to the heart and soul of ethnography. As we have discussed, ethnographic research depends on cultivating social relationships created and nurtured for months or years. Ethnographers cannot simply observe because, by definition, we must *participate* in the fieldsite. Building sustainable human relationships on a foundation of deception is antithetical to participant observation, which presupposes trust and rapport, both predicated on openness and honesty. Deceptive practices such as undisclosed video or audio recording that might support a covert approach are outside ethical ethnographic practice.

Assuming a false identity, perpetuating deceptions required to pose as someone we are not, may become increasingly untenable as we attempt to manage a web of lies that introduce contradictions and falseness to our presentation of self. Ethnography presents sufficient challenge without adding the need to keep track of a series of falsehoods. The moment of revelation of our true identity—and there will always be one—is almost certain to provoke bad feeling, whether we unmask ourselves in the field or an informant reads an account in which she recognizes the research. The very basis of the data gathering activity of ethnography is compromised, if not destroyed, through deception.

Deceptive practice may also lead to a more widespread "poisoning of the well" for the research community. If informants learn that we have lied about our identity, they may refuse to participate in the future studies with us, other ethnographers, or researchers from other disciplines. The offended parties may spread the word to those in their social groups. Deceptive practice thus bears potential consequences not only for individual ethnographers, but for colleagues as well. Community integrity is at stake.

Methodologically, "experimentation" under the false pretenses of an assumed identity is a sort of Frankenstein's monster that ends, ultimately, in unethical practice. If faking an identity, we are ostensibly immersed in the authentic cultures taking place around us yet seek to control one variable—identity. Given the complexity and dynamism of human culture, it is impossible to make claims under such a pseudo-experimental regime on the order of "I know what it's like to be a woman because I had a female avatar." In the absence of extensive trials in multiple conditions controlling for changes in a multitude of possible variables in a virtual world (which could include, for example, technological, legal, social, and regulatory variables), the researcher cannot say with confidence that being a woman "caused" an observed behavior. Behaviors might just as easily have arisen in response to the variables mentioned above, or others including the ethnographer's age, gender, social class, and so on. Lacking a fully worked out experimental design, the researcher cannot formulate a principled logic for meaningful analysis.

In addition to inadequate study design for proper experimentation, such ethnographic poseurs are unlikely to do a good job of simulating the identity they seek to study. Ethnography is a social enterprise in which ethnographers speak and act. If we are not who we say we are, our words and actions will fail to reflect the sensibilities and accumulated life experience of the type of person we claim to be. The presentation of self will be inauthentic, eliminating our possibility for discovering, say, "how a woman is treated in a virtual world."

Such varied and serious methodological problems originating in bad field experiments constitute a clear violation of research ethics. Claims made are almost certain to be wrong, misrepresenting the persons and communities studied. We discuss the dangers of inaccurate portrayals of our informants' lives below, but for the moment we note that misrepresentation betrays the most fundamental principles of ethnographic research. For several reasons—methodological, logistical, ethical—field experiments remain "an uncommon method of social science research" (Pager 2009:39).

In short, ethical ethnographic investigation avoids deception. Ethnographic work is grounded in sustaining relations of honesty, openness, respect, and consideration: this is a source of methodological strength. These dispositions enable us to care for informants and, by extension, the larger scientific communities in which we participate.

8.6 SEX AND INTIMACY

As we have indicated, ethnographic research relies on the embodied researcher (including one's virtual embodiment) devoting significant time and energy, including emotional energy, to the communities and activities under study. By definition, participant observation entails a certain level of intimacy with informants, in the sense of closeness and deep rapport. Such closeness naturally has the potential, under certain circumstances, to eventuate in sexual activity. Historically, sex between researchers and informants has been informally acknowledged but rarely discussed. In the last few decades, the topic has received more attention (Kulick and Willson 1995; Markowitz and Ashkenazi 1999). Our goal is not to offer strict rules of comportment, because every case is different, but to suggest that as a general heuristic (construed in the broadest sense), sexual activity with informants is best avoided. This has been the traditional advice given to ethnographers (even if it is not always followed).

We make this suggestion for two reasons. First, we often do not know the meanings our informants attach to sex. Particularly given the asymmetric power dynamics between researcher and informant, there is significant potential to generate misunderstandings, unrealistic expectations, and broken hearts (on either side)—none of which are conducive to getting the job of ethnography done. Second, since sexual activity (especially when first initiated) is by nature unpredictable, it may be difficult to anticipate possible consequences to our research or careers, and to our informants' feelings and lives. Sexual or romantic encounters, if revealed, can compromise our status, or that of our informants, in the social group with which we interact.

Sex with informants may introduce deception in relation to others, as ethnographer and informant attempt to conceal the activity. A degree of subterfuge can emerge, placing both ethnographer and informant outside the bounds of the openness and honesty that constitute good ethnographic practice. And though it may seem far-fetched, journalists are always looking for sensationalist stories about virtual worlds. We do not want to see our names in a headline reading "Virtual World Researcher Has Sex with Subjects." The ethnographer and informant may become caught up in complicated machinations, and so might our institution and funding agencies, if journalists reveal activities others judge to be inappropriate.

We started with the issue of sex, but intimacy is an ethical issue that arises far more frequently. Sex is pretty easily avoided if we so choose, but intimacy in some form is central to the very practice of ethnography. The "participation" component of participant observation often involves emotionally charged exchanges of words and deeds. Interviews may move toward highly personal topics. Informants may invite us to participate in special activities not generally shared with outsiders. Intimacy may thus give ethnographies potency and explanatory power through the data capture they permit, distinguishing them from the products of other research paradigms.

The question is how to best prepare for and respond ethically to intimacies (Kendall 2009). As we have discussed, protecting informant anonymity is important, and issues seen as intimate are clearly cases in which we should ensure confidentiality. Writing up the material gained through encounters seen to be intimate in some fashion requires extreme sensitivity and tact. Each case is different; there are no cookbook rules we can propose. In general, if we feel hesitation or pangs of guilt or concern as we write, it is probably wise to move to other topics. It is never worth failing to care for informants, no matter how compelling the data. Care may require withholding information. Ethnography in certain circumstances demands restraint, and judgments regarding the release of information are sometimes best rendered conservatively.

Since most persons participating in virtual worlds are comfortable with technology, as researchers we should consider in advance what kinds of online boundaries we wish to set with those we study. For example, it is likely we will want to "friend" people we meet within the virtual world, but what if we receive a friend invitation to a social network site like Facebook, or a request to follow our private Twitter feed? What if the groups we are studying are using a social network site themselves in an important way? To be consistent with our informants, we suggest deciding on a policy before beginning fieldwork, and if changing our policy at some point, to do so across the board.

It is important to think through the implications of social network sites. Informants may feel slighted if they find we have friended someone they know in a guild or other social group and not them. Friending may inappropriately expose our social network or those of our informants. Because many social networking sites allow for the possibility of "friends of friends" accessing comments on others' posts, we should consider the forms of privacy protections such systems afford and how they align with our broader ethical standards.

However, once the research is complete, if we have become friends with informants and are willing to expose our networks, social network sites can be a convenient way to stay in touch. In many cases, a blog, Facebook page, or Twitter feed for our research project might provide a way to show we care about our informants while keeping our private lives, and the private lives of informants, reasonably separate.

In all matters pertaining to sex and intimacy, as in every aspect of ethnography, the principle of care should be our touchstone. We must take into consideration possible harm or embarrassment that can be brought about through romantic, sexual, and intimate activities, just as when conducting ethnographic research in the physical world. We should think such activities through—very carefully—before setting forth on potentially troublesome adventures or revealing information acquired in close encounters.

8.7 DOING GOOD AND COMPENSATION

At a minimum ethnographers should seek to have a neutral impact on the communities we study, but we should go beyond neutral effect to strive for positive impact. "Doing good" creates a favorable impression of researchers in general and ethnographers in particular, paving the way for future research by ourselves and others, as well as giving back to those who make our work possible.

It is important to be realistic about appropriate involvement. For instance, in Second Life Tom has advised or participated in the activities of several groups, but without taking a leadership role. Celia was given a community service award by Uru refugees in There.com for her role as an ambassador in telling their story to the outside world through the many public lectures and writings she has presented on the Uru diaspora.

A host of informal opportunities for doing good may arise during research, and we should take advantage of them. Bonnie sometimes listened (in whispers or a private voice channel) when guildmates experienced hurt feelings or were upset at something that happened during the course of World of Warcraft play. She was able to provide a sympathetic ear as well as a bit of advice (her subject position as an older person with life experience was useful). Celia's interviews with Uru refugees often had a benefit to informants, many of whom felt traumatized by the closure of Uru. Listening provided a sense of empowerment for a community that felt ignored or forgotten. Some persons Tom interviewed in Second Life used the opportunity to talk through problems ranging from romantic difficulties to gender identity.

These forms of doing good are ways to provide at least some recompense for the invaluable contributions of informants' time and thoughts. But what about more tangible benefits? Should we give gifts to compensate informants; can this be a way to do good? Beginning ethnographers often feel the need to provide informants with something, hoping a gift will stimulate interest and ensure cooperation. In our experience giving gifts does neither. The best informants have a genuine desire to talk to ethnographers, and those just turning up for the free virtual t-shirt are likely to be lackadaisical and unmotivated. However, gift giving may be a normal part of the life of the community in which the ethnographer operates. In Bonnie's experiences in Papua New Guinea and Western Samoa, frequent gifting (of food, small household items, and inexpensive clothing) was part of ordinary existence, not a special marker of the research relationship. In gaming guilds people often share virtual items just as New Guineans share yams. Bonnie did the same, in both contexts, as part of participant observation.

Some ethnographers give gifts after an interview to signal appreciation. Such gifts are a gracious way to offer thanks; they are usually small tokens, though it depends on the situation. Gifts can sometimes be given that benefit the whole community. Celia made donations to the Uru community island in There.com, aware that its real estate fees and the purchase of decor (all costs paid in U.S. dollars) were being carried at considerable personal expense to the group's leaders. When working with high-status informants (such as Bonnie's research with brain surgeons in a hospital study), there is no gift that is not a token, though such tokens may be appreciated.

Despite these scenarios in which some form of compensation may be appropriate, in many cases the best gift is simply thanks and appreciation. Informants want to know their words meant something. They light up when they see that we have learned from them, found our conversations with them significant and useful, and paid close attention to the details and nuances of their lives and experiences.

8.8 TAKING LEAVE

An inequality between ethnographer and informant is that fieldwork is never a lifelong endeavor. Even in cases where we return to a fieldsite many times over decades, each individual period of research has a beginning and an end. However, with only a few exceptions (like migration), informants do not leave. Even in virtual worlds, where movement is more common and entire virtual worlds can go out of existence (as documented in Celia's work on diasporic communities), informants usually have a greater investment in their virtual world than do the researchers who study them. Ethnographers rightly seek to embed themselves into communities via significant investments of time and energy, but participants may feel confused, betrayed, or abandoned if we simply disappear one day, never to log on again.

As a result, it is helpful during the final month or so of research to prepare informants for our departure, letting them know that the primary data collection phase is drawing to a close. Unless we do a full-fledged follow-up or longitudinal study at a later date, we must accept the fact that save perhaps for correspondence with a few informants who have become friends, an intensive relationship to any particular fieldsite will come to an end. Of course, online research does afford the freedom to not entirely terminate our relationships with informants; this can allow us access to new phenomena we may wish to study, as well as maintaining valued friendships. Tom has made presentations about his research on multiple occasions in Second Life, which has provided opportunities to reconnect with informants. There may also be cases where maintaining ongoing connections can become an entrée into future studies, as was the case with Celia's University of There research.

8.9 ACCURATE PORTRAYAL

It is imperative that we work to create the fairest and most accurate portrayal of informants' lifeworlds. Most ethnographers would agree with Malinowski's classic conclusion that the goal of an ethnographic study is "to grasp the native's point of view, his relation to life, to realize *his* vision of *his* world" (1922:25; emphasis in original). The general principle is to forge a sympathetic depiction of informants' lives, even when discussing aspects of informants' lives that some might find troubling—for instance, the existence of discrimination or violence. This approach does not entail agreeing with all the beliefs and actions of our informants, but it does mean laboring to grasp informants' own visions of their worlds.

We are aware of critiques of ethnography that point to its potential for inaccurate portrayal (Clifford and Marcus 1986), but in our view the resolution of these debates is not particularly vexing, as summed up some time ago in Geertz's dictum that ethnography is "not an experimental science in search of law but an interpretive one in search of meaning" (1973:5). As anthropologist Franz Boas noted over a century ago during the origins of ethnography, the ethnographic approach "considers every phenomenon as worthy of being studied for its own sake" (Boas 1887:642). An ethnography is an interpretation; it is neither God's truth nor the final word. Yet this does not cast us into a postmodern morass in which all interpretations are equal. Like field sciences from astronomy to zoology, the fact that the value of ethnographic research is not predicated on replication does not mean there are no standards for assessment. It is up to us, ethically, as scholars to create, seek out, propagate, and defend adequate standards.

There is significant value, then, in accurate portrayals of the cultures and peoples we study; they result from the investments of time and energy the ethnographic method demands. What other practitioners tread so diligently, carefully, and respectfully in their human encounters? The work of ethnography pushes us far from familiar modes of being, as we "remain in close and continuing relations with the natural social order" (Blumer 1954:10). While ethnographers of virtual worlds are spared some of the disease and discomfort of our physical world colleagues, accurate portrayal of virtual worlds may require a commitment to very long hours at the computer and the disruption of other activities. Family members may not understand the need to log on to a virtual world immediately after dinner, spend many hours on a weekend in raid sessions, or stay up until three a.m. doing fieldwork. But if we are to find out how raiders really behave, or what happens in the wee hours in that dance club in Second Life, we must commit, ethically, to whatever it takes to experience the activities where the data we require are generated.

A final issue in terms of accurate portrayal concerns accessibility of writing, which we discuss further in chapter 11. In general, we argue for writing in the most accessible manner possible and see no conflict between clarity and incisiveness or theoretical power. There certainly have been ethnographies written so that they are difficult to understand without being part of a small group of researchers sharing a particular technical vocabulary. We discourage this approach. However, we emphasize as well the existence of genre. There are genres of ethnographic writing (journal articles, for instance) where, owing to the need for concision or a desire to advance a specific theoretical conversation, researchers may write in a manner that is not immediately accessible to everyone. The point is not that everything we write should be readable by the communities studied, or by any and all academic communities; it is that we should write in the clearest manner possible that is appropriate for a particular genre. Additionally, ethnographers should be able to write in a range of genres, including some that are accessible to at least some people in the communities from which we have drawn data, insight, and inspiration, as well as multiple interdisciplinary communities who may find the work interesting and productive.

Overall, then, the ethnographic enterprise hinges on engaging others in ethical conversation and preparing careful, accurate accounts that do not compromise informants. As indicated at the beginning of this chapter, the ability to do this rests on the foundational principle of care. Ethnographers must be expert at creating human encounters that give back to informants through the agency of satisfying human contact, in a spirit of respect and regard. Most of our informants will never read what we write about them, and few will have even an inkling of the academic contestations with regard to which we toil. Informants will, however, remember us, the ethnographers. They will recall our gifts of listening, the deep interest displayed in the smallest details of their lives, and the way we took care to discern and follow the complexities and enigmas of their everyday pursuits and dreams.

CHAPTER NINE

HUMAN SUBJECTS CLEARANCE AND INSTITUTIONAL REVIEW BOARDS

9.1 INSTITUTIONAL REVIEW BOARDS (IRBs)

Institutional Review Boards, often known as "IRBs" or "Human Subjects Offices," are administrative bodies that monitor research ethics. They can be part of a university, corporation, nonprofit organization, or government entity that conducts or sponsors human subjects research. They are prevalent throughout the United States, where IRB approval is typically mandatory for all research involving human subjects (whether biological or behavioral). In other countries ethical guidelines may not be governed by an internal IRB, but operate via a mix of institutional and national regulations, professional association guidelines, and national data protection offices (Respect Project 2004; CESSDA 2011).

IRBs arose out of abuses in experimental research that occurred between the 1930s and 1970s, as discussed in section 8.2 (see Schrag 2009a). The Declaration of Helsinki, which builds on the Nuremberg Code, was adopted in 1964 by the World Medical Association and constitutes a set of standards for biomedical research ethics (WMA 1964). This document established protection for "human subjects," namely, any human person in a biomedical experiment, as well as consideration of special risks to vulnerable populations such as children, prisoners, and persons with mental illness.

While concerns regarding experimentation with human subjects are well founded and essential to ethical biomedical research practice, the biomedical model on which IRB procedures are built is largely inappropriate for social scientific field-based research. The two research paradigms have little in common. IRB protocols and procedures reflect the particular ways in which biomedical experimentation is conducted. Biomedical research is typically organized in controlled experiments structured to test a series of hypotheses. Experiments are carried out in a sampled population whose size and characteristics are known at the outset. Contact between study subjects and researchers (principal investigators) rarely occurs; generally procedures are undertaken by staff who do not analyze or write up data. Deception is not only allowed, it is obligatory if a study utilizes placebos. In biomedical research, study subjects rarely interact with one another as in ethnographic research. Cassell observed, "[Ethnographic] fieldwork does not place human interaction outside the research paradigm; instead, the paradigm is based upon human interaction" (1980:31).

While the analytical unit in biomedical research is the individual, in ethnographic research it is the group. We maintain extended contact over time with study participants, while biomedical researchers usually do not. We rarely know exactly how many informants we will observe or interview, or in which demographic categories; nor can we produce a precise schedule within which observations or interviews will occur. With reference to human subjects review, Margaret Mead, who thought the idea of IRB review absurd for ethnographers, observed, "Anthropological research does not have subjects. We work with informants in an atmosphere of trust and mutual respect" (1969:361).

Given such profound differences in research paradigms, it is no wonder that social scientists often chafe at IRB protocols. Because these protocols are predicated on a biomedical model, IRB staff often require firm numbers regarding samples and may demand periodic updates on how many people have been interviewed or observed. If estimated numbers are not met, IRB staff may ask why. Such interrogations can be difficult for ethnographers, who do not organize their studies around the precise numbers or the timetables required for certain statistical treatments.

Increasingly social scientists have critiqued the biomedical orientation of IRB procedures and philosophies, raising the possibility of social science research oversight taking place independently from IRB review (Schrag 2009b). These critiques recall how in the United States social scientists came close to escaping IRB regulation. In 1980, in the context of debates regarding the purview of IRBs over social science research, Edward Pattullo, director of the Center for the Behavioral Sciences at Harvard and chair of Harvard's IRB, stated, "[T]here should be no requirement for prior review of research utilizing legally competent subjects if that research involves neither deceit, nor intrusion upon the subject's person, nor denial or withholding of accustomed or necessary resources" (1980:15). Sadly, this viewpoint did not prevail, and the social sciences fell under the hegemony of biomedically focused institutional review bodies.

For the moment, then, social scientists (at least in the United States) must work within the constraints of the IRB system. In contexts where universities or other organizations are federally mandated to oversee research carried out by faculty and students, ethnographers cannot begin their work prior to receiving IRB approval. Many nonprofit organizations and commercial companies that employ ethnographers also have IRBs, either as a requirement for eligibility for federal grants or for legal protection, or both. Sometimes ethnographers must contend with more than one IRB, for example, if they work for a corporation that has a federal research grant, or through a subcontract.

Although IRBs typically derive their authority from federal law, they operate with a high degree of independence and can establish rules and procedures beyond those that stem from federal mandate. Each IRB has unique protocols and concerns pursuant to the disciplinary foundations of its institution, past legal challenges that have led to policy decisions, and particularities of the submission process. In the United States IRBs sometimes prioritize shielding institutions from litigation over protecting human subjects or supporting research. In consequence, many ethical considerations regarding ethnographic research are not recognized by IRBs because they hold no legal risk. Conversely, many of the liability and bureaucratic concerns of IRBs have little to do with ethical ethnographic inquiry. As a result, it is incorrect to assume that IRB approval means our work is ethical, or that because our work is ethical it will pass IRB muster.

9.2 PREPARING A PROTOCOL FOR IRB REVIEW

Following an initial online training course (which is often outdated in terms of internet research), IRBs require that researchers submit a protocol that follows a strict format (although that format can vary between IRBs). Submitting a protocol can be laborious, depending on the procedures and software of the institution. Some corporations require only a single document containing all the required elements. Universities typically have an online submission system comprised of a series of forms, with the protocol broken down into various subsections. The general format usually appears as follows:

- The purpose of the research, including the research question, in lay terms.
- A list of the research personnel, all of whom must have training certification. Working with collaborators from other institutions may require documenting their IRB certification at their own institutions, though some allow for multiple institutions to share a single IRB protocol.

- Research methods, including a detailed description of the research protocol. It is seldom sufficient to simply say "participant observation," for instance; IRB staff will want to see a specific explanation of what such an approach will entail.
- The places where we will conduct the research. For many IRBs this will imply laboratory or other physical locations. We should take the time to explain online fieldsites; clarifying their nature can help avoid time-consuming confusion.
- Number and description of the research subjects, including whether or not they fall into legally specified categories of vulnerable populations. Enumerating and describing research subjects in this manner can be difficult for ethnographers; we must provide the best estimates we can.
- Recruitment method and deployment strategy, including specific language of recruitment materials. IRBs may request permission from forum moderators or even game companies in order to approve recruitment protocols.
- The text of informed consent documents, and a description of how we will obtain informed consent.
- Potential risks and benefits to subjects.
- How we will maintain the confidentiality of research data.
- Level of review. While there is variation, IRBs have differing categories reflecting the degree to which they scrutinize proposed projects, with the highest attention to research that involves experimentation, particularly medical experimentation. Ethnographic research often is not subject to this level of review but is usually classed as "expedited," "excused," or "exempt." In some cases "exempt" protocols can greatly simplify IRB approval, such as no longer requiring a signed consent form for interviews. Ethnographic research may carry only "informational" risk (regarding personal data) rather than psychological or physical risk. However, even if the research is low risk, full review may be required if the study includes groups defined as vulnerable (for instance, children, incarcerated persons, or mentally disabled individuals). Note that even research with only informational risk may continue to come under IRB oversight in annual reviews and audits.

Overall we should always strive to write our IRB protocol so that individuals with no prior knowledge of ethnography or virtual worlds can understand it. It is advisable to look at the format before writing the protocol, paying special attention to question phrasings and character limits. Otherwise we can find ourselves rewriting the entire protocol several times.

9.3 WORKING WITH IRBs

IRBs are often staffed with experienced analysts or administrators with whom it is wise to have a conversation before even beginning to write an application. (We might think of them as informants from an unknown culture.) Staff often vet protocols before they are passed to faculty reviewers and may request changes before formal submission. It is helpful to assess how well IRB staff understand virtual worlds. We can educate our IRBs: "a well-informed IRB will better understand the ethical issues in virtual worlds research and will be able to issue strong recommendations to improve an inadequate proposal" (Fairfield 2011:85). We should not assume, for instance, that IRB staff (or academic reviewers) know the difference between a web site, a forum, and a virtual world, or that they are familiar with terms like "avatar." We must be careful with words like "embodied" because staff or reviewers might assume there is a biological component to the research. Many IRBs require that parts of the protocol that will be seen by human subjects (like consent forms) be written at a particular grade level, sometimes tested using the automatic grade-level checker in Microsoft Word. Avoid jargon, discipline-specific terms, excessive theory, and "academese" at all costs.

It is helpful to begin the IRB review process early. It is not unusual for IRBs to reject a protocol the first time, often requiring several rounds of revision before approval. Revision may involve anything from minor inconsistencies in the text to major modifications. Some IRBs meet every month, but others meet less frequently or may have a backlog of applications, meaning that approval can take three to six months or more. Some virtual world research projects will be deemed so low risk as to qualify for "expedited" or "exempt" review, but this is not guaranteed. We favor the "submit early and often" approach. This is particularly important if the project must be completed within a fixed time frame, such as a graduate thesis project. Studying the successful IRB protocols of colleagues and peers from our institutions is a good way to begin the process.

In terms of approval, IRBs tend to err on the side of caution. Responding to requests for revision can be challenging, particularly when IRB personnel and reviewers are not familiar with ethnographic research, virtual worlds research, or both. One of us once provided a careful summary of the virtual nature of a planned research project but was then asked, "Will you be raiding together face to face?" We checked the text, and we had spelled out the circumstances, but unfamiliarity with virtual worlds provoked the question. Another one of us encountered a problem with a member of a corporate IRB who had apparently read accounts of online rape and was concerned that subjects might be assaulted during a research session.

IRBs typically use terms like "risk," "benefit," and "vulnerable populations" to calculate the danger a research project poses to human subjects. Virtual worlds research is often considered low risk because it cannot cause immediate physical harm to participants. If the research is conducted exclusively online, the physical world identity of the subject can be hidden and may in fact never be known. Even so, IRB reviewers may mistakenly see risk based on alarmist mass media reporting. A reviewer for one of our projects was concerned that the subject might undergo a traumatic experience during a research session. This concern was addressed by emphasizing that participants could log off if they felt uncomfortable (this is now a common clause in many IRB consent forms for virtual worlds research). In another case one of us encountered concern from an IRB that felt that we should not ask parents about their children's play of World of Warcraft because it is "a violent game." We explained that the parents had already decided to allow their children to play, and that we did not view World of Warcraft as "violent." One of us had a study blocked by the IRB because of the inclusion of a vulnerable population for which the board had no experienced reviewers, even though the research was extremely low risk and potentially even beneficial to the participants. These kinds of misunderstandings underscore the importance of continuing dialogue with IRB personnel.

9.4 INFORMED CONSENT AND ANONYMITY

Most IRBs require that human subjects provide informed consent. This often means that subjects sign a paper form saying that they understand what data are being collected about them and give permission for the data to be used in the research. However, under "exempt" status, simply providing the subject with a "Study Information Sheet" that outlines the purpose and risks of the research is sufficient; a signed form is not needed, and the information can even be gone over verbally. When IRBs refuse to consider exempt status for online research, the mandate for signed consent forms can present such a high hurdle as to make the research infeasible. In some cases, as with Tom's research in Second Life, Celia's in There.com, and T.L.'s early work, ethnographers can successfully argue that avatar-name-only consent using an online form is sufficient, so long as we protect subject anonymity. When a physical world interview is involved, however, IRBs may insist on a physically signed consent form, although this requirement can sometimes be waived to maintain participant anonymity. With regard to telephone or email-only interviews, IRBs vary widely in their requests, ranging from verbal (recorded) consent, to electronically "signed" forms, to a simple email assent.

Minors are a tricky issue; they are considered a vulnerable population, so requests to include them in a study will raise concern. However, the position of IRBs toward minors varies. In one case we have experienced, members of an IRB requested that we include minors in a study from which they were originally excluded, because their inclusion would improve the study. Depending on the context, minors are usually asked to fill out an assent form, and a parental consent form is also typically required. In some of our online research, parental consent has been waived because it compromises subject anonymity, requiring researchers to obtain real names and addresses of subjects. In the case of face-to-face research, a parental consent form will always be required in addition to the assent, and it is likely that the IRB will restrict video recording, for instance, not allowing subjects' faces to be recorded.

In addition to informed consent from research subjects, IRBs might also require consent from representatives of entities such as forum moderators and website administrators. On several occasions IRBs have asked us to obtain permission from the game companies who owned the virtual worlds we were studying. Game companies are often uncooperative with researchers, so when we responded that this would make the research impossible, they withdrew the request. In some cases we have argued that virtual worlds constitute "public" places. On occasion some IRBs might require a clause in a protocol that we will agree to abide by the Terms of Service or End User Licensing Agreement of the virtual world we are researching.

IRBs usually ask researchers to anonymize all results and identifiers, including the names of avatars, physical world persons, servers, and groups. Of particular concern are personal identifiers like full names, addresses, and social security numbers (although it would be unusual for us to collect such information). There have been incidents of researchers having laptops with personal data stolen. If possible, we avoid collecting such personal identifier information in the first place, since it is typically unnecessary. If collected, personal data do not necessarily have to be shared with all members on a team. For instance, in one of Celia's collaborative projects, the team conducting face to face lab protocols collected physical world names but did not share them with the team doing inworld participant observation, who only had avatar names. Regardless of what data storage methods we use, we must ensure the data are safeguarded in line with the human subjects requirements of our institutions. Data must generally be stored on a secure server or locked in a cabinet in a private office.

We can ease the work of fulfilling IRB demands by beginning the process early, studying examples of colleagues' successful protocols, making personal contacts at our IRB office to ask questions, and promptly supplying answers to staff questions or requests for changes in the protocol. We suggest being flexible and cooperative; however, there may be rare cases where we need to be firm. One of us has experienced two instances in which the IRB suggested a complete change of research topic or subject pool. In both cases getting IRB approval required significant compromises that were largely deleterious to the research. While such interventionist moves are uncommon, they lie within the realm of possibility; we can mitigate them by educating our IRBs.

IRBs seem to work well with precedent. Some of us have had success with setting up standards, such as a precedent for an approved online consent form, which can be used as a template for multiple projects. Celia's lab has formed a human subjects research working group that maintains a library of methods books and articles, as well as an online knowledge base that includes links to IRB training sites, previously approved consent forms and protocols, and other resources that help to build on prior work and streamline the IRB process.

CHAPTER TEN

DATA ANALYSIS

10.1 ETHNOGRAPHIC DATA ANALYSIS: FLEXIBILITY AND EMERGENCE

The work of data analysis is often forgotten in discussions of ethnographic research. Ethnographers write about their experiences "in the field," discussing data collection in great detail. Particularly since the publication of *Writing Culture* (Clifford and Marcus 1986), ethnographers have also explored the process of writing itself. Both forms of reflexivity have been valuable, and of course this book addresses them. However, ethnographers have been far less transparent about the intermediate step of data analysis that makes possible the transition from data to text. Too often this step is treated as a black box, as if it is simply the brilliant minds of individual researchers that make connections and draw conclusions.

Like participant observation itself, data analysis is highly emergent and contextual (Bernard 1998). There is no one way to come up with the broad insights and claims that give ethnographic analyses their unique stamp and which ensure that the texts produced will be cited and discussed by others. But we can offer some practical advice. The most fundamental approach to data analysis is to engage in a rigorous intellectual process of working deeply and intimately with ideas. Analysis is not primarily about tuning coding schemes or tweaking data analysis software packages. It is about finding, creating, and bringing thoughtful, provocative, productive ideas to acts of writing.

This process is deeply personal, almost idiosyncratic, but begins with stretching our cognitive and perceptual horizons to encounter, absorb, and react to relevant literatures and conversations. We discover ideas through a systematic process of reading the literature, discussing our research with colleagues, and taking note of whatever strikes us as interesting and pertinent as we experience it in the field. Students in particular must learn to develop and trust their instincts, which will be improved by engaging with the literature and wider research community. A sustained passion for talking, thinking, and reading, for forging collegial discussions in domains of interest—these activities are the source of the good ideas that populate the ethnographic literature. At the same time, ethnographic research is profoundly exploratory and deeply identified with discovery. It is up to us to develop sound, persuasive arguments about what we find interesting, and to convince others that these arguments illuminate our data and speak to crucial concerns and debates.

One of the biggest differences between ethnographic data analysis and other paradigms centers on the temporal flow of the research. Most research paradigms establish coding and other analytic schemes *before* undertaking data collection. To conduct a survey, for instance, we must decide ahead of time if we will ask people to identify their age in terms of "under 20, 20–39, 40 and up," or "under 15, 15–29, 30–44, 45 and up," and so on. We must decide if we are going to ask about age, gender, or income. In contrast, while ethnographers formulate plans before conducting research (as discussed in chapter 4), we also try to be responsive and open to shifting our interests as we encounter the unexpected. We modify methods and research questions to respond to what we find in the field. Such shifts entail reshaping plans for data analysis.

As a result, we often construct significant portions of our data analysis protocols *after* we have completed field research. For someone conducting ethnographic research for the first time—and, on occasion, even for the experienced ethnographer—this flexibility may feel like a disconcerting lack of structure, out of step with common expectations for scientific research. Yet recall how a virtue of participant observation and other ethnographic methods is that they allow us to treat data as culturally situated: the value of the data is linked to the contexts of its collection. We cannot know those contexts in advance. An ethnographic methodology extends this kind of flexible approach into the data analysis phase.

10.2 PRELIMINARY REFLECTIONS WHILE IN THE FIELD

There is a general timeline to ethnographic research, from research design through data collection, data analysis, and the writing of research results. However, some stages may overlap, including data collection and data analysis. The classic scenario is to leave the field after a year of research to return home and, comfortably seated in one's office or library, pour over fieldnotes, interviews, and all the other data amassed during that long year. In this scenario, the "fieldnotes" produced during data collection and the "ethnography" produced through data analysis are rigidly sequential. However, this idealized scheme of observing, recording, and analyzing oversimplifies the realities of ethnographic research: "distinguishing these three phases of knowledge-seeking may not, as a matter of fact, normally be possible; and, indeed, as autonomous 'operations' they may not in fact exist" (Geertz 1973:20; see also Gupta and Ferguson 1997).

Thus, although there is a typical sequence to ethnographic work, the process can also have an iterative quality. Ethnographers may sometimes begin data analysis before data collection is complete (LeCompte and Schensul 1999). Since to varying degrees we do not know what we seek until we find it, it is not only possible but also desirable to engage in preliminary reflection on our data while in the field. We are not simply acting as recording robots while doing our fieldwork; it is normal (and beneficial) to be engaged in some low-level reflection as we proceed. This can help inform fieldwork and allow us to be responsive to emerging insights. In graduate school Tom was advised to leave his Indonesia fieldsite every few months for a weekend, travel to a nearby town (or even just a hotel in the same town), and try some preliminary review of his material to see what themes were emerging and where he might want to focus further data collection efforts. As recommended by Mills (1959), Celia kept a research journal throughout her fieldwork on the Uru diaspora; this allowed her to capture personal insights and revelations in situ, which informed her data collection and later her analysis. She also made notations on her actual fieldnotes if she noticed something that might represent a pattern or wanted to follow up on something she had seen or heard during participant observation or interviews. Given that in ethnographic work research questions and topical foci are to some degree emergent, preliminary reflections in the field can help modify data collection to better account for issues of which we were unaware prior to the research itself.

A strength of virtual world ethnography is that it is particularly amenable to weaving together data collection and some early reflections on where we are in the work. Sitting at our desks, we can alternate between looking at piles of collected data around us and stepping back into our virtual world fieldsite. While conducting fieldwork in Second Life, Tom would sometimes not log into the virtual world for a couple days to write summary discussions of his findings. T.L. remembers sitting around waiting at a gaming event, sketching out ideas in her notebook, when she stumbled upon a breakthrough in how to think about her data. As she mapped the various actors and activities she was seeing (Clarke 2005), noting their interrelations, she came to realize the diverse domains of data not as a barrier for analysis and something to overwhelm her, but as the heart of the story. This led her to broaden her gaze for the remainder of that event undaunted.

It is thus important to be open to the possibility of preliminary reviews of our data while in the field, so long as two dangers are kept in mind. First, the bulk of analysis should take place after fieldwork, or after a significant portion of fieldwork in a multi-year study. Preliminary analysis is counterproductive if it is so time-consuming that it detracts from data collection. Second, it is necessary to understand that the preliminary labeling of data as they are gathered is not the same as data analysis. In addition to using these moments to tweak our data collection, we can consider the early work we do in looking over our data while still in the field as opportunities to leave ourselves waypoints for future in-depth analysis.

10.3 THE ROLE OF THEORY IN DATA ANALYSIS

In chapter 3 we noted that ethnography differs from grounded theory and ethnomethodology in that it often builds on prior theoretical work. We discussed the notion that ethnographers draw from varying types of theory—whether philosophical or social scientific—as lenses through which to understand patterns of social activity. But how can such theories be applied; how do we even know where to begin? Being conversant in a number of different theoretical approaches is helpful; however, it is of course impossible to have a comprehensive knowledge of all available theories. Furthermore, it is mistaken to use theories simply because they are in vogue or we have a particular axe to grind. The theoretical frameworks we select should be responsive to the data and research interests.

This may seem to contradict traditional notions of scientific inquiry. However, ethnographers typically place theories in dialogue with data, sometimes drawing theoretical approaches from unexpected places if they suit the analytical task at hand. This approach is especially apt when "grand theories" such as activity theory are used as broad conceptual grounding. Such theorizing invariably needs to be rounded out with more focused "middle-range" theories in closer contact with the data. Bonnie has used theories of innovation and computer-mediated communication in her publications, while keeping activity theory as an orienting framework. For example, she used Seay and Kraut's notion of "problematic usage" of games to discuss debates about "addiction" in regard to World of Warcraft, but she also used the more abstract, higher-level theories of John Dewey and activity theory (Nardi 2010).

Understanding this back-and-forth relationship between data and theory in ethnographic analysis is important because all too frequently we have seen students and researchers asserting that their work is valuable because it is theoretically unprecedented. Such claims of absolute novelty are both unnecessary and misleading. Of course the dangers of false claims to originality in ethnographic research are hardly limited to studies of new technologies. The continuing influence of that mindset can be seen in pressures to not research a virtual world that has already been studied, as if building a research community were a bad thing and being the ostensibly first person to describe a new online environment was valuable by definition (Fairfield 2011). This orientation obscures the fact that research is an intersubjective enterprise, founded in the cumulative theoretical work of numerous forebears and colleagues.

There are several approaches to weaving theory into our analyses. One way to begin is to look at the work of other researchers in our disciplinary areas to see which theories they have found most productive. Celia arrived at the application of de Certeau's notion of consumption as a creative practice through the work of sociologist Paul Willis (1981), as well as Henry Jenkins's foundational studies of fan culture (1992). She built on this concept in theorizing how members of the Uru diaspora were forging a "fictive ethnicity" through their transplantation of Uru culture and artifacts to other virtual worlds (Pearce and Artemesia 2008). As ethnographers we should feel free to engage flexibly with a range of disciplines in developing our theoretical perspectives. For instance, Celia has drawn from the psychological theory of flow (Csíkszentmihályi 1990) and Goffman's (1974) sociological theory of frame analysis. Broader theoretical orientations, such as Marxist, feminist, or queer theory, can also act as conceptual resources for better understanding the phenomena we encounter in our fieldwork.

An example from Tom's work that highlights this scholarly principle of "standing on the shoulders of giants" is the concept of techne. Tom noticed that Second Life residents kept talking about how making things was important to them. He also saw such crafting take place, often collaboratively, during participant observation, and he joined in these activities. Over time he also realized that these ideas about crafting extended to how people modified their avatars and homes, how they talked about "building" community, even questions of fashioning identity and worldview. This inspired Tom to research the idea of "crafting." He was stunned to discover that one ancient Greek word for crafting, *techne*, was the root of the contemporary term "technology." He knew right away he was on to something. Then he discovered not only that Aristotle had discussed the distinction between *techne* and *episteme* (knowledge), but that important theorists including Félix Guattari, Michael Foucault, Martin Heidegger, and Bernard Stiegler had explored how the concept of techne could shed light on human relations to technology. Techne ended up becoming a central theoretical framework of Tom's analysis, but not because he had stated in his original research design "I want to use the concept of techne" or "I need to cite Foucault in my book so people will think I am smart." Through an iterative relationship to his ethnographic research, Tom forged a theory in dialogue with his fieldsite. That he could analyze aspects of Second Life culture through the lens of Aristotle by way of Foucault suggests new forms of online sociality. Without such understandings of how our work fits into broader scholarly debates, we cannot make a truly original contribution to the field.

T.L. has, for example, drawn theoretical concepts from actor network theory into her analysis of gaming. In her work on modding, she built upon Latour's formulation of the role of nonhuman actors (1992) to discuss how user-created software came to act as a powerful member of raiding teams. She analyzed mods not just as tools, but as social actors that carry with them particular agency, values, and expectations. Inspired by the work of Rabinow (2003), as well as Deleuze and Guattari (1987), she developed, in engagement with her data, a notion of the "assemblage of play" as a way of understanding how diverse components well beyond the packaged game software co-constitute experience in these spaces (Taylor 2009). She found resonance in this approach to what Bowker and Star (1999) identified as an "ecological understanding," a useful frame for that stage of ethnographic work when we begin to comb through our fieldnotes, looking for interrelations and piecing together a rich picture of the life of a virtual world.

10.4 BEGINNING DATA ANALYSIS: SYSTEMATIZE AND THEMATIZE

In this section we discuss techniques for analyzing data to move toward developing broader insights, but we want to emphasize at the outset that while this task is a necessary step in data analysis, it is not the hard part. The hard part is developing *original* insights and ideas with wider relevance to our research communities. From our fieldwork we collect a staggering range of materials. During data analysis we get to survey this material, looking for the patterns and relationships that will lead to important insights and arguments. This process is slow: there are no shortcuts. "Becoming friends" with the data is a way to think of this journey; it is just as immersive, in its way, as fieldwork: "The ethnographer begins concentrated analysis and writing by reading his fieldnotes in a new manner, looking closely and systematically at what has been observed and recorded. In so doing, she treats the fieldnotes as a data set, reviewing, re-experiencing, and reexamining everything that has been written down, while self-consciously seeking to identify themes, patterns, and variations within this record" (Emerson, Fretz, and Shaw 1995:144). We must give ourselves over to the data—minimizing interruption, ensuring concentration, and finding the quiet in which the data will speak to us. We will provide some details for analyzing various forms of data, but we start with general guidelines.

A first step is systematizing our data. This reveals patterns that can lead to larger insights when combined with other concepts and principles. Systematization is done by going through all the material, sorting it, marking it up, and annotating it where needed. This process usually involves some form of tagging; that is, labeling data with micro-units such as "gender," "conflict," "alts," then moving to coding. The distinction between tagging and coding is heuristic, but coding usually refers to a systematic categorizing of data with higher-level constructs such as "player notions of work/play" or "the relationship between temporality and romance." Note that coding and tagging require actually reading a text, not just doing word searches. For instance, notions of work and play might be stated in language that does not include the words "work" or "play." An exclamation like "crap, have to leave for my shift in 15 minutes :(" typed into guild chat reveals attitudes about work that may be juxtaposed to particular events taking place at the time, yielding important data that we can interpret with nuance because we were on the scene, knew the participants, and had extensive background knowledge of the social group or activity in question.

If working with material digitally, we could in principle use a range of qualitative data analysis programs (such as Atlas.ti). While some researchers employ such programs, it is striking that none of us has ever used them. Our experience has been that they typically require a steep learning curve and are frequently constrained by analytical assumptions built into the software. There may also be a tendency to believe that qualitative analysis software is somehow more "objective" than hand coding and analysis, and that such software may help overcome the myth that ethnography is "undermined by subjectivity," discussed in chapter 3. But the situated and contextual nature of ethnographic research and analysis defies standardization and mechanization. It is erroneous to assume that a piece of technology (which, incidentally, is made by people) can do the interpretive work of a thoughtful human mind.

Instead we opt for the flexibility of standard word processing, database, and spreadsheet programs—and even paper and pen—to comment on, highlight, move, and search for data. Thus, while not in any way discouraging the use of qualitative data programs, we emphasize that they do not, in themselves, perform the work of analysis. The key to data analysis is to interact with the dataset: read it, study it, immerse oneself within it, and let the data paint a portrait of the culture we are studying. Answers to research questions lie within the data—and furthermore, new questions inhabit the data as well, questions that stood outside the universe of the thinkable when we originally designed the project. No data analysis software will ever lead us to such questions; it is through intensive engagement with the data that these questions (and their answers) will become apparent.

Coding is an early stage of data analysis, not its culmination. Sometimes researchers think that once coding is done, the work of data analysis is complete. However, by definition coding misses the big picture: the overarching meanings, histories, and linkages between cultural domains will not be rendered intelligible within schemes that label, tag, or segment. For instance, applying the code "learning episode" to an event in which a player teaches another player a gaming technique tells us nothing about how the persons involved understood what learning means, the dynamics of collaborative learning, the motivations behind learning in a play context, how learning is subjectively experienced, or the contexts that shape the learning interaction.

This second level of analysis thus involves building out from our initial phase to thematizing the data. During this stage we are looking for patterns, critical moments where a phenomenon is echoing through the culture in a significant way. While it may begin with noting a simple argument over a virtual billboard, a brief lamentation about the impending demands of a player's job, or a phrase that appears independently in multiple interviews, thematic development is about moving beyond the notation of single incidents. The work we do in systematizing helps leverage our data in finding recurrences. While it is from often seemingly minor details that our most important findings sometimes arise, they come as well from the overview of data writ large, engaging with theoretical and conceptual arguments in the literature, and developing new arguments when necessary. We must establish that our data reveal wider patterns.

As we sort our data to develop themes, it will often prove helpful to arrange the data into "piles" or sections with subject headings. These subject headings can include emic concepts (like "avatar customization" or "mods in raiding"), as well as etic concepts (like "social stratification" or "hegemony"). As noted earlier, our most important analytical tool is ideas. We bring them in from theory, generate them from the data, and build on emic constructs to perform our analyses.

For viewing, some ethnographers print out key materials. Others rely on virtual piles—cutting and pasting relevant data into a Word document, for instance. Some do both. T.L. first sorts through her digital materials, then prints out a portion so that she can shuffle the data around in physical piles, marking things up with pens and highlighters. Tom prefers to keep all his data in digital form, using the "outline" function of Word to thematically organize the data, or entering data into a Filemaker Pro database where it can be easily sorted and regrouped. Bonnie first prints out and reads all her fieldnotes and interview transcripts like a novel, then goes back over the data more analytically, armed with colored pens, Post-it notes, and the original digital files to facilitate searching for specific words and phrases. Celia has used a combination of all these approaches, as well as the "old school" technique of organizing concepts and patterns on index cards.

Whatever procedures we employ, the goal is to organize the data into manageable pieces we can thematically analyze and easily locate when writing up research results. Using folders and subdirectories on a computer can be helpful. As piles or sections of data accumulate, we can refine them. Some will get so large and unwieldy that we will be forced to split them up into two or more topics. In other cases we may find a section with only a few items in it; this can prompt us to consider combining it with another section.

Ethnographers develop higher-level themes by linking or juxtaposing coded units, such as "the way informants talk about crafting objects shares features with the way they talk about falling in love." Critical incidents or events that reveal cultural propensities, connections, conflicts, or problems may also yield themes, such as Bonnie's assessment of the agency of gaming software in altering social relations, which she analyzed in light of events surrounding changes in raiding requirements following a software expansion in World of Warcraft.

In practice, tags, codes, and themes are not mutually exclusive and should inform each other. Often we begin to notice higher-level units as we work with lower-level units. We may, for example, be searching for instances of talk related to gender and discover that distinct formulations significantly structure game discourse and activity. Ultimately these first two stages of data analysis—systematization and thematization—are in close conversation with each other and are iterative. As we develop thematic threads through the data we may find ourselves polishing coding schemes or finding new angles we did not spot when we began. As we indicated at the start of this section, the process of analysis is as immersive as the fieldwork itself, and we should, while attending to the data in a rigorous way, also let it lead us to important critical areas. Before we continue and discuss the move from thematizing to narrativizing and building arguments, we want to talk about some specific issues that can arise with various forms of data.

10.5 WORKING WITH PARTICIPANT OBSERVATION DATA

While the guidelines above apply to all forms of data gathered during fieldwork, different kinds of data often require special approaches. Given that participant observation is the pivotal data collection method of ethnographic research, it follows that fieldnotes should be central to analysis. Fieldnotes will include not just major incidents, but a range of mundane interactions and episodes. In many cases the commonplace and everyday may prove more informative than events that occasioned explicit commentary.

Ethnographic research is fundamentally about understanding a culture from the inside out. However, by the time we get to the data analysis phase, we are often so acculturated to the fieldsite that we take its cultural logics for granted, just as our informants do. Analyzing participant observation data helps to "make strange" (Bell, Blythe, and Sengers 2005) our fieldsite once again; this allows us to retrace the ethnographic journey from outsider to insider, chronicling key moments of curiosity, befuddlement, and insight.

Whether working with fieldnotes digitally, physically, or both, the goal of analyzing data collected via participant observation is to discover patterns that illuminate the research question and develop new insights. A good first step is to read everything and look for core themes. This is admittedly something of a black art, but knowledge of the literature and understandings of what is important and interesting guide the process.

Issues of contention may be important, but so are widespread norms, consensus, and repeated scenarios and routines: ethnography is probably the science most dedicated to the normal and the quotidian.

Two concepts that provide a useful way to think about analysis are Mills' notion of "the sociological imagination" and Richardson's metaphor of "crystallization." Mills reminds us that we can move in and out of the data, observing it at different scales, from the most minute detail to the broadest overall pattern of culture. To achieve this "you try to think in terms of a variety of viewpoints and in this way to let your mind become a moving prism catching light from as many angles as possible" (1959:214). Richardson also invokes the prism in her metaphor of crystallization; this can highlight the multifaceted nature of our data, since crystals possess "symmetry and substance with an infinite variety of shapes. . . . What we see depends on our angle of repose" (1994:934).

Just as with participant observation, we should not conceptualize working through fieldnotes as a distanced process. Our deep embodied knowledge of the fieldsite is an asset, and it is through (not despite) such engagement that we produce our best work. We should "participate" in our participant observation data as we analyze it, watching for things that catch our eye and incidents we find important. Of course, what may catch our eye are things that leave us perplexed, or that challenge some hunch or argument we are developing.

When faced with these conundrums, we must be diligent to avoid the trap of dismissing data that do not fit the argument we are trying to build. We should look for places in our fieldnotes where we noted being confused by something we encountered, or where we identified exceptions to patterns. Contradictions in the data often open up the possibility of new and unexpected discoveries or serve to illuminate our understanding of cultural norms. There is no need to fear discovering something that appears to disprove our ideas: this situation usually represents an opportunity to clarify and deepen the analysis. Since there are always variable attitudes and practices in any culture we study (Romney, Weller, and Batchelder 1986), there often exist two or three dominant understandings of an issue. Discovering this complexity can bring new insights and open new problematics. For instance, Bonnie noticed a bimodal distribution in player attitudes regarding real money trading (RMT), in other words buying and selling virtual items for conventional currencies among World of Warcraft players. The heated emotions offered up by players on this topic led her to analyze portrayals of "Chinese gold farmers" who retail virtual items for physical world currencies. During data analysis Tom found evidence that in Second Life some residents liked having more than one avatar (an alt), while others disagreed with the practice. Learning about these multiple perspectives did not disprove his ideas about avatars but helped him craft a more robust theory of virtual embodiment. T.L. noticed differing opinions about "powergamers" during her EverQuest research that spoke to deeper themes about how people understood distinctions between play and work. Following the trail of divergent responses in the data allowed her to push her own initial thinking on the subject.

10.6 WORKING WITH INDIVIDUAL AND GROUP INTERVIEW DATA

Next to participant observation data, the most significant body of data will usually come from individual and/or group interviews. The process of converting interviews from their raw audio or video form into transcribed text is not just a practical procedure. It is an analytical journey as well. As mentioned earlier, there are unglamorous, mechanical aspects to transcription. However, what must not be forgotten is that when working with the texts of our interviews, even in apparently rote tasks of transcription, we are engaging in a deeply analytic practice. Many researchers (including some of us) have transcribed interviews while still in the field, to ensure data are not lost and to see what topics might need further investigation. However, all of us have transcribed interviews after completing primary fieldwork. The value in having at least some transcription take place after fieldwork is that we can use the process of transcribing analytically. It can allow us to simultaneously look back on our fieldwork with the benefit of hindsight and engage with the data in a focused and intimate manner. When outside transcribers produce transcripts of audio interviews, it is imperative that we read them slowly and carefully, since we will not have had the benefit of listening closely to the interviews during transcription. In this case, if needed, we should go back to portions of the original audio to listen for nuances of intonation and other aural cues that may help us grasp the data more fully.

In ethnographic research interview data are not analyzed in isolation. A unique affordance of ethnographic methods is that they allow us to compare what people *do* with what they *say* about what they do. While ethnographers are concerned with what people are up to, we are also concerned with their emic understandings of what they are doing and its significance to them. An important aspect of data analysis therefore involves comparing the interactions observed in participant observation with participants' own understandings and interpretations of these activities. In some cases we may find contradictions; in others we may find that a particular action takes on new meaning when looked at through a particular cultural lens. Informants may be more or less self-reflective, more or less critical of their cultures and the individuals within them. In Celia's work with the Uru diaspora, activities and artifacts in virtual worlds often had hidden meanings informed by players' history in Uru, as revealed through interviews. Fountains, a book on a pedestal, a decorated egg, or a certain style of tall pine tree had special meaning among Uru refugees in There.com that could be drawn out only through interviews.

As we sit down with our interview transcriptions, the process of data analysis does not differ substantially from the approach to dealing with participant observation data. The goal is immersion in the material: watching for themes and points where informants make insightful comments, notating useful passages, and highlighting quotable lines. Data analysis may be oriented toward broader themes, or it may be at the level of detailed tagging of small analytical units (such as the use of a particular word or phrase). One approach can be to re-listen to recorded interviews with the transcription before us, annotating the transcription as we go along. Often we have particular participants who are especially informative and articulate; working closely with those interviews is very useful. The ultimate goal is to distill from the hours of conversations the core concepts, themes, and issues around which we will build our ethnographies.

The words of our informants are a powerful part of the final work, and we should attend not only to the issues they raise, but to their way of speaking about them. Do particular words, phrases, or ideas recur? Are there moments of strong sentiment or ambivalence? Are there places where the informant's words do not align with the concepts and ideas we are developing, challenging our understandings of the data? Are there specificities of language use that reveal aspects of culture? Are informants introducing terms, concepts, or ideas that are especially unique?

All these suggestions apply equally to group interviews. There are, however, a few minor additional issues. When analyzing group interview data, it is important to attend both to moments of consensus—when participants agree on some issue of interest—and moments of debate, as these disagreements can illuminate the range of opinions and practices regarding some domain of human action. For instance, in the months before the introduction of voice into Second Life, residents participating in group interviews with Tom had lively discussions about its risks and benefits. This included the issue of voice possibly making social interactions too linked to physical world identities, and how voice would effect persons with hearing disabilities versus visual disabilities. Tracking this range of debate through group interviews helped Tom understand the cultural meanings of voice in Second Life; indeed, the image in his book of a resident with a "no voice" protest sign was taken in his Second Life home during a group interview.

One final important point: while all our transcriptions form a core corpus of our data, we will end up using direct quotes from only some of our conversations. Direct quotes bring our participants to life, foreground the specificity of ethnographic research, and add authenticity to our characterization of cultures. However, long interview quotes without analysis or interpretation do not "speak for themselves." Thus part of our job as scholars is to comb through the mass of data and identify and analyze effective excerpts to share with readers. As we examine our data we should pay careful attention to (and notate so we can rediscover!) particularly strong passages or quotes we can use to ground our arguments as we move into the writing stage.

10.7 WORKING WITH IMAGES, VIDEO, AND TEXTUAL DATA

Most ethnographers gather images, video, and textual data. If a research project is concerned with video, imagery, or questions of archives and history, these kinds of data will be central to the analysis, and we should approach them using the same fine-grained attention to detail and thematics described above with reference to participant observation and interview data. However, if (as is often the case) such data supplement participant observation and interview data, then the question is how to use images, video, and textual data in a manner that effectively supports and illustrates key points without overwhelming the analysis.

Sometimes a short segment of inworld video yields rich data. For example, Bonnie analyzed the properties of text in World of Warcraft by studying a one-minute video segment of a raid encounter. She observed that in-game texts were quite different from the typical printed page or webpage; the texts were ephemeral and mobile, occurring all over the screen, and were positioned by players according to their own personal preferences. The texts were rendered in blazing colors, often with accompanying audio. They were multi-authored, originating from the game software as well as multiple software modifications. To analyze such texts it was necessary to use video data, as many properties of the text could be observed only by watching the shifting of the texts as they moved across the screen and viewing the texts' temporal flow as they alternated between visibility and invisibility during a raid encounter.

We might want to go through screenshots after making an initial pass at the written material, watching for images that might usefully illustrate a theme or point. In some cases (as when Tom discussed basic features of Second Life or Celia described the avatar creation mechanism of each of the games in her study), we might return to the fieldsite to take screenshots that will clearly reflect the overall narrative. T.L. tends to print out particularly evocative images so she can add them to thematic piles; the images help her remember related points in the fieldwork data. Screenshots of player-created artifacts played a major role in Celia's research on the productive play practices of members of the Uru diaspora. They enabled her to compare multiple user-created instantiations of the same Uru artifact alongside those from the original game, revealing the emergence of a hybrid style that replaced the realism of Uru with the cartoon aesthetic of There.com.

The kinds of textual data gathered during virtual world fieldwork can be very diverse, including text from popular press articles, FAQs, forums, blogs, wikis, books, news aggregators, and virtual world newspapers and magazines. Regardless, during data analysis we should organize this material thematically, highlight key phrases and statements, and link it to other forms of data.

In some cases analysis hinges on gathered textual materials, such as Bonnie's studies of digital documents regarding Chinese gold farmers or her analysis of World of Warcraft theorycrafting. Here analysis proceeds much as it does with fieldnotes: we assemble a corpus of texts and scrutinize them in detail. It may be necessary to limit the corpus of online materials since many websites contain vast stores of data. The general procedure is to discover what the websites are about (which may involve reading them for months) and then to use exemplars from the texts to illustrate key points.

Even when focusing on video recordings or texts, our analysis should be deeply informed by the cultural knowledge we have gained through participant observation. As in Bonnie's example above about analyzing raid video, it is far easier to understand why raid texts are coming and going so quickly when we understand the activity of raiding itself. Sound participant observation research acts as the core of an ethnographic approach and can thus link a range of analyses that draw on data collected through other methods.

10.8 THE END OF THE DATA ANALYSIS PHASE: FROM THEMES TO NARRATIVES AND ARGUMENTS

At what point should we consider our data analysis complete and move on to the final synthesis of our findings? One effective way to know when we have reached this point is that as we review the data, we are not seeing new patterns emerge. We are nearing the end of data analysis when we know the key themes to which our data speak, and even such details as which pile or section contains certain quotes or stories, or which folder on our computer holds prized images. Reaching this point is no small feat, and we should not shortchange this stage of ethnographic research. Our journey of data analysis moves from systematizing our data, to generating core thematics, to developing narratives and arguments that bring us to larger theoretical and conceptual points.

For instance, during preliminary analysis of his participant observation data, Tom noted when place and time shaped Second Life resident interactions—an argument over an ugly billboard next to someone's virtual home, or lag causing people at a dance to get out of sync with the music. But this examination of the data was merely a first step. Only after extensive analysis did Tom realize he wanted to claim that place and time are as central to virtual sociality as identity or embodiment. This broad conclusion arose not just from Tom's notations about virtual billboards and discos, but because of his knowledge of literatures on identity and embodiment. His participant observation enabled him to evaluate and critique notions in that literature and to develop, with the rigor of a sound empirical base, new conceptions of what constitutes social experience in virtual worlds.

Bonnie's analysis regarding how World of Warcraft players view work and play began late one night when she noticed a player discussing, with dread, her work schedule, noting the exact time she had to be at her job in the morning and how little time she had left for the pleasurable activity of playing World of Warcraft. The emotion in the player's chat conversation struck Bonnie as interesting and led her to Dewey's critique of aspects of modernity (including notions of work and school), which was surprisingly similar to sentiments expressed by many World of Warcraft players, as documented in Bonnie's corpus of interviews and chatlogs.

One of the most significant findings of Celia's Uru research was the discovery of "intersubjective flow." This concept merged Csíkszentmihályi's psychological theory of "flow" (1990), play theorist Bernie DeKoven's concept of co-liberation (1992), and the principle of "intersubjectivity" (Blumer 1969) to create a more social interpretation of how the psychological phenomenon of "flow," or optimal experience, is enhanced through group play.

As T.L. came to see the ways players invested their time, energies, and passions into the game of EverQuest, she became struck by the game developer's use of the phrase "You're in our world now!" which was meant to evoke a sense of stepping into a fantasy space. Yet it signaled something more. Players spoke of their investment and connection to their digital characters, experiences, and communities yet also at times wrestled with the idea that the game was in some sense not fully theirs, that it was still owned by a company. As she read literature around intellectual property and cultural life, T.L. found herself more fully exploring this critical theme, reflecting on otherwise disparate data piles (avatar auctions, game tag lines, end user license agreements, fan fiction, player investment) in a more cohesive way to link up with this much broader contemporary conversation ranging well beyond virtual worlds.

Much of what we have described in terms of data analysis involves systematically reviewing our data and moving to discrete thematic formulations. The final step is crafting a narrative around these themes, presenting evidence and argumentation to convey larger points to our readers. This process of distillation facilitates "getting our head around the data"—realizing what we have and how we might organize our insights and supporting evidence to craft the ethnography itself. A helpful technique for this initial stage of identifying a key argument is devising an "elevator pitch"—a few sentences to try out on a partner, colleague, friend, or whoever will listen. If we cannot succinctly and effectively sum up what we want to address, further clarification of the ideas is needed. For example, Bonnie's book on World of Warcraft is about "the aesthetics of play in a digital medium." Tom was eventually able to say, "My book is about what culture in a virtual world tells us about culture more generally." We move toward deciding what our written account will emphasize. Given the page limits of conference papers and journal articles—and the need to not spend the rest of our life writing that book!—we must make decisions. What is the argumentative heart of what we want to say? What do readers really need to know about what we have discovered? These decisions can be bittersweet because a well-executed ethnographic project will produce more data and insights than can appear in any written work.

To facilitate this process it is helpful to sit down and brainstorm outlines of the argument, mapping out potential sections of an article or book. T.L. sketches out possible components of the argument, linking outlined points to the themed piles of data she has already organized. Bonnie starts by writing out key points she wants to make in a few sentences each, and then deriving sections and subsections from the points. Tom's favorite approach is to use the outline function of Microsoft Word to group related points, examples, and references together since this makes it easy to move items around and also to collapse the outline so as to see the overall flow of an argument. Celia begins by writing a brief description of the key patterns that have emerged from the data analysis.

From these outlines and sketches, we feed in material from our fieldwork and interviews to bring life to arguments. This is where extensive and well-marked data gained through fieldwork provide robust evidence. Our data serve as the raw material, but we lean as well on our knowledge of the literature and provocative ideas we glean from informants themselves. Central to establishing the value of ethnographic data is linking it to broader analyses. Ethnographic evidence and argumentation presents itself in the form of compelling incidents, cases, stories, quotations, and vignettes, interwoven with theoretical and conceptual points. It is through the rich detail of our fieldwork in concert with rigorous argumentation that we create social scientific knowledge out of our ethnographic practice. We discuss various forms of ethnographic writing in more detail in chapter 11.

10.9 GENERALIZATION AND COMPARISON

When analyzing ethnographic data we focus on the rich specificity of fieldwork: persons, events, memorable statements, arresting images. However, from that specificity we craft an analysis whose value goes beyond the particular incidents we encountered. We seek patterns and logics—the ways of thinking, believing, and doing that make cultures and societies possible. This scoping outward need not end at the boundaries of the culture or cultures we study, not least because cultures are never neatly bounded in the first place. From the earliest days of fieldwork practice, ethnographers have extended their claims past any one culture. We have sought to generalize. As the eminent anthropologist Edmund Leach noted, "When we read Malinowski we get the impression that he is stating something which is of *general* importance" (1961:1, emphasis in original).

This analytic move is perhaps one of the most misunderstood by those unfamiliar with ethnographic research, who still sometimes see such research as limited to a small locality. This misunderstanding, linked to the myths we discussed in chapter 3, is problematic because it can lead to devaluing ethnographic work as simply providing "local color," or illustrative anecdotes for other methodological approaches that would presumably provide the generalizations. For this reason an important analytic task is to think about how our work speaks to broader contexts and cultural conversations. If we study a single server, or even a single guild, on what basis can we say that the research also applies to similar entities? If we undertake an in-depth project on avatars in one virtual world, does what we find apply to other spaces? How do the processes of cultural production inworld help us speak about offline issues? In this section we discuss three issues relevant to this question of generalization: situating and scoping the fieldsite, comparison, and falsifiability.

Situating and scoping the fieldsite

Any fieldsite is an example of a larger class of similar entities: guilds, servers, online universities, and so on. Ethnographers will need to think through how their fieldsite links up to more general issues and phenomena present in the larger class. Are we making claims about our own guild, or the larger class "guilds," or perhaps a more restricted set, for example, family guilds in that specific game? A claim is a statement that we can substantiate with our findings with respect to the scoped entity. The data must be robust enough to sustain claims as new data (collected by us or other researchers) are added to the record. Our data regarding the general issues and phenomena we wish to link to must be at the right level of generality. We should be wary of overgeneralizing, but at the same time we should not be afraid to point to phenomena that are likely to have broader implications.

One argument that frequently shapes concerns with regard to ethnographic generalization involves statistical significance. Many quantitative methods are designed to account for generalization via the statistical technique of random sampling. If (and this is often a bigger "if" than commonly acknowledged) there exists a discrete population from which a random sample can be drawn, and if the target population meets the assumptions underlying a particular statistical test, quantitative researchers can state with a degree of confidence that their claims are generalizable to the population as a whole. However, random samples or large-scale projects are not the only approaches available to researchers. Ethnographers generally seek to explain a holistic unit such as a community or activity—a learning activity in a classroom, skilled performance in a raid, guild interactions, or the operation of a photography club in Second Life.

Because we do not deal in "variables" but in relations between people and things, our sample is not random in the statistical sense.

Because we are not relying on a random sample, we situate our fieldsites by explaining their historical specificity and describing aspects that may be relatively idiosyncratic versus representative of broader patterns (Markham 2009). It is up to us as ethnographers to develop a sense of the universe of possibilities, and to locate the work within that universe. For instance, if we study a single guild on a single server we may learn something valuable, but we must also be careful to explain the kind of guild, the type of server, and other matters delineating the study group. Tom worked in his data analysis to situate Second Life in the context of other virtual worlds (including those structured as online games), video games, and other internet-related phenomena like social networking sites and blogs. It is noteworthy that all four of us have traveled across various regions of cyberspace in our investigations, examining our questions of interest in multiple contexts.

Once we understand the universe of phenomena of which our fieldsite is an example, we can appropriately scope our claims. For instance, it may be reasonable to say that players of fantasy-themed multi-user virtual worlds form certain player typologies (Bartle 1996), but it would be unsatisfactory to generalize this model without a consideration (through either primary or secondary data) of players in other game genres, or even within the fantasy genre. In some cases we may scope our claims in the sense of focusing on the specific communities we have studied. Often we forget the value in careful, detailed analysis of specific cultures without any claim to broad generalization.

Another way to scope our claims is to use "moderatum generalizations" (Williams 2000; Payne and Williams 2005). These are moderate claims, "not attempts to produce sweeping sociological statements that hold good over long periods of time, or across ranges of cultures . . . they are moderately held, in the sense of a political or aesthetic view that is open to change. This latter characteristic is important because it leads such generalizations to have a hypothetical character. They are testable propositions that might be confirmed or refuted through further evidence" (Payne and Williams 2005:297). Recognizing this middle ground between speaking only of individuals, on the one hand, and making sweeping statements, on the other, is very effective to help scope our claims. For example, during his Second Life research Tom became interested in the phenomenon of being "away from keyboard," or "afk." This occurred when residents left their computers for a time without shutting down the Second Life program, so that their avatar remained in the virtual world. Tom observed afk practices in many social contexts and discussed it in individual and group interviews. Indeed, afk was so pervasive that it was coded into the Second Life client, both as an alert that residents could use to indicate they were away and as an automated animation in which avatars appeared to nod off. In addition, it was clear that afk had implications—for instance, the possibility of presence without immersion—that were not only highly revealing about Second Life but relevant to other virtual worlds, where afk was also pervasive. When Bonnie did her research on U.S. servers, she used North America as the delimiter for her claims about World of Warcraft because she played on several North American servers. She consistently observed common patterns across the servers and reported her findings as pertaining to the United States and Canada.

Another issue of scope is that ethnographers excel at discovering dimensions or variables of interest that may be useful to other researchers using a variety of qualitative or quantitative techniques (see Fidel 2012). For example, an ethnographer could learn about the existence of gay guilds in a virtual world. That could lead other ethnographers to look for that possibility in other virtual worlds, or for a statistician to include a question about gay guilds on their survey. In other words, the "scope" is not merely a single site where an ethnographer has conducted research, but the discovery of important dimensions of the community or activity under study. Dimensions of social life that ethnographers discover can be analyzed with qualitative techniques, or they can be operationalized as variables for statistical treatment (such as correlating age, gender, player type, and time in-game; see, e.g., Debeauvais et al. 2011).

Overall, then, when ethnographers make claims, we are balancing two sets of considerations. On one hand we do not wish to argue that all those we study believe or act in the same way. Rather we are able to show that a cultural logic or norm is widely shared and teaches us something of value beyond the specific individuals we studied. On the other hand we realize the circumscribed character of our fieldsite in relation to all other possible sites (and thus, indeed, the entire world). We stay attuned to the specificities of our research yet simultaneously seek moments of larger cultural generalization where viable.

Comparison

Drawing on the work of other researchers, particularly other ethnographers, can also be useful for building arguments. Generalization is not the only valid path to scientific inquiry; ethnographers can also contribute through comparison (Paccagnella 1997). While a quantitative researcher might conduct research in a large number of virtual worlds, this is impractical for ethnographers, though it is of course possible to do research in more than one virtual fieldsite during a given project (as Celia did with her Uru research).

However, to study every instance of anything is impossible. Ethnographers can also generate valuable insights by working in a comparative mode, analyzing similarities and differences between our research and the work of our colleagues. Science is cumulative: it is by the accretion of new data and analyses that we formulate a better picture of the phenomena under study. One reason the notion of the "lone ethnographer" is false is that even in those cases where we are not working as part of a team, we should draw comparatively on the work of others when formulating generalizations. For instance, when developing his generalizations about the afk phenomenon, Tom not only analyzed patterns in his own data but corroborated his findings by consulting scholarly discussions of the phenomenon in other virtual worlds.

Falsifiability

Finally, it is worth noting that as we think through the question of generalization and ethnographic research, we grapple as well with broader issues of falsifiability in social science. In this case we are talking not about how we might generalize, but how we might use our work to problematize existing generalizations, even our own. In such contexts our work may provide a valuable counterpoint to that of other researchers whose overgeneralized claims may be in need of better specification. Ethnographic research is particularly well suited to contribute to this fundamental aspect of social scientific theory building. Indeed the grounding of such research in everyday experience can provide theoretical and conceptual rigor: "[Karl] Popper himself used the now famous example 'all swans are white' and proposed that just one observation of a single black swan would falsify this proposition and in this way have general significance and stimulate further investigations and theory building. The case study is well suited for identifying 'black swans' because of its in-depth approach: What appears to be 'white' often turns out on closer examination to be 'black' " (Flyvbjerg 2006:228).

For example, T.L. identified forms of speech and patterns of behavior in her early work on virtual worlds that indicated embodied experiences within them. At a time when the dominant rhetoric was of disembodied minds floating in cyberspace, this was a solid research finding to complicate emerging theories about life online (Taylor 2002). Ethnographic work is well suited for falsifying established claims because ethnographers deal with emergent social situations during research and must be prepared to rethink original assumptions and research design based on what we encounter. This stance makes us open to recognizing behaviors or cultural patterns that act as "black swans," problematizing existing generalizations. Such counterexamples that trouble established paradigms are sometimes termed "critical cases" (Flyvbjerg 2006; see also Kitayama and Cohen 2007).

This discussion of situating and scoping the fieldsite, comparison, and falsifiability shows that as ethnographers, we should not assume that we cannot speak with authority about broader patterns in the cultures we study, or about more global issues. We need not cede generalizations to other disciplines and approaches that face methodological conundrums of their own. With critical reflection and appropriately delimiting our claims (essential practices for researchers employing any methodology), an ethnographic study of a virtual world will say much about that virtual world, and if done effectively it will also have value for thinking broadly about virtual worlds and other online social forms, and even social practices outside virtual worlds. This movement between the rich specificity of ethnographic data and various forms of generalization is in fact a classic strategy, a "continuous dialectical tacking between the most local of local detail and the most global of global structure in such a way as to bring them into simultaneous view" (Geertz 1983:68).

CHAPTER ELEVEN

WRITING UP, PRESENTING, AND PUBLISHING ETHNOGRAPHIC RESEARCH

11.1 THE EARLY STAGES OF WRITING UP: CONFERENCES, DRAFTS, BLOGS

The process of writing up and presenting research is a key step in the crafting of the ethnographic work. As anthropologist Rena Lederman observed, a "written ethnography is not just a summary or selection of 'what's in the notes' . . . the point of ethnography is . . . to enable one's audience to understand something of interest about a corner of the world they have not experienced directly themselves" (Lederman 1990:82). In *A Thrice-Told Tale* (1992), Margery Wolf provided three descriptions of her fieldwork in Taiwan: once as raw fieldnotes (including notes taken by her native assistant), once as an ethnographic text, and once as a short story in which she reflected on the mystical nature of events (Wolf 1992). This work and the work of other ethnographers has helped reveal the varied ways ethnographic data can be transformed into written texts.

As indicated by its etymology, "ethno-graphy" (culture-writing), writing is the primary output of ethnographic research. Genres include both analytical prose and narrative text. Ethnographic writing and presentation can take other forms as well, including visual components such as pictures and film. The writing process itself has been described as a method of inquiry, as it is often through the articulating of the outcomes of our analysis that we arrive at our most important insights (Richardson 1994). As part of this process of articulating our work, ethnographers often bring key arguments, ethnographic evidence, and relevant literatures together into preliminary drafts. In disciplines like anthropology and sociology, conferences provide venues for speakers to present preliminary versions of their ethnographic work. In some computer science subdisciplines, such as human-computer interaction and computer-supported collaborative work, certain conferences are highly selective and accepted papers are considered publications on par with journal articles. These conferences may still present opportunities for presenting work in progress, along with other conferences and workshops. For instance, Bonnie's first World of Warcraft papers appeared in 2006, though she continued field research long afterwards. Both T.L. and Celia published a number of papers and book chapters while writing up their larger monographs.

Regardless of our disciplinary areas, it is important to present work with a minimum of jargon, reminding the audience of key points and including memorable illustrative examples. After being tested in a presentation context, these virtues can hopefully find their way into the written ethnography as well. Presenting at venues where the audience has less familiarity with virtual worlds is particularly useful. This can provide valuable hints as to how an argument might be crafted so as to anticipate misunderstandings and make the ethnography accessible to the widest possible audience. It may also prompt fruitful comparisons outside the specific domain of virtual worlds. We have all been surprised, for instance, at the differing ways our research has been received at anthropology or sociology conferences in comparison to science and technology studies conferences, or human-computer interaction conferences. Presenting for diverse audiences has helped us improve our written work.

Another time-honored way for researchers to improve early drafts is to circulate them to colleagues. In the internet age it is simple to email a draft chapter or article to fellow scholars well versed in virtual worlds, as well as to those less familiar with the topic but knowledgeable about good ethnographic writing. A variation on this technique can involve posting drafts on a blog or other online forums; this practice creates the opportunity for a broad range of commentary and feedback. Some authors have even posted entire book drafts online in installments (Wardrip-Fruin 2009). Given pressures to get one's work out swiftly, it can be tempting to skip the stage of circulating early drafts—but we guarantee that taking time to get peer feedback will make the final product of more lasting value.

While we recommend these two useful methods—informal conferences and sharing of drafts—we also urge care with regard to the distribution of pre-publication material. At conferences, for instance, it is not unusual for an audience member to ask for a copy of the talk. In such a circumstance it is important to recall that once a draft has been emailed to even one person or posted to a single blog, there is no way to bring it back and it can circulate online indefinitely. In our experience, while plagiarism is of course an ever-present danger, it is less an issue than with other methodological approaches because ethnographic research requires such a significant time investment. People who have never played World of Warcraft are unlikely to advance themselves by claiming as their own some insight based on our research in the game (although, of course, anything can happen). Often, just as with anthropology and sociology, individuals are associated with a particular theme or context, such as Tom's research with gay Indonesians or Celia's work on emergent behavior with the Uru diaspora and in There.com. The greater danger in our view (a danger some of us have experienced) is that when an earlier draft starts to circulate, it will sometimes be cited instead of the final, published version, leading to confusion and misinterpretation.

Every researcher thus has to weigh the pluses and minuses of releasing drafts. One technique is to save a draft as a PDF with a "do not cite or circulate" watermark and "This draft only for John Doe" on the footer of each page. This practice makes it easier to share work in progress while declaring that it is not ready for general circulation. It is also wise to personally request in email that colleagues do not circulate drafts. Usually fellow researchers are sensitive to the need to sometimes restrict access, but it is easy to forget the contexts in which one received a draft and circulate it anyway (in which case the watermark is a big help). If we wish to be particularly cautious, we can even more fully safeguard early drafts by distributing only printed copies, which will be harder (though not impossible) to circulate.

An additional form of feedback, which is not standard to all research but which some of us have used, involves showing drafts to selected informants. Three caveats should be kept in mind. First, we do not want to use the fact that we received informant comments as a means to claim "ethnographic authority" (Clifford 1983). In other words, we do not want to assert that "the people I studied agree with my interpretation, so no one can disagree with any aspect of my conclusions." Second, if we share drafts, we must be prepared for the possibility that informants will disagree with our analysis in some way. Of course this could offer the possibility of revising our claims to make them more valid. However, no culture is unanimous. Informants may wish to present an account with which we do not agree, and it is important to be able to preserve our own interpretations. Third, because feedback is from selected informants only, the possibility of bias increases.

Some ethnographers take informant feedback one step further, not only soliciting commentary but integrating some of that commentary into the final text. Such texts, in which the participants being studied are able to contribute to the text itself via forums and other online methods, have been used in internet studies since the 1990s (e.g., Fisher 1990). They can sometimes add another dimension of texture and perspective in studies of communities that are particularly self-reflective and engaged in the research process. Celia used this technique by posting chapters of her book on a blog and asking for participant commentary. The informant comments were included verbatim as annotations in the final work, augmenting Celia's own analysis. This practice made the informants visible in another way, since they participated in the analysis itself.

11.2 WRITTEN GENRES

While there are many different forms of dissemination (including non-textual forms), there are three primary genres for formal ethnographic writing: the book, the essay (which usually appears as a journal article, a book chapter, or conference paper), and the research report (which may appear as a conference paper, journal article, book chapter, full-length report, or Ph.D. dissertation). The genres in which we choose to publish, and the order in which we do so, will be based not just on intellectual goals but also on our institutional location and larger career trajectories. These considerations are particularly important for ethnographers of virtual worlds since many of us work outside contexts such as anthropology or sociology departments where ethnographic writing is well understood.

Historically the gold standard for published ethnographies has been the book-length monograph (indeed, when people say they are reading "an ethnography," they often mean a book). A book-length text is ideal because it allows us to present the rich social and historical contexts we have studied. Like no other form of writing, a full-fledged ethnography affords exploring divergent points of view, examining multiple cultural domains (for instance, gender, religion, or identity), and linking the research to a broad range of relevant literatures. However, while book-length monographs can be extremely effective (all four of us have written books for precisely that reason), they entail a slow, time-consuming cycle. In academic disciplines such as computer science, it is expected that scholars will produce shorter publications (conference and journal papers in particular), with book-length texts coming after tenure, if at all. In others, such as anthropology or most humanities disciplines, a singly authored published book is a requirement for tenure. Industrial researchers, particularly consultants, may opt for the book genre as it serves as a calling card and a means of lending credibility to one's expertise.

In contrast to a book, the essay forces us to focus on an aspect of our analysis that we find compelling, link it to relevant literatures, and devise an argument that pushes forward a conceptual conversation. The essay is a genre of delimited and focused claims and serves readers through this brevity. It is for this reason that, for many ethnographers, the essay has "seemed the natural genre in which to present cultural interpretations and the theories sustaining them" (Geertz 1973:25). An example of an ethnographic essay is Nardi and Kow's (2010) "Digital Imaginaries: How We Know What (We Think) We Know about Chinese Gold Farming," in which ethnographic data are used to develop a concept of "digital imaginaries." Celia and T.L. have published numerous essays on their online game research, some of which, such as T.L.'s paper on female EverQuest players (Taylor 2003b) and Celia's article on "productive play" (Pearce 2006), present concepts that were later further developed in their books. Tom's essay "A Ludicrous Discipline" discussed the applications of ethnography in the study of virtual worlds (Boellstorff 2006).

In comparison to essays, the research report tends to emphasize empirical findings over a novel conceptual contribution. Research reports can vary in length from a short, journal-length publication, to a full-length report, to a short book (100–200 pages.) A full-length research report is sometimes required by a funder, corporate employer, or client and may come burdened with publishing restrictions. An example of a short research report is Celia's study of the University of There (Pearce 2009b).

11.3 DISSEMINATION

The form in which we choose to convey our results will be determined by the audience to whom we wish to disseminate our research and the value placed on different forms of conveyance within our fields. This will vary depending on disciplinary areas, as well as career goals. In most academic fields peer-reviewed articles and books are the currency of the realm; but other disciplines or regions also value lectures, conference presentations, and even, in some cases, performances and exhibitions as modes of ethnographic conveyance.

In terms of text-based works, as our discussion above indicates, there are many genres of ethnographic writing, each with its own advantages and disadvantages, and each with its own disciplinary impact. The decision as to what genre to write and where to publish may be driven by a number of considerations, including career goals, positioning, or even constraints presented by funders, employers, or clients. Equally important will be the mechanism of publication, such as peer review, which may have bearing on the promotion process of our institution or how our work is viewed by colleagues.

Selecting the appropriate venue for publication entails a number of considerations. The main two are appropriateness for the field and the ability of the venue to accommodate virtual worlds research. Virtual worlds research has been published in journals and conferences across a diverse range of disciplines and subdisciplines, including computer science, behavioral science, sociology, anthropology, communication, game studies, human-computer interaction, computer-supported collaborative work, and internet studies, to name a few.

Journal and conference publications provide three advantages. One is faster turnaround. Conference publications run on a tight cycle and are especially effective at publishing up-to-date results. Journal papers vary depending on the journal, from publication within a year to longer cycles, sometimes up to two years. Another advantage is peer review; in addition to being a primary measure of scholarly achievement in academia and a common requirement for tenure, peer review helps improve the quality of publications through feedback from reviewers and editors. Third, as pointed out earlier, conference papers and journal articles offer concision and focus, which may be harder to accomplish in a full monograph. Practitioners and industrial researchers may also publish in journals and conference proceedings.

As mentioned, the full book-length monograph has been the gold standard for ethnographic research results. Books, however, take time to write and publish (at least two years, in most cases). While some might see this as meaning the analysis will be dated, writing a book forces ethnographers step back from current controversies and craft analyses with an eye toward longer-term debates. Particularly given the relative novelty of virtual worlds, a broader historical perspective can be useful. Identifying an appropriate publisher will be an important decision, especially for junior scholars. Again this should be determined based on which publisher provides status and visibility in our field. Many publishers have expanded their purview to virtual worlds research. Junior scholars should be aware, however, that university presses carry more prestige in academia than do trade or technical presses.

Book publishers often produce not only monographs, but edited volumes in which a series of authors write chapters or essays on some shared topic. Each chapter in such an edited volume is roughly the length of a journal article, and the genres are quite similar (indeed, some edited volumes originate as special issues of journals). Edited volumes can sometimes be produced more swiftly than monographs and can be highly visible. At the same time, while peer-reviewed publications are often available via the internet, book chapters are hard to obtain online short of ordering the book itself. In addition, by and large book chapters do not carry as much weight in academia as do peer-reviewed journal articles. On the other hand, a book chapter can be an excellent outlet for industry researchers or practitioners for whom tenure is not an issue, as well as a way for academics to introduce a signature theme or theory, a writing genre, or a think piece that might not easily find a place in a peer-reviewed conference or journal.

The distribution of white papers and full-length research reports varies depending on the funding source or context. Some private research institutions, such as the Rand Corporation and SRI International, regularly publish research reports and white papers that are sold or distributed for free. In some cases these types of documents may be tied to a nondisclosure agreement that forbids public dissemination of the work. Some grantors publish research reports from their own websites, and some may even require researchers to obtain permission to disseminate results in peer-reviewed journals.

The internet affords many forms of self-publication. These have the advantage of accelerating the dissemination process but also lack the credibility of book publishers, peer-reviewed publications, or even institutionally published reports. Blogs, for instance, allow authors to instantaneously publish their work online and can permit useful forms of commentary and intellectual engagement. There are also more formal venues for self-publishing working documents and white papers, such as the Social Science Research Network (SSRN). For ethnographers of virtual worlds, blogs can serve to disseminate research findings with colleagues and also the communities we study. This is why we have sometimes published informal discussions of our research findings on blogs, including creating private access blogs that allow informants to annotate our findings. There are, however, reasons to be wary of forms of non-peer-reviewed online publication (including self-published books or presses without a significant editorial function). Without peer review it will be difficult for readers to distinguish our work from the thousands of writings about virtual worlds that circulate on the internet. The peer review process also helps writers improve their manuscripts so as to clarify arguments and anticipate possible misunderstandings. Additionally, non-peer-reviewed publications do not usually count for tenure or promotion in academic contexts.

Both anthropology and sociology have long traditions of alternative forms of conveyance. Although ethnography, by definition, has a strong textual emphasis, non-textual forms of presenting research—such as photography, film, museum exhibits, and even performance—have been used to convey ethnographic work. The decision about when to use these alternative genres will be driven by both disciplinary and ethical considerations. Public and invited lectures have long had cachet in academia and carry different value in different contexts. All of us have given such lectures. Celia and Tom have also experimented with performance by presenting relatively traditional academic lectures via their avatars. Tom once gave a presentation at a center for the arts in San Francisco during which his avatar spoke before an audience of about fifty people in Second Life, which was streamed onto a screen in the arts center, while Tom's physical world body and the arts center audience were streamed back into Second Life so they could be seen and heard by the virtual audience. We have also given inworld talks and interviews. All these forms are acceptable, but each carries different value in a given field.

Visual anthropology and media studies have used both still photography and cinema to report ethnographic research results. However, as discussed in chapter 8, ethical issues may preclude their use in order to protect informant confidentiality. Performance ethnography, which merges ethnographic text with performance, is recognized in performance studies circles as a hybrid of art practice and research. Norman Denzin argued that performance-based approaches, which are closely tied with action research, are an innovative form of intervention, foregrounding those who have historically been relegated to "otherness" (2003:4–8). He traced the performative turn in the presentation of ethnographic texts to initiatives in the 1990s by Schechner (1998) and Conquergood (1998) to include performance as a mode of using ethnographic insights to artistically explore themes of colonialism and racism. Regardless of the form of conveyance we use, it is important to remember that novel presentation genres do not exempt us from the need for methodological rigor and ethical practice.

As with any other form of dissemination, the decision will rest in part on our disciplinary context and what it values. Many university departments (for instance, studio art or media studies departments) are accustomed to assessing non-textual forms of scholarly production, but social science, communications, and computer science departments are less familiar with evaluating such work. Ethnographers must decide if their own data set and analytical goals suggest non-textual forms of publication or not. It bears emphasizing that most ethnographers work in multiple genres—it is less a matter of choosing one genre than matching genres to our goals: what we want to say and to whom, and what will draw the broadest audience in our fields.

11.4 THE WRITING PROCESS

With these issues in mind, we turn to our experiences in writing ethnographies of virtual worlds. Ethnographic writing is less formulaic than some forms of scientific writing, but regardless of the genre, it generally involves bringing together four key components: data analysis, theory, relevant literatures, and method.

By the time we begin to write in earnest, we should have identified during the data analysis phase the principal arguments we wish to make, topics we wish to discuss, useful theoretical frameworks from other scholars and our own work, and previously published scholarship from a range of disciplines that we find useful in analytical and comparative terms.

In terms of the process of writing itself, there is no one right way to craft an ethnography. We typically begin with the topics that seem easiest to tackle: issues and themes that appeared with great frequency, or that were somehow surprising or interesting. Any ethnography should have some kind of historical discussion that engages with relevant literatures and locates the fieldwork in the context of previous research. This is particularly important for virtual worlds since they are a novel domain of inquiry and can in principle be related to a wide range of scholarship. Whether or not to include this as a stand-alone literature review or integrate it into the text itself is a stylistic choice and may be shaped by disciplinary conventions or genres.

In addition, part of composing any ethnography is deciding on the order in which topics will be presented. In some cases we may wish to use a narrative to lead into our findings; in others the narrative may follow the findings to support our arguments. Balance may also be a consideration. If one section is much longer than others, this may be a sign that it should be broken into two sections, so that there is pacing and flow to the overall argument.

While the view that ethnographic writing is nothing but anecdotes or vignettes misrepresents the work ethnographers do, it is true that the power of ethnographic writing inheres in our ability to link our conceptual claims to rich data, showing how these claims play out in the everyday lives of those we have studied. Quotations, narrative episodes, and case studies from fieldwork are often what readers remember the most and can play a critical role in convincing others of the veracity of our claims. As Emerson, Fretz, and Shaw point out: "thematic narratives use fieldnotes not as illustrations and examples of points that have already been made, but as building blocks for constructing and telling the story in the first place. . . . [T]he excerpts in an ethnographic story are not so much evidence for analytic points as they are the core of the story" (1995:171). Multiple quotations and narratives, ideally from differing data collection methods (including images in some cases), are particularly helpful for substantiating central or counterintuitive findings.

A number of stylistic questions arise around questions of authority, including the balance between our own voices and those of our informants. The balance between direct quotes and ethnographer observation is also a consideration. Because a good deal of the data we collect is textual, it can often be beneficial to support a particular analytical point with informants' own words. Celia used a variety of techniques for integrating direct quotes from her informants into her Uru ethnography, including user-created poetry, quotes taken from participant observation and interview sessions, and inviting players to annotate her final results. Some of her most salient findings were best expressed through the words of informants themselves: a player's observation that "we create our avatars, and our avatars create us," for instance, provided a succinct way to describe the dynamic feedback loop between physical world players and avatar construction (Pearce and Artemesia 2009:215–216). Direct quotes bring our informants to life, foreground the specificity of ethnographic research, and add authenticity to our characterization of cultures.

We will also want to consider how to best summarize our methods with the sometimes limited word count afforded by many of the genres discussed earlier. Although we might be tempted to skip a discussion of methods, including it will help sharpen our arguments. Method is often rendered invisible in writings on virtual worlds research. This might include discussing contexts where we conducted participant observation and the kinds of questions we asked during interviews. Such discussion is important because the use of ethnographic methods in virtual worlds remains poorly understood, but also because ethnographic methods vary significantly depending on the cultural contexts being investigated. It is useful to mention how we addressed ethical concerns such as informed consent and anonymity, given the heightened awareness of privacy concerns online.

11.5 A QUICK TRIP BACK TO THE FIELD?

Overall, we have presented three distinct phases of ethnographic research: (1) data collection, (2) data analysis, and (3) writing up research results. In practice these phases can sometimes productively overlap. For instance, as noted in chapter 10, it may be helpful to engage in some preliminary data reflection during fieldwork. Another kind of overlap can occur between data analysis and writing; often it is only when actually composing the ethnography that researchers realize some pivotal aspect of the culture they are studying. E. M. Forster's adage "How can I tell what I think till I see what I say?" (1956:101) goes to the heart of this connection between conceptualizing an argument and writing it down.

We call for caution, however, in combining the first and third phases (that is, combining data collection with writing an ethnography). In the traditional model of ethnographic research associated with Malinowski and the British tradition (as well as in the French tradition associated with Claude Lévi-Strauss, among others), these phases were definitively distinct: the ethnographer went on a long journey to a strange land to conduct fieldwork, then returned home to write up the results. In the American tradition associated with Franz Boas and his students, multiple visits to a fieldsite were more common, raising the possibility of additional fieldwork while writing one's ethnography.

This potential for returning to the field while writing takes on new dimensions when conducting ethnographic research in virtual worlds. The very device we are most likely using to write—a computer—is that through which we access the fieldsite. As ethnographers of virtual worlds, we can thus return to the fieldsite without even leaving our desks! This is tempting indeed, and all of us did spend time in our virtual fieldsites while writing our ethnographies. This practice can be useful—not so much because it allows us to update the ethnography (since ethnographies are always located in particular times and places), but because it permits us to gather additional data about issues we later realize are of special importance. When writing a series of research reports or essays, interspersing periods of fieldwork with periods of data analysis and writing can be highly beneficial. For ethnographers who participate in informatics and computer science subdisciplines, research reports and papers at major conferences may be a primary form of writing. Therefore the cycle of research-analysis-writing is shorter in these disciplines than for ethnographers who produce a book every few years.

Despite these benefits, we urge moderation in returning to the virtual fieldsite to gather additional data while writing. Fieldwork has its own structure, with a beginning and an end (even if we return for new, follow-up research at a later date). The danger is that too many return visits will slow down the writing process and introduce tangents that compromise the flow and integrity of the ethnography. So although conducting additional research while writing up can be helpful, as a rule of thumb we recommend acknowledging the fact that research is structured by a timeline, and moving toward closure by completing the ethnographic writing itself.

11.6 TONE, STYLE, AND AUDIENCE

No piece of writing speaks to all readers. Audiences can be relatively broad or focused, but they are always delimited. Depending on the points to be made, it is entirely acceptable to write for an audience of fellow specialists, and in doing so to make use of theoretical terms and references that will be difficult for those outside that research community to understand.

However, it is most effective to avoid thinking of such focused research communities as our primary audience. There is a general need for ethnographic research, particularly with regard to the relatively new domain of virtual worlds, to be more recognized and valued, and thus institutionally supported. A basic effort to explain key terms on first use (so they are not seen as jargon), remind readers about key authors being cited, and provide rich ethnographic detail can transform writing that might otherwise be of narrow interest into a highly accessible and lively read. Tom, for instance, included a section entitled "Terms of Discussion" in the first chapter of his ethnography about Second Life, so that key ideas were explained as clearly as possible from the outset. Celia and T.L. make it a habit of defining terms in everyday language to make their writing more accessible to a wider audience.

Writing in a clear manner is emphatically not the same thing as "dumbing down." Too often it remains the case that researchers produce deliberately opaque and obfuscating texts, turgidity standing in for insightfulness. The furthest thing from our minds is an anti-intellectual attack on anything not deemed "plain speech." Instead our point is, first, that in most cases there need be no incompatibility between clarity and theoretical rigor, and second, that it behooves us as ethnographers of virtual worlds to reach the broadest audience possible—across academic disciplines but also outside the university, to designers, players, and readers of all kinds, including our informants. This is particularly the case because the popularity of virtual worlds has made research on them fascinating to many users and practitioners outside academia. We should not be surprised to discover readers drawn to our work due to their experiences participating in—or even helping to design—the virtual worlds we study.

Virtual worlds research spans a broad variety of disciplines, from computer science, to anthropology, to the humanities, each with its own unique, and sometimes impenetrable jargon. A seasoned and educated computer science scholar may find some of the idiosyncratic language of anthropology to be incomprehensible, and vice versa. Our research can have broader impact and influence across disciplines if written in such a way that transcends disciplinary linguistic silos.

For these reasons of clarity, we encourage ethnographers to avoid what is sometimes termed the "ethnographic present" (for instance, "the Balinese like to eat rice"). While using the present tense to refer to ethnographic data collected in the past was once commonplace (favored by chroniclers of other cultures going all the way back to Herodotus), it has been correctly criticized for presenting informants as living in a timeless culture (Fabian 1983:80). The ethnographic present is particularly inelegant for writing about virtual worlds, as they are characterized by rapid change. In looking over our past work, all of us certainly feel relieved that we used the past tense. World of Warcraft no longer has sixty levels. Second Life no longer allows communication only through text. At this writing There.com had closed and was about to reopen, and Uru had closed and reopened three times since Celia began her initial research with the Uru diaspora. The value of ethnographic writing lies in the analysis of cultures, including virtual world cultures, at particular historical points in time. All ethnography inevitably becomes history.

Many of our readers will not have a familiarity with the worlds we study. Even game studies scholars have specific foci, and a console-based researcher may not be familiar with the mechanics or representation of World of Warcraft or Second Life. Our challenge, then, is to provide sufficient context and nuance without overwhelming the reader with details. A brief summary of the core mechanics of the virtual world, as well as its size and audience, is often helpful. Bonnie wrote a chapter section called "A Short WoW [World of Warcraft] Primer" in her book on World of Warcraft to acquaint readers with basic game mechanics and social organization. But how much vivid detail of the space must we convey to effectively make our conceptual points? It is tempting to "geek out" on details about conventions or the history of the world we are studying. The extent to which we explicate a world depends on the intended audience and analytical points we wish to make. If publishing in a journal like *Games and Culture*, we do not need to spend time defining virtual worlds. If the outlet is a journal focused on human-computer interaction, or a journal in sociology or anthropology, we should set aside more space for background explanation. It may be useful to have someone unfamiliar with virtual worlds read a draft to ensure that the explanation is sufficient.

Regardless of the genre, publication, and audience, we strongly encourage concision. By virtue of their limited word count, journal articles and conference submissions force us to be focused and organized in our thinking. Authors who complain to journal editors that their ethnographic material is so rich, or their theoretical insights so profound, that they cannot possibly abide by the word limits every other author faces are missing the point; they should be writing a book or, at the very least, an extended book chapter. (For tips on writing journal articles, see Boellstorff 2008b, 2010, 2011). Another approach is to isolate findings and devote a paper to one aspect of the study, laying aside insights that might be better suited for future publishing opportunities. Even when dealing with something as long as a book, concision is a virtue. Researchers typically gather far more data than they can reasonably fit in an ethnography, a state of affairs only magnified for virtual worlds ethnographies by the deluge of data made possible by the ability to save vast amounts of digital information. In the early periods of ethnographic research, when the (impossible) goal was to present a holistic portrait of a culture, ethnographies grew long indeed. Raymond Firth's *We, the Tikopia* (1936), for instance, "runs to almost 600 pages, and . . . one wonders almost why Firth stopped when he did" (Kuper 1996:70). This tactic is rarely useful in the contemporary period. The job of the ethnographer is thus to distill from a massive body of data an account that provides insight rather than overwhelms. When we craft our ethnographies with care, whatever form they take, our work can contribute to a range of scholarly conversations and even attract interest beyond the halls of academia. Ethnographic research on virtual worlds provides a perspective no other approach to technology and society can offer: it can demonstrate imbrications of technology, culture, and selfhood with significant and enduring social consequences.

CHAPTER TWELVE

CONCLUSION: ARRIVALS AND NEW DEPARTURES

Historically, ethnographic texts have typically used the devices of arrival and departure to begin and end their narratives. For a handbook on ethnographic methods, the tropes of arrival and departure can be reversed. We began not with an arrival but a departure into issues of research design; this included dispelling myths about ethnography that can short-circuit an appreciation of its value. We then discussed a wide palette of methods for data collection, paying special attention to the central method of participant observation. We also addressed questions of ethics and IRBs before discussing data analysis and ways to write up research results.

All these topics represent points of departure, pathways toward the practice of ethnographic research. Now, with these discussions "in hand," we hope that you arrive at your own ethnographic research projects with a set of tools and concepts that make your work more enjoyable and productive. Even if your focus is not on virtual worlds, we can think of no greater compliment than the thought that you arrive at your research with some points or insights we have worked to provide.

In a sense this handbook is highly reflexive: while drawing on the work of many talented colleagues, we have turned primarily to examples from our own research since that allowed us to go "behind the curtain" and show how we conducted our ethnographic work. In the interest of keeping this handbook succinct—something the reader could actually lift with one hand—we have spoken less about the crafting of this text itself. Here we note briefly that, for the four of us, writing this handbook was enormously gratifying, and not only because it allowed us to speak about questions of method too often relegated to office corridors and the lobbies of conference hotels. The method of writing this handbook (about method) was itself a fascinating journey.

At the outset of this project, we made a pivotal decision to craft not an edited volume nor a text in which each of us had our own chapter to speak in isolation of our own fieldwork practice. Instead we opted to write this handbook collectively. You will search in vain for any part of this text that is "Bonnie's section," "T.L.'s section," "Tom's section," or "Celia's section." In the earlier stages of writing, we broke into pairs and worked on individual chapters. These individual chapter drafts were then passed to the other authors via email and circulated numerous times before being combined into a single document that did not reside on any single machine but was located online.

We envy those authors who are able to escape to a research center for a working retreat. During the writing of this handbook, all four of us were busy with teaching, research, other writing projects, and conferences. We had no choice but to work from a distance, with only a few opportunities for physical world meetings. For several months we worked on this single document from four different physical world locations via Google Docs, an online word processing tool, covering three different time zones. Often we wrote asynchronously, one person revising a section and then moving to something else before the next person worked on that section of the document. We left hundreds of comments for each other, discussing issues in turn before coming to agreement and "resolving" the comment thread (using a feature that would then delete the editorial note). In other cases we wrote synchronously, sometimes while on a Skype call, and using the software's text chat feature. Google Docs allowed us to see where the other authors' cursors were placed in the document, and even to jump to their spot so we could all attend to the same place in the text. It did not escape our notice that this started to feel like the kinds of social interaction that we had been observing in virtual worlds, and we playfully referred to our cursors as our "avatars."

But while we were thankful to be able to use online technologies to facilitate our work, we could have used those technologies to produce a text in which we spoke separately, or an edited volume for that matter. The decision to have the four of us write with a single authorial voice for an entire book-length text about methodology was a real risk, pushing us into uncharted waters of deep collaboration. In our view the risk has paid off in ways we could not have imagined when we began this project. By collectively comparing and contrasting our varied approaches in varied virtual world fieldsites, but from the perspective of a single textual voice, we feel we have provided methodological insights that would have been impossible with segregated individual chapters. Each of us contributed to the overall plan for the book in distinctive ways that resulted eventually in the single voice that speaks within the final product, yet which reflects our diverse experiences and perspectives.

Our personal intellectual dispositions and interests entered the book in a multitude of ways. We also encountered ways in which our differing disciplinary backgrounds shaded the literatures or points to which we were attuned. The synergies of four different researchers working together generated not only a rich experience of growth and understanding as we engaged each other in debate and discussion, but a rhetorically and conceptually settled version of the specificities and realities of ethnographic study of virtual worlds as we see them. While all versions of anything are, in the long run, provisional, we devoted great effort to achieving an account of ethnography in virtual worlds that we believe illumines our subject in the contemporary moment.

With all the resources four scholars could muster from our collective decades' worth of ethnographic experience in virtual worlds (as well as other contexts of human activity), and the guidance of our anthropological and sociological forebears, we discovered, and rediscovered, notable stability and continuity in the enduring project of ethnography. As a result, this book, while specific, can be broadly applied to a variety of virtual world contexts—including, we hope, those that might arise in the future. It is our objective that no matter what your fieldsite or research question, you will find something from this book that will be usefully at hand as you conduct your ethnographic work.

As ethnographers we are part of a community of scholarly debate and collaboration that can support and challenge us in our research practice. As a research community, we can also look outward as we collectively continue to advocate for our methodological approach. We strongly assert that ethnography will continue to have an important role to play in the study of virtual worlds. The place of ethnographic research in this emerging body of work is bright, to say the least: understanding the new cultures of virtual worlds is vitally important, and it cannot happen without the contributions of ethnographers. As we have indicated on multiple occasions in this handbook, the relevance of ethnographic research extends to social science in the broadest sense. And beyond: we also have key insights to offer with regard to questions of design, to the place of technology in society, and to social theory.

To continue to participate in broad public and academic discourses on crucial matters of design, theory, and technology in society, as ethnographers we are charged with doing even more to reach out and communicate lucid understandings of what we do, how we do it, and why we do it. This commitment is a challenge. Ethnographers tend to harbor a renegade pride in not fearing to tread in unknown places; we think nothing of arriving in an unfamiliar culture to establish intensive, long-term interactions with the persons whose lifeworlds we seek to understand (and who are sometimes initially bewildered by our presence), and to move among them without at first knowing very much at all. More often than not, we manage to extract something of value from the uncontrollable hubbub that is life, which we record in our ethnographies. But we often do all this without saying exactly how we did it. In casual conversation we may claim to have accomplished the work by "hanging out" with informants "in the field." This bit of posturing points to our embodied expertise, but it is also an evasive maneuver that fails to reveal what lies "under the hood" of ethnographic investigation.

We have labored in this handbook to reveal the details of ethnographic research in the most sustained and comparative manner with regard to virtual worlds. We have tried to sweep away persistent epistemological cobwebs, emphasized the indispensable role of participant observation, insisted on the ethical responsibilities inherent in ethnographic practice, provided what we hope will be useful tips and techniques, and argued for the unique contributions of ethnography to the scientific study of humankind. It is our sincere wish that this handbook aid and sustain ethnographers of virtual worlds as they strive to communicate with new audiences, confident and sure of their own practice.

To remain in the center of conversations about technology and society in this manner, the topic of ethnography in virtual worlds (and beyond) can never be divorced from the issue of methodology. Good research practice is key; without it the validity and significance of research results, and the cumulative, collective processes of science that yield a corpus of sound scientific works, are impossible. As we have seen, ethnographic research on virtual worlds can sometimes be marginalized. In some cases at the root of the problem are myths about ethnography itself. In other cases misconceptions arise when individuals claiming to "do ethnography," with little or no training, have spent a brief period wandering about some virtual world collecting superficial anecdotes, lacking both the careful design and ethical practice required of ethnographic research. We hope to have shown throughout this handbook that good ethnographic research is a rigorous undertaking, and that rigor is fundamentally linked to the way the method is pursued through a steady accumulation of intensive, contextualized data sought in the multitude of places our informants conduct their everyday lives.

Current trends suggest that ethnographic research will have much to contribute in the years to come as we increasingly engage in online socialities. The generations that grew up playing online games or spending time in virtual worlds will both demand and invent interesting and sophisticated digital spaces. Intense interest in the study of virtual worlds comes from both established academics seeking to incorporate these environments into their research portfolios, and a new generation of researchers for whom virtual worlds will be a central part of their scholarship. All these trends indicate that interest in the study of virtual worlds will only gain momentum. We, as ethnographers, are at the center of debates over the role of online technologies in the human journey, in both its fascinating variations and its surprising commonalities. With this knowledge in hand, you have arrived at an exciting point: a point of arrival for new departures into ethnographic adventures.

REFERENCES

Abdelnour-Nocera, J. 2002. Ethnography and Hermeneutics in Cybercultural Research Accessing IRC Virtual Communities. *Journal of Computer-Mediated Communication* 7(2). http://onlinelibrary.wiley.com.doi/10.1111/j.1083-6101.2002.tb00146.x/full.

Abu-Lughod, L. 1991. Writing against Culture. In *Recapturing Anthropology*. R. Fox, ed. Pp. 137–162. Santa Fe: School of American Research Press.

Agar, M. H. 2008. *The Professional Stranger*. 2nd edition. Bingley, UK: Emerald Publishing.

Ahmad, M., B. Keegan, J. Srivastava, D. Williams, and N. Contractor. 2009. Mining for Gold Farmers: Automatic Detection of Deviant Players in MMOGs. *Proceedings of the International Conference on Computational Science and Engineering*. Pp. 340–345. August 29–31, Vancouver, Canada.

Algeo, J. 1993. Desuetude among New English Words. *International Journal of Lexicography* 6(4):281–293.

American Anthropological Association (AAA). 1986. Statement on Ethics. http://aaanet.org/stmts/ethstmnt.htm.

Anderson, B. 1983. *Imagined Communities: Reflections on the Origin and Spread of Nationalism*. London: Verso.

Appadurai, A. 1988. *The Social Life of Things: Commodities in Cultural Perspective*. Cambridge: Cambridge University Press.

Appelcline, S. 2000–2009. *Trials, Triumphs & Trivialities*. http://www.skotos.net/articles/show-ttnt.phtml.

Asad, T., ed. 1973. *Anthropology and the Colonial Encounter*. London: Ithaca Press.

Association of Internet Researchers (AoIR). 2002. *Ethical Decision-making and Internet Research Recommendations from the AoIR Ethics Working Committee*. http://aoir.org/reports/ethics.pdf.

Au, W. J. 2008. *The Making of Second Life: Notes from the New World*. New York: Harper Collins.

Balkin, J., and B. Noveck, eds. 2006. *The State of Play: Law, Games, and Virtual Worlds*. New York: New York University Press.

Barnard, A. 2000. *History and Theory in Anthropology*. Cambridge: Cambridge University Press.

Bardzell, S., and J. Bardzell. 2007. Docile Avatars: Aesthetics, Experience, and Sexual Interaction in Second Life. *Proceedings of the 21st British HCI Group*

Annual Conference on People and Computers. Swinton, UK: British Computer Society.

Bartle, R. 1996. *Hearts, Clubs, Diamonds, Spades: Players Who Suit MUDs*. http://www.mud.co.uk/richard/hcds.htm.

———. 2004. *Designing Virtual Worlds*. Indianapolis: New Riders.

Bateson, G., and M. Mead. 1946. *Balinese Character: A Photographic Analysis*. New York: New York Academy of Sciences.

Baym, N. 2009. What Constitutes Quality in Qualitative Internet Research? In *Internet Inquiry: Conversations about Method*. A. Markham and N. Baym, eds. Pp. 173–189. Los Angeles: Sage Publications.

Baym, N., and A. Markham. 2009. Introduction: Making Smart Choices on Shifting Ground. In *Internet Inquiry: Conversations about Method*. A. Markham and N. Baym, eds. Pp. vii–xix. Los Angeles: Sage Publications.

Beck, U., and E. Beck-Gernsheim. 2008. Global Generations and the Trap of Methodological Nationalism for a Cosmopolitan Turn in the Sociology of Youth and Generation. *European Sociological Review* 25(1):25–36.

Becker, H. 1963. *Outsiders: Studies in the Sociology of Deviance*. New York: Free Press.

Behar, R. 1993. *Translated Woman: Crossing the Border with Esperanza's Story*. Boston: Beacon Press.

———. 1996. *The Vulnerable Observer: Anthropology That Breaks Your Heart*. Boston: Beacon Press.

Behar, R., and D. A. Gordon. 1995. *Women Writing Culture*. Berkeley: University of California Press.

Bell, G., M. Blythe, and P. Sengers. 2005. Making by Making Strange: Defamiliarization and the Design of Domestic Technologies. *ACM Transactions on Computer-Human Interaction* 12(2):149–173.

Benedict, R. 1946. *The Chrysanthemum and the Sword: Patterns of Japanese Culture*. Boston: Houghton Mifflin.

Berger, P. L., and T. Luckmann. 1966. *The Social Construction of Reality: A Treatise in the Sociology of Knowledge*. Garden City, NY: Doubleday.

Bernard, H. R. 1998. *Handbook of Methods in Cultural Anthropology*. Walnut Creek, CA: AltaMira Press.

———. 2006. *Research Methods in Anthropology: Qualitative and Quantitative Methods*. 4th edition. Walnut Creek, CA: AltaMira Press.

Bloomfield, R. 2009. How Online Communities and Flawed Reasoning Sound a Death Knell for Qualitative Methods. *Terra Nova* blog, March 31. http://terranova.blogs.com/terra_nova/2009/03/do-online-communities-sound-a-death-knell-for-qualitative-methods.html.

Blumer, H. 1954. What Is Wrong with Social Theory. *American Sociological Review* 18:3–10.

———. 1969. *Symbolic Interactionism: Perspective and Method*. Berkeley: University of California Press.

Boas, F. 1887 [repr. 1940]. The Study of Geography. In *Race, Language, and Culture*. Pp. 639–647. New York: Macmillan.

Boellstorff, T. 2002. Ethnolocality. *Asia Pacific Journal of Anthropology* 3(1):24–48.

———. 2005. *The Gay Archipelago: Sexuality and Nation in Indonesia*. Princeton: Princeton University Press.

———. 2006. A Ludicrous Discipline? Ethnography and Game Studies. *Games and Culture* 1(1):29–35.

———. 2008a. *Coming of Age in Second Life: An Anthropologist Explores the Virtually Human*. Princeton: Princeton University Press.

———. 2008b. How to Get an Article Accepted at *American Anthropologist* (or Anywhere). *American Anthropologist* 110(3):281–283.

———. 2009a. Method and the Virtual: Anecdote, Analogy, Culture. *Journal of Virtual Worlds Research* 1(3):4–7.

———. 2009b. Experimenting with Virtual Worlds: The Phantom Rebuttal. Published on the *Virtual Cultures* blog, March 8. http://virtualcultures.typepad.com/virtualcultures/2009/03/experimenting-with-virtual-worlds-the-phantom-rebuttal.html.

———. 2010. Queer Techne. In *Queer Methods and Methodologies: Intersecting Queer Theories and Social Science Research*. K. Browne and C. J. Nash, eds. Pp. 215–230. Surrey: Ashgate Publishing.

———. 2011. Submission and Acceptance: Where, Why, and How to Publish Your Article. *American Anthropologist* 113(3):383–388.

Book, B. 2006. *Virtual Worlds Review*. http://www.virtualworldsreview.com/.

Bortolotti, L., and M. Mameli. 2006. Deception in Psychology: Moral Costs and Benefits of Unsought Self-Knowledge. *Accountability in Research* 13(3):259–275.

Bosk, C. 1979. *Forgive and Remember: Managing Medical Failure*. Chicago: University of Chicago Press.

Bourdieu, P. 1998. *Practical Reason: On the Theory of Action*. Palo Alto: Stanford University Press.

Bowker, G. C., and S. L. Star. 1999. *Sorting Things Out: Classification and Its Consequences*. Cambridge: MIT Press.

boyd, d., and K. Crawford. 2012. Critical Questions for Big Data. *Information, Communication & Society*. iFirst article, 1–18.

Bremer, R. 1987. *Indian Agent and Wilderness Scholar: The Life of Henry Rowe Schoolcraft*. Mount Pleasant: Clarke Historical Library, Central Michigan University.

Bruckman, A. 1992. *Identity Workshop: Emergent Social and Psychological Phenomena in Text-Based Virtual Reality*. Ms. http://www.cc.gatech.edu/~asb/papers/misc/identity-workshop.rtf.

———. 1998. Community Support for Constructionist Learning. *Journal of Computer Supported Collaborative Work* 7(1/2):47–86.

Bruckman, A. 2002. Studying the Amateur Artist: A Perspective on Disguising Data Collected in Human Subjects Research on the Internet. *Ethics and Information Technology* 4(3):217–231.

———. 2006. Teaching Students to Study Online Communities Ethically. *Journal of Information Ethics* 15(2):82–98.

Bruyn, S. 1966. *The Human Perspective in Sociology: The Methodology of Participant Observation*. Englewood Cliffs, NJ: Prentice-Hall.

Buchanan, E., ed. 2004. *Readings in Virtual Research Ethics*. Hershey, PA: Information Science Publishing.

Buchanan, E., and C. Ess. 2009. Internet Research Ethics and the Institutional Review Board: Current Practices and Issues. *SIGCAS Computers and Society* 39(3):43–49.

Bunzl, M. 1996. Franz Boas and the Humboldtian Tradition: From *Volksgeist* and *Nationalcharakter* to an Anthropological Concept of Culture. In *Volksgeist as Method and Ethic: Essays on Boasian Ethnography and the German Anthropological Tradition*. G. W. Stocking, Jr., ed. Pp. 17–78. Madison: University of Wisconsin Press.

———. 2004. Boas, Foucault, and the "Native Anthropologist": Notes toward a Neo-Boasian Anthropology. *American Anthropologist* 106(3):435–442.

———. 2005. Anthropology Beyond Crisis: Toward an Intellectual History of the Extended Present. *Anthropology and Humanism* 30(2):187–195.

Burawoy, M., et al. 1991. *Ethnography Unbound: Power and Resistance in the Modern Metropolis*. Berkeley: University of California Press.

Burk, D. 2010. Authorization and Governance in Virtual Worlds. *First Monday* 15(5). http://firstmonday.org/htbin/cgiwrap/bin/ojs/index.php/fm/article/view/2967.

Candea, M. 2009. Arbitrary Locations: In Defence of the Bounded Field-site. In *Multi-Sited Ethnography: Theory, Praxis, and Locality in Contemporary Research*. M.-A. Falzon, ed. Pp. 25–45. Surrey, UK: Ashgate.

Carter, D. 2005. Living in Virtual Communities: An Ethnography of Human Relationships in Cyberspace. *Information, Communication, and Society* 8(2):148–167.

Cassell, J. 1980. Ethical Principles for Conducting Fieldwork. *American Anthropologist* 82(1):28–41.

Castells, M. 2000. *The Information Age: Economy, Society, and Culture. Volume 1: The Rise of the Network Society*. Boston: Blackwell.

Castronova, E. 2001. Virtual Worlds: A First-Hand Account of Market and Society on the Cyberian Frontier. *The Gruter Institute Working Papers on Law, Economics, and Evolutionary Biology* 2(1). http://www.bepress.com/giwp/default/vol2/iss1/art1.

———. 2006. On the Research Value of Large Games: Natural Experiments in Norrath and Camelot. *Games and Culture* 1(2):163–186.

Chan, P. 2010. Narrative Participation within Game Environments: Role-Playing in Massively Multiplayer Online Games. M.S. thesis, Digital Media Graduate Program, Georgia Institute of Technology.

Charmaz, K. 1991. *Good Days, Bad Days: The Self and Chronic Illness in Time*. New Brunswick, NJ: Rutgers University Press.

Chee, F., and R. Smith. 2005. Is Electronic Community an Addictive Substance? In *Interactive Convergence: Critical Issues in Multimedia*, S. Schaffer and M. Price, eds. Pp. 137–155. Oxford: Inter-Disciplinary Press.

Chen, M. 2009. Communication, Coordination, and Camaraderie in World of Warcraft. *Games and Culture* 4(1):47–73.

Cherny, L. 1999. *Conversation and Community: Chat in a Virtual World*. Palo Alto: Stanford Center for the Study of Language and Information.

Choontanom, T., and B. Nardi. 2012. Theorycrafting: The Art and Science of Using Numbers to Interpret the World. *Games, Learning, and Society*. C. Steinkuehler, ed. London: Cambridge University Press.

Clarke, Adele E. 2005. *Situational Analysis: Grounded Theory after the Postmodern Turn*. Thousand Oaks, CA: Sage Publications.

Clifford, J. 1983. On Ethnographic Authority. *Representations* 1(2):118–146.

———. 1986. Introduction: Partial Truths. In *Writing Culture: The Poetics and Politics of Ethnography*. J. Clifford and G. Marcus, eds. Pp. 1–26. Berkeley: University of California Press.

———. 1992. Travelling Cultures. In *Cultural Studies*. L. Grossberg, G. Nelson, and P. Treichler, eds. Pp. 96–116. New York: Routledge.

Clifford, J., and G. Marcus. 1986. *Writing Culture: The Poetics and Politics of Ethnography*. Berkeley: University of California Press.

Connors, R. 1997. *Composition-rhetoric: Backgrounds, Theory, and Pedagogy*. Pittsburgh: University of Pittsburgh Press.

Conquergood, D. 1998. Beyond the Text: Toward a Performative Cultural Politics. In *The Future of Performance Studies: Visions and Revisions*. S. J. Dailey, ed. Washington, DC: National Communication Association.

Coombe, R. J. 1998. *The Cultural Life of Intellectual Properties: Authorship, Appropriation, and the Law*. Durham: Duke University Press.

Copier, M. 2005. Connecting Worlds. Fantasy Role-Playing Games, Ritual Acts and the Magic Circle. *Proceedings of Digital Games Research Association Conference: Changing Views—Worlds in Play*, Vancouver, Canada.

Council of European Social Science Data Archives (CESSDA). 2011. *Rights and Confidentiality: Research Ethics*. http://www.cessda.org/sharing/rights/4/.

Csíkszentmihályi, M. 1990. *Flow: The Psychology of Optimal Experience*. New York: Harper and Row.

Curtis, P. 1992 [repr. 1997]. Mudding: Social Phenomena in Text-Based Virtual Realities. In *Culture of the Internet*. Sara Kiesler, ed. Pp. 121–142. Mahwah, NJ: Lawrence Erlbaum Associates.

Cushing, F. 1979. *Zuñi: Selected Writings of Frank Hamilton Cushing*. J. Green, ed. Lincoln: University of Nebraska Press.

———. 1986. *Zuni Folk Tales*. Tucson: University of Arizona Press, first published 1901.

Damer, B. 1998. *Avatars!: Exploring and Building Virtual Worlds on the Internet.* Berkeley: Peachpit Press.

Debeauvais, T., B. Nardi, D. Schiano, N. Ducheneaut, and N. Yee. 2011. If You Build It They Might Stay: Retention Mechanisms in World of Warcraft. *Foundations of Digital Games Conference*, June 28–July 1, Bordeaux, France.

de Certeau, M. 1984. *The Practice of Everyday Life.* Berkeley: University of California Press.

Deegan, M. 2001. The Chicago School of Ethnography. In *Handbook of Ethnography.* P. Atkinson, A. Coffey, S. Delamont, J. Lofland, and L. Lofland, eds. Pp. 11–25. London: Sage Publications.

DeKoven, B. 1978. *The Well-Played Game: A Player's Philosophy.* New York: Anchor Books.

———. 1992. "CoLiberation." *Deep Fun.* http://www.deepfun.com/colib.htm.

Deleuze, G., and F. Guattari. 1987. *A Thousand Plateaus: Capitalism and Schizophrenia.* B. Massumi, trans. Minneapolis: University of Minnesota Press.

de Munck, C., and E. Sobo, eds. 1998. *Using Methods in the Field: A Practical Introduction and Casebook.* Lanham, MD: AltaMira Press.

Denzin, N. K. 2001. *Interpretive Interactionism.* 2nd edition. Thousand Oaks, CA: Sage Publications.

———. 2003. *Performance Ethnography: Critical Pedagogy and the Politics of Culture.* Thousand Oaks, CA: Sage Publications.

DeWalt, K., and B. DeWalt. 2002. *Participant Observation: A Guide for Fieldworkers.* Walnut Creek, CA: AltaMira Press.

DeWalt, K., B. DeWalt, and C. Wayland. 1998. Participant Observation. In *Handbook of Methods in Cultural Anthropology.* H. Bernard, ed. Pp. 259–299. Walnut Creek, CA: AltaMira Press.

Dibbell, J. 1993. A Rape in Cyberspace. *Village Voice* 38(51):36–42.

———. 1998. *My Tiny Life: Crime and Passion in a Virtual World.* New York: Henry Holt.

———. 2006. *Play Money: Or, How I Quit My Day Job and Made Millions Trading Virtual Loot.* New York: Basic Books.

DiPaola, S., and C. Collins. 2003. A Social Metaphor-Based 3D Virtual Environment. In *Proceedings ACM SIGGRAPH 2003*, July 27–31, San Diego, California.

Dirks, N. 2001. *Castes of Mind: Colonialism and the Making of Modern India.* Princeton: Princeton University Press.

Dourish, P. 2001. *Where the Action Is: The Foundations of Embodied Interaction.* Cambridge: MIT Press.

Duranske, B. 2008. *Virtual Law: Navigating the Legal Landscape of Virtual Worlds.* Chicago: ABA Press.

Edwards, P. 1997. *The Closed World: Computers and the Politics of Discourse in Cold War America.* Cambridge: MIT Press.

Einstein, A. 2009. *Einstein on Cosmic Religion and Other Opinions and Aphorisms*. Mineola, NY: Dover Publications, first published 1931.

Ellis, J., B. Nardi, and C. Pearce, eds. 2009. *Productive Play* (special issue). *Artifact* 2(2).

Elm, M. 2009. How Do Various Notions of Privacy Influence Decisions in Qualitative Internet Research? In *Internet Inquiry: Conversations about Method*. A. Markham and N. Baym, eds. Pp. 69–87. Los Angeles: Sage Publications.

Emerson, M., R. Fretz, and L. Shaw. 1995. *Writing Ethnographic Fieldnotes*. Chicago: University of Chicago Press.

Evans-Pritchard, E. E. 1940. *The Nuer: A Description of the Modes of Livelihood and Political Institutions of a Nilotic People*. Oxford: Oxford University Press.

Fabian, J. 1983. *Time and the Other: How Anthropology Makes Its Object*. New York: Columbia University Press.

Fairfield, J. 2011. Avatar Experimentation: Human Subjects Research in Virtual Worlds. *Washington & Lee Public Legal Studies Research Paper Series*, accepted paper no. 2010–14. http://papers.ssrn.com/sol3/papers.cfm?abstract_id=1717057.

Fidel, R. 2012. *Human Information Interaction: An Ecological Approach to Information Behavior*. Cambridge: MIT Press.

Fielding, N., R. Lee, and G. Blank. 2008. *The Sage Handbook of Online Research Methods*. Los Angeles: Sage Publications.

Fine, G. 1993. Ten Lies of Ethnography: Moral Dilemmas of Field Research. *Journal of Contemporary Ethnography* 22(3):267–294.

Firth, R. 1936. *We, the Tikopia: A Sociological Study of Kinship in Primitive Polynesia*. London: Allen and Unwin.

Fisher, M. 1990. *Debating Muslims: Cultural Dialogues in Postmodernity and Tradition, New Directions in Anthropological Writing*. Madison: University of Wisconsin Press.

Flyvbjerg, B. 2006. Five Misunderstandings about Case-Study Research. *Qualitative Inquiry* 12(2):219–245.

Forster, E. M. 1956. *Aspects of the Novel*. Orlando, FL: Mariner Books, first published 1927.

Forsythe, D. 1999. "It's Just a Matter of Common Sense": Ethnography as Invisible Work. *Journal of Computer Supported Cooperative Work* 8(1/2):127–145.

Fox News. 2011. Chinese Prisoners Forced to Play World of Warcraft, Detainee Says. *Fox News*, May 26. http://www.foxnews.com/scitech/2011/05/26/chinese-prisoners-forced-play-world-warcraft-detainee-says/.

Frazer, J. G. 1922. *The Golden Bough*. New York: Macmillan.

Frege, G. 1959. *Foundations of Arithmetic*. Oxford: Basil Blackwell, first published 1884.

Fron, J., T. Fullerton, J. F. Morie, and C. Pearce. 2007a. Playing Dress-Up: Costume, Roleplay, and Imagination. *Philosophy of Computer Games Conference*, January 25–27, University of Modena/Reggio Emilia, Italy.

Fron, J., T. Fullerton, J. F. Morie, and C. Pearce. 2007b. The Hegemony of Play. *Proceedings of the Digital Games Research Association Conference: Situated Play*, September 24–28, Tokyo, Japan.

Fujimura, J. 1997. *Crafting Science: A Sociohistory of the Quest for the Genetics of Cancer*. Cambridge: Harvard University Press.

Gaines, R. 2010. Roman Rhetorical Handbooks. In *A Companion to Roman Rhetoric*. W. Dominik and J. Hall, eds. Pp. 163–180. Oxford: Blackwell.

Gamson, J. 1999. *Freaks Talk Back: Tabloid Talk Shows and Sexual Nonconformity*. Chicago: University of Chicago Press.

Garfinkel, H. 1991. *Studies in Ethnomethodology*. Cambridge, UK: Polity Press.

Garfinkel, H., and H. Sacks. 1970. On Formal Structures of Practical Action. In *Theoretical Sociology*. J. McKinney and E. Tiryakian, eds. Pp. 338–366. New York: Appleton-Century-Crofts.

Geertz, C. 1973. Thick Description: Toward an Interpretive Theory of Culture. In *The Interpretation of Cultures*. Pp. 3–32. New York: Basic Books.

———. 1983. "From the Native's Point of View": On the Nature of Anthropological Understanding. In *Local Knowledge: Further Essays in Interpretive Anthropology*. Pp. 55–72. New York: Basic Books.

Gerlholm, T., and U. Hannerz. 1982. Introduction: The Shaping of National Anthropologies. *Ethnos* 47(1/2):5–35.

German Government. 1949. Regulations and Ethical Guidelines: The Nuremberg Code. In *Trials of War Criminals before the Nuremberg Military Tribunals under Control Council Law No. 10, Vol. 2*. Pp. 181–182. Washington, DC: U.S. Government Printing Office.

Gibson, W. 1984. *Neuromancer*. New York: Ace Books.

Gilmore, L. 2010. *Theater in a Crowded Fire: Ritual and Spirituality at Burning Man*. Berkeley: University of California Press.

Glaser, B., and A. Strauss. 1967. *The Discovery of Grounded Theory*. New York: Aldine.

Goffman, E. 1961. *Asylums: Essays on the Social Situation of Mental Patients and Other Inmates*. New York: Doubleday.

———. 1974. *Frame Analysis: An Essay on the Organization of Experience*. New York: Harper and Row.

Gold, R. 1997. The Ethnographic Method in Sociology. *Qualitative Inquiry* 3(4):388–402.

Golub, A. 2010. Being in the World (of Warcraft): Raiding, Realism, and Knowledge Production in a Massively Multiplayer Online Game. *Anthropological Quarterly* 83(1):17–45.

Goodman, L. A. 1961. Snowball Sampling. *Annals of Mathematical Statistics* 32(1):148–170.

Gravity. 2009. GMG Partners with Gravity Interactive for Prepaid Cards. *GMG Entertainment*. http://www.gmg-entertainment.com/press/gmg-partners-with-gravity.php?iframe=true&width=980&height=600.

Grimmelmann, J. 2006. "Virtual Borders: The Interdependence of Real and Virtual Worlds." *First Monday* 11(2). http://firstmonday.org/htbin/cgiwrap/bin/ojs/index.php/fm/article/view/1312/1232.

Guest, T. 2007. *Second Lives: A Journey through Virtual Worlds.* London: Hutchinson.

Guimarães, M. 2005. Doing Anthropology in Cyberspace: Fieldwork Boundaries and Social Environments. In *Virtual Methods: Issues in Social Research on the Internet.* C. Hine, ed. Pp. 141–156. New York: Berg.

Gupta, A. 1998. *Postcolonial Developments: Agriculture in the Making of Modern India.* Durham: Duke University Press.

Gupta, A., and J. Ferguson. 1997. Discipline and Practice: "The Field" as Site, Method, and Location in Anthropology. In *Anthropological Locations: Boundaries and Grounds of a Field Science.* A. Gupta and J. Ferguson, eds. Pp. 1–46. Berkeley: University of California Press.

Gygax, G., and D. Arneson. 1974. *Dungeons & Dragons.* Lake Geneva, WI: TSR Games.

Hacking, I. 1982. Experimentation and Scientific Realism. *Philosophical Topics* 13(1):71–87.

Hall, S. 1996. When Was "The Post-Colonial"? Thinking at the Limit. In *The Post-Colonial Question: Common Skies, Divided Horizons.* Ian Chambers and Lidia Curti, eds. Pp. 242–260. London: Routledge.

Haniff, N. 1985. Toward a Native Anthropology: Methodological Notes on a Study of Successful Caribbean Women by an Insider. *Anthropology and Humanism Quarterly* 10(4):107–113.

Haraway, D. 1988. Situated Knowledges: The Science Question in Feminism and the Privilege of Partial Perspective. *Feminist Studies* 14(3):575–599.

Heeter, C. 2008. *investiGaming: Research Findings on Gender and Games.* Self-published research report.

Herman, L. 2001. *Phoenix: the Fall and Rise of Videogames.* 3rd edition. Springfield, NJ: Rolenta Press.

Hillery, G. 1955. Definitions of Community: Areas of Agreement. *Rural Sociology* 20(4):111–122.

Hine, C. 2000. *Virtual Ethnography.* London: Sage Publications.

———. 2005. Virtual Methods and the Sociology of Cyber-Social-Scientific Knowledge. In *Virtual Methods: Issues in Social Research on the Internet.* C. Hine, ed. Pp. 1–16. New York: Berg.

———. 2009. How Can Qualitative Internet Researchers Define the Boundaries of Their Projects? In *Internet Inquiry: Conversations about Method.* A. Markham and N. Baym, eds. Pp. 1–20. Los Angeles: Sage Publications.

Hinsley, C. 1983. Ethnographic Charisma and Scientific Routine: Cushing and Fewkes in the American Southwest, 1879–1893. In *Observers Observed: Essays on Ethnographic Fieldwork.* G. W. Stocking, ed. Pp. 53–69. Madison: University of Wisconsin Press.

Hofer, T. 1968. Comparative Notes on the Professional Personality of Two Disciplines. *Current Anthropology* 9(4):311–15.

Hoskins, J. 1998. *Biographical Objects: How Things Tell the Stories of Peoples' Lives*. London: Routledge.

Hothersall, David. 2004. *History of Psychology*. New York: McGraw-Hill.

Howard, R. E. 1932. The Phoenix on the Sword. *Weird Tales* 20(6).

Howison, J., K. Crowston, and A. Wiggins. 2012. Validity Issues in the Use of Social Network Analysis with Digital Trace Data. *Journal of the Association for Information Systems*.

Huberman, A., and M. Miles. 1994. *Qualitative Data Analysis: An Expanded Sourcebook*. 2nd edition. Thousand Oaks, CA: Sage Publications.

Humphreys, S. 2004. Commodifying Culture: It's Not Just about the Virtual Sword. Paper presented at the Other Players conference, Center for Computer Games Research, IT University of Copenhagen, Denmark.

Hurston, Z. 1935. *Mules and Men*. New York: Harper and Row.

International Game Developers Association (IGDA). 2005. *Game Developer Demographics: An Exploration of Workforce Diversity*. San Francisco: IGDA.

Jackson, J. E. 1990. "I am a Fieldnote": Fieldnotes as a Symbol of Professional Identity. In *Fieldnotes: The Makings of Anthropology*. R. Sanjek, ed. Pp. 3–33. Ithaca: Cornell University Press.

Jacobs, G., ed. 1970. *The Participant Observer*. New York: George Braziller.

Jakobsson, M. 2006. Virtual Worlds and Social Interaction Design. Ph.D. dissertation, Umeå University, Sweden.

Jakobsson, M., and T. L. Taylor. 2003. The Sopranos Meets EverQuest: Social Networking in Massively Multiplayer Online Games. *FineArt Forum* 17(8). http://hypertext.rmit.edu.au/dac/papers/Jakobsson.pdf.

Jenkins, H. 1992. *Textual Poachers: Television Fans and Participatory Culture*. New York: Routledge.

Kaberry, P. 1957. Malinowski's Contribution to Field-work Methods and the Writing of Ethnography. In *Man and Culture: An Evaluation of the Work of Bronislaw Malinowski*. R. Firth, ed. Pp. 71–91. London: Routledge and Kegan Paul.

Kafai, Y. 1995. Gender Differences in Children's Constructions of Video Games. In *Interacting with Video*. P. Greenfield and R. Cocking, eds. Pp. 39–52. New York: Ablex Publishing.

Kafai, Y., C. Heeter, J. Denner, and J. Sun, eds. 2008. *Beyond Barbie® and Mortal Kombat: New Perspectives on Gender and Gaming*. Cambridge: MIT Press.

Kaptelinin, V., and B. Nardi. 2006. *Acting with Technology: Activity Theory and Interaction Design*. Cambridge: MIT Press.

Katz, J., and T. Csordas. 2003. Phenomenological Ethnography in Sociology and Anthropology. *Ethnography* 4(3):275–288.

Kendall, L. 2002. *Hanging Out in the Virtual Pub: Masculinities and Relationships Online*. Berkeley: University of California Press.

———. 2009. Question Four: How Do Issues of Gender and Sexuality Influence the Structures and Processes of Qualitative Internet Research? In *Internet Inquiry: Conversations about Method*. A.N. Markham and N.K. Baym, eds. Pp. 99–118. London: Sage Publications.

Kent, S. 2001. *The Ultimate History of Video Games*. Roseville, CA: Prima Publishing.

King, B., and J. Borland. 2003. *Dungeons and Dreamers: The Rise of Computer Game Culture from Geek to Chic*. New York: McGraw-Hill.

Kitayama, S., and D. Cohen. 2007. *Handbook of Cultural Psychology*. New York: Guilford Press.

Kivits, J. 2005. Online Interviewing and the Research Relationship. In *Virtual Methods: Issues in Social Research on the Internet*. C. Hine, ed. Pp. 35–49. New York: Berg.

Knorr-Cetina, K. 1999. *Epistemic Cultures: How the Sciences Make Knowledge*. Cambridge, MA: Harvard University Press.

Kolko, B. 1995. Building a World with Words: The Narrative Reality of Virtual Communities. *Works and Days* 13(1–2):105–126.

Kolko, B., L. Nakamura, and G. Rodman, eds. 2000. *Race in Cyberspace*. New York: Routledge.

Koster, R. 2004. *A Theory of Fun for Game Design*. Scottsdale, AZ: Paraglyph Press.

Kow, Y. M. 2011. Rethinking Participation. Ph.D. dissertation, University of California, Irvine.

Kow, Y. M., and B. Nardi. 2009. Culture and Creativity: World of Warcraft Modding in China and the U.S. In *Online Worlds: Convergence of the Real and the Virtual*. B. Bainbridge, ed. Pp. 21–42. Heidelberg: Springer.

———, eds. 2010. User Creativity, Governance, and the New Media. *First Monday* 15(5). http://firstmonday.org/htbin/cgiwrap/bin/ojs/index.php/fm/issue/view/312/showToc.

———. 2010. Who Owns the Mods? *First Monday* 15(5). http://firstmonday.org/htbin/cgiwrap/bin/ojs/index.php/fm/article/view/2971/2529.

———. 2011. Forget Online Communities? Revisit Cooperative Work! *Proceedings of the ACM Conference on Computer-Supported Cooperative Work*, March 19–23, Hangzhou, China.

Kratz, C. 2010. In and Out of Focus. *American Ethnologist* 37(4):805–826.

Krueger, M. 1983. *Artificial Reality*. Reading, MA: Addison-Wesley.

Krueger, R. 1994. *Focus Groups: A Practical Guide for Applied Research*. 2nd edition. Thousand Oaks, CA: Sage Publications.

Kuhn, T. 1962. *The Structure of Scientific Revolutions*. Chicago: University of Chicago Press.

Kuklick, H. 2011. Personal Equations: Reflections on the History of Fieldwork, with Special Reference to Sociocultural Anthropology. *Isis* 102(1):1–33.

Kulick, D., and M. Willson, eds. 1995. *Taboo: Sex, Identity and Erotic Subjectivity in Anthropological Fieldwork*. New York: Routledge.

Kuper, A. 1996. *Anthropology and Anthropologists*. 3rd edition. London: Routledge.

Lastowka, G. 2010. *Virtual Justice: The New Laws of Online Worlds*. New Haven, CT: Yale University Press.

Lastowka, G., and D. Hunter. 2004. The Laws of the Virtual Worlds. *California Law Review* 92(1):3–73.

Latour, B. 1992. Where Are the Missing Masses? The Sociology of a Few Mundane Artifacts. In *Shaping Technology/Building Society: Studies in Sociotechnical Change*. W. E. Bijker and J. Law, eds. Pp. 225–258. Cambridge: MIT Press.

———. 1993. *The Pasteurization of France*. Cambridge: Harvard University Press.

Latour, B., and S. Woolgar. 1979. *Laboratory Life: The Social Construction of Scientific Facts*. London: Sage Publications.

Law, J. 2004. *After Method: Mess in Social Science Research*. London: Routledge.

Layton, R. 1997. *An Introduction to Theory in Anthropology*. Cambridge: Cambridge University Press.

Leach, E. 1961. *Rethinking Anthropology*. London: Althone.

LeCompte, M., and J. Schensul. 1999. *Designing and Conducting Ethnographic Research*. Thousand Oaks, CA: AltaMira Press.

Le Dantec, C., R. Farrell, J. Christensen, M. Bailey, J. Ellis, W. Kellogg, and K. Edwards. 2011. Publics in Practice: Ubiquitous Computing at a Shelter for Homeless Mothers. *Proceedings of the Computer Human Interaction Conference*, May 7–12, Vancouver, Canada.

Lederman, R. 1990. Pretexts for Ethnography: On Reading Fieldnotes. In *Fieldnotes: The Makings of Anthropology*. R. Sanjek, ed. Pp. 71–91. Ithaca: Cornell University Press.

Lessig, L. 1999. *Code and Other Laws of Cyberspace*. New York: Basic Books.

Lewis, C., and N. Wardrip-Fruin. 2010. Mining Game Statistics from Web Services: A World of Warcraft Armory Case Study. *Foundations of Digital Games Conference*, June 19–21, Monterey, CA.

Lim, T., and B. Nardi. 2011. A Study of Raiders with Disabilities in World of Warcraft. *Foundations of Digital Games Conference*, June 28–July 1, Bordeaux, France.

Lohman, J. 1937. Participant-Observation in Community Studies. *American Sociological Review* 2(6):890–898.

Lowood, H. 2008. Game Capture: The Machinima Archive and the History of Digital Games. *Mediascape*, Spring. http://www.tft.ucla.edu/mediascape/Spring08_GameCapture.pdf.

Ludlow, P., and M. Wallace. 2007. *The Second Life Herald: The Virtual Tabloid That Witnessed the Dawn of the Metaverse*. Cambridge: MIT Press.

Mackay, W. 1995. Ethics, Lies and Videotape. *Proceedings of ACM CHI '95 Human Factors in Computing Systems*. Pp. 138–145. New York: ACM Press.

Malaby, T. 2009. *Making Virtual Worlds: Linden Labs and Second Life*. Ithaca: Cornell University Press.

Malinowski, B. 1922. *Argonauts of the Western Pacific*. New York: E. P. Dutton.

———. 1944. The Functional Theory. In *A Scientific Theory of Culture and Other Essays*. Pp. 147–176. Chapel Hill: University of North Carolina Press.

Marcus, G. 1995. Ethnography in/of the World System: The Emergence of Multi-Sited Ethnography. *Annual Review of Anthropology* 24:95–117.

———. 1998. The Problem of the Unseen World of Wealth for the Rich: Toward an Anthropology of Complex Connections. In *Ethnography Through Thick and Thin*. Pp. 152–160. Princeton: Princeton University Press, first published 1989.

———. 2003. On the Unbearable Slowness of Being an Anthropologist Now: Notes on a Contemporary Anxiety in the Making of Ethnography. *XCP: Cross-cultural Poetics* 12:7–20.

Margolis, J., and A. Fisher. 2002. *Unlocking the Clubhouse: Women in Computing*. Cambridge: MIT Press.

Markham, A. 1998. *Life Online: Researching Real Experience in Virtual Space*. Walnut Creek, CA: AltaMira Press.

———. 2009. How Can Qualitative Researchers Produce Work That Is Meaningful across Time, Space, and Culture? In *Internet Inquiry: Conversations about Method*. A. Markham and N. Baym, eds. Pp. 131–155. Los Angeles: Sage Publications.

Markham, A., and N. Baym, eds. *Internet Inquiry: Conversations about Method*. Los Angeles: Sage Publications.

Markowitz, F., and M. Ashkenazi, eds. 1999. *Sex, Sexuality, and the Anthropologist*. Urbana: University of Illinois Press.

Mason, B. 1996. Moving toward Virtual Ethnography. *American Folklore Society News* 25(2):4–5.

Masterson, J. 1994. *Ethnography of a Virtual Society, or How a Gangling, Wiry Half-Elf Found a Way to Fit In*. Missoula: University of Montana. http://www.johnmasterson.com/ethno.html.

Maynard, M., and J. Purvis. 1994. *Researching Women's Loves from a Feminist Perspective*. London: Taylor & Francis.

McCall, G., and J. Simmons, eds. 1969. *Issues in Participant Observation: A Text and Reader*. Reading, MA: Addison-Wesley.

McDonough, J. 1999. Designer Selves: Construction of Technologically Mediated Identity within Graphical, Multiuser Virtual Environments. *Journal of the American Society for Information Science* 50(10):855–869.

McKee, H., and J. Porter. 2009. Playing a Good Game: Ethical Issues in Researching MMOGs and Virtual Worlds. *International Journal of Internet Research Ethics* 2(1):1–24.

McRae, S. 1997. Flesh Made Word: Sex, Text, and the Virtual Body. In *Internet Culture*. D. Porter, ed. Pp. 73–86. New York: Routledge.

Mead, M. 1928. *Coming of Age in Samoa*. New York: Mentor Books.

———. 1935. *Sex and Temperament in Three Primitive Societies*. New York: Mentor Books.

———. 1969. Research with Human Beings: A Model Derived from Anthropological Field Practice. *Daedalus* 98(2):361–386.

Meadows, M. 2008. *I, Avatar: The Culture and Consequences of Having a Second Life*. Berkeley: New Riders.

Milgram, S. 1974. *Obedience to Authority*. New York: Harper and Row.

Millen, D. 2000. Rapid Ethnography. *Proceedings of the Conference on Designing Interactive Systems: Processes, Practices, Methods, and Techniques* (DIS '00):280–286.

Miller, D., ed. 2005. *Materiality*. Durham: Duke University Press.

Miller, K. A. 1998. Gender Comparisons within Reenactment Costume: Theoretical Interpretations. *Family and Consumer Sciences Research Journal* 27(1):35–61.

Mills, C. W. 1959. *The Sociological Imagination*. New York: Oxford University Press.

Milroy, L., and M. Gordon. 2003. *Sociolinguistics: Method and Interpretation*. Oxford: Wiley-Blackwell.

Mnookin, J. 1996. Virtual(ly) Law: The Emergence of Law in LambdaMOO. *Journal of Computer-Mediated Communication* 2(1). http://jcmc.indiana.edu/vol2/issue1/lambda.html.

Monette, D., T. Sullivan, and C. DeJong. 2010. *Applied Social Research: A Tool for the Human Services*. Florence, KY: Brooks Cole.

Morgan, D. 2001. Focus Group Interviewing. In *Handbook of Interview Research: Context & Method*. J. Gubrium and J. Holstein, eds. Pp. 141–160. Thousand Oaks, CA: Sage Publications.

Morningstar, C., and R. Farmer. 1991. The Lessons of Lucasfilm's Habitat. In *Cyberspace: First Steps*. M. Benedikt, ed. Pp. 273–301. Cambridge: MIT Press.

Mortensen, T. 2003. Pleasures of the Player; Flow and Control in Online Games. Ph.D. dissertation, Volda College and University of Bergen, Norway.

Murnane, R., and J. Willett. 2011. *Methods Matter: Improving Causal Inference in Educational and Social Science Research*. Oxford: Oxford University Press.

Nader, L. 1972. Up the Anthropologist: Perspectives Gained from Studying Up. In *Reinventing Anthropology*. D. Hymes, ed. Pp. 284–311. New York: Pantheon Books.

Nakamura, L. 2002. *Cybertypes: Race, Ethnicity and Identity on the Internet*. New York: Routledge.

Nardi, B. 1984. The Height of Her Powers: Margaret Mead's Samoa. *Feminist Studies* 10(2):323–337.

———. 2005. Beyond Bandwidth: Dimensions of Connection in Interpersonal Interaction. *Journal of Computer-Supported Cooperative Work* 14(2):91–130.

———. 2010. *My Life as a Night Elf Priest: An Anthropological Account of World of Warcraft*. Ann Arbor: University of Michigan Press.

Nardi, B., and Y. M. Kow. 2010. Digital Imaginaries: How We Know What (We Think) We Know about Chinese Gold Farming. *First Monday* 15(6). http://firstmonday.org/htbin/cgiwrap/bin/ojs/index.php/fm/article/viewArticle/3035/2566.

Nardi, B., S. Ly, and J. Harris. 2007. Learning Conversations in World of Warcraft. *Proceedings Hawaii International Conference on Systems Science*, January 3–6, 2007, Waikoloa, Big Island, HI.

Nardi, B., R. Vatrapu, and T. Clemmensen. 2011. Comparative Informatics. *Interactions* 18(2):28–33.

Neisser, U. 1976. *Cognition and Reality: Principles and Implications of Cognitive Psychology*. New York: W. H. Freeman.

OED (Oxford English Dictionary). 2011. "Intuitive." http://www.oed.com/viewdictionaryentry/Entry/98801, accessed March 3, 2012.

Office of Human Subjects Research, http://ohsr.od.nih.gov/.

Ondrejka, C. 2004. Escaping the Gilded Cage: User Created Content and Building the Metaverse. *New York Law School Law Review* 49(1):81–101.

Orgad, S. 2009. How Can Researchers Make Sense of the Issues Involved in Collecting and Interpreting Online and Offline Data? In *Internet Inquiry: Conversations about Method*. A. Markham and N. Baym, eds. Pp. 33–53. Los Angeles: Sage Publications.

O'Rouke, M. 1998. Fencing Cyberspace: Drawing Borders in a Virtual World. *Minnesota Law Review* 82:609–704.

Ottenberg, S. 1990. Thirty Years of Fieldnotes: Changing Relationships to the Text. In *Fieldnotes: The Makings of Anthropology*. R. Sanjek, ed. Pp. 139–160. Ithaca: Cornell University Press.

Paccagnella, L. 1997. Getting the Seat of Your Pants Dirty: Strategies for Ethnographic Research on Virtual Communities. *Journal of Computer-Mediated Communication* 3(1). http://jcmc.indiana.edu/vol3/issue1/paccagnella.html.

Pager, D. 2009. Field Experiments for Studies of Discrimination. In *Research Confidential*. E. Hargittai, ed. Pp. 38–60. Ann Arbor: University of Michigan Press.

Pargman, D. 2000. The Fabric of Virtual Reality: Courage, Rewards, and Death in an Adventure Mud. *M/C: A Journal of Media and Culture* 3(4). http://journal.media-culture.org.au/0010/mud.php.

Pascoe, C. 2007. *Dude, You're a Fag: Masculinity and Sexuality in High School*. Berkeley: University of California Press.

Pattullo, E. 1980. Who Risks What in Social Research? *The Hastings Center Report* 10(2):15–18.

Paul, C. 2010. Welfare Epics: The Rhetoric of Rewards in World of Warcraft. *Games and Culture* 5(2):158–176.

Payne, G., and M. Williams 2005. Generalization in Qualitative Research. *Sociology* 39(2):295–314.

Pearce, C. 1997. *The Interactive Book: A Guide to the Interactive Revolution.* Indianapolis: Macmillan Technical Publishers.

———. 2006. Productive Play: Game Culture from the Bottom Up. *Games and Culture* 1(1):17–24.

———. 2008a. The Truth about Baby Boomer Gamers. *Games & Culture* 3(2):142–174.

———. 2008b. Spatial Literacy: Reading (and Writing) Game Space. *Proceedings of the Future and Reality of Gaming Conference*, October 17–19, Vienna, Austria.

———. 2009. Collaboration, Creativity and Learning in a Play Community: A Study of the University of There. *Proceedings of the Digital Games Research Association Conference*, September 1–4, London, England.

Pearce, C. and Artemesia. 2008. Identity-as-Place: Trans-Ludic Identities in Mediated Play Communities—The Case of the Uru Diaspora. *Proceedings of the Internet 9.0: Association of Internet Researchers Conference*, October 15–18, Copenhagen, Denmark.

———. 2009. *Communities of Play: Emergent Cultures in Online Games and Virtual Worlds.* Cambridge: MIT Press.

Pelto, P., and G. Pelto. 1973. Ethnography: The Fieldwork Enterprise. In *Handbook of Social and Cultural Anthropology. J. Honigmann, ed.* Pp. 241–88. Chicago: Rand McNally and Company.

Pink, S. 2007. *Doing Visual Ethnography.* 2nd edition. London: Sage.

Pollner, M., and R. Emerson. 2001. Ethnomethodology and Ethnography. In *Handbook of Ethnography.* P. Atkinson, A. Coffey, S. Delamont, J. Lofland, and L. Lofland, eds. Pp. 118–135. London: Sage Publications.

Poole, S. 2000. *Trigger Happy: The Aesthetics of Videogames.* London: Fourth Estate.

Poovey, M. 1998. *A History of the Modern Fact.* Chicago: University of Chicago Press.

Popper, F. 1993. *Art in the Electronic Age.* New York: Harry Abrams.

Povinelli, E. 2002. *The Cunning of Recognition: Indigenous Alterities and the Making of Australian Multiculturalism.* Durham: Duke University Press.

Powdermaker, H. 1966. *Stranger and Friend: The Way of the Anthropologist.* New York: Norton.

Rabinow, P. 1977. *Reflections on Fieldwork in Morocco.* Berkeley: University of California Press.

———. 2003. *Anthropos Today: Reflections on Modern Equipment.* Princeton: Princeton University Press.

Ragin, C., J. Nagel, and P. White. 2004. *NSF Workshop on the Scientific Foundations of Qualitative Research.* Arlington, VA: National Science Foundation.

Reed-Danahay, D. 1997. *Auto/ethnography: Rewriting the Self and the Social.* Oxford: Berg.

Reid, E. 1996. Informed Consent in the Study of On-Line Communities: A Reflection on the Effects of Computer-Mediated Social Research. *The Information Society* 12(2):169–174.

———. 1999. Hierarchy and Power: Social Control in Cyberspace. In *Communities in Cyberspace*. M. Smith and P. Kollock, eds. Pp. 107–133. London: Routledge.

Reiter, R., ed. 1975. *Toward an Anthropology of Women*. New York: Monthly Review Press.

Respect Project. 2004. *RESPECT Code of Practice for Socio-Economic Research*. http://www.respectproject.org/code/.

Restrepo, E., and A. Escobar. 2005. "Other Anthropologies and Anthropology Otherwise": Steps to a World Anthropologies Framework. *Critique of Anthropology* 25(2):99–129.

Reverby, S. 2009. *Examining Tuskegee: The Infamous Syphilis Study and Its Legacy*. Chapel Hill: University of North Carolina Press.

Rheingold, H. 2000. *The Virtual Community: Homesteading on the Electronic Frontier*. Cambridge: MIT Press.

Richardson, L. 1994. Writing: A Method of Inquiry. In *Handbook of Qualitative Research*. N. Denzin and Y. Lincoln, eds. Pp. 923–948. Thousand Oaks, CA: Sage Publications.

Romney, A. K., S. Weller, and W. Batchelder. 1986. Culture as Consensus: A Theory of Culture and Informant Accuracy. *American Anthropologist* 88(2):313–338.

Rosaldo, M., and L. Lamphere, eds. 1974. *Woman, Culture, and Society*. Palo Alto: Stanford University Press.

Rosaldo, R. 1993. *Culture and Truth: The Remaking of Social Analysis*. Boston: Beacon Press.

Rosenberg, M. 1992. *Virtual Reality: Reflections of Life, Dreams, and Technology. An Ethnography of a Computer Society*. Ms.

Said, E. 1978. *Orientalism*. New York: Pantheon.

Salamone, F. 1979. Epistemological Implications of Fieldwork and Their Consequences. *American Anthropologist* 81(1):46–60.

Sambasivan, N., N. Rangaswamy, K. Toyama, and B. Nardi. 2009. Under Development: Encountering Development Ethnographically. *Interactions* 16(6):20–23.

Sanjek, R., ed. 1990. *Fieldnotes: The Makings of Anthropology*. Ithaca: Cornell University Press.

Schaap, F. 2002. *The Words That Took Us There: Ethnography in a Virtual Reality*. Amsterdam: Aksant Academic Publishers.

Schechner, R. 1998. What Is Performance Studies Anyway? In *The Ends of Performance*. P. Phelan and J. Lane, eds. Pp. 357–362. New York: New York University Press.

Schegloff, E. 1997. Whose Text? Whose Context? *Discourse & Society* 8(2):165–187.

Schensul, J. 1999. Focused Group Interviews. In *Enhanced Ethnographic Methods: Audiovisual Techniques, Focused Group Interviews, and Elicitation*

Techniques. J. Schensul, M. LeCompte, B. Nastasi, and S. Borgatti, eds. Pp. 51–114. Walnut Creek, CA: Altamira Press.

Schiano, D., B. Nardi, T. Debeauvais, N. Ducheneaut, and N. Yee. 2011. A New Look at World of Warcraft's Social Landscape. *Foundations of Digital Games Conference*, June 28–July 1, Bordeaux, France.

Schieffelin, E. 1976. *The Sorrow of the Lonely and the Burning of the Dancers*. New York: St. Martin's Press.

Schoolcraft, H. 1851. *Historical and Statistical Information Respecting the History, Condition, and Prospects of the Indian Tribes of the United States*. Bureau of Indian Affairs. Philadelphia: Lippincott, Grambo.

Schrag, Z. 2009a. *Ethical Imperialism: Institutional Review Boards and the Social Sciences, 1965–2009*. Baltimore: Johns Hopkins University Press.

———. 2009b. How Talking Became Human Subjects Research: The Federal Regulation of the Social Sciences, 1965–1991. *Journal of Policy History* 21(3):3–37.

Schubert, D. 2003. The Lighter Side of Meridian 59's History. In *Developing Online Games: An Insider's Guide*. J. Mulligan and B. Patrovsky, eds. Pp. 361–371. Indianapolis: New Riders.

Schutz, A. 1967. *The Phenomenology of the Social World*. Evanston: Northwestern University Press.

Seay, A., B. Fleming, K. Lee, and R. Kraut. 2004. Project Massive: A Study of Online Gaming Communities. In *Computer Human Interaction '04: Extended Abstracts on Human Factors in Computing Systems*, 1421–1424. New York: ACM Press.

Simmel, G. 1908. The Stranger. In *Georg Simmel on Individuality and Social Forms*. 1972 edition. D. N. Levine, ed. Chicago: University of Chicago Press.

Skeggs, B., ed. 1995. *Feminist Cultural Theory: Production and Process*. Manchester: Manchester University Press.

———. 1997. *Formations of Class and Gender: Becoming Respectable*. London: Sage Publications.

Spencer, B., and F. J. Gillen. 1899. *The Native Tribes of Central Australia*. London: Macmillan.

Spinuzzi, C. 2008. *Network*. Cambridge: Cambridge University Press.

Spradley, J. 1979. *The Ethnographic Interview*. Belmont, CA: Wadsworth.

Spyer, P., ed. 1997. *Border Fetishisms: Material Objects in Unstable Spaces*. London: Routledge.

Squire, K. 2005. Changing the Game: What Happens When Video Games Enter the Classroom? *Innovate: Journal of Online Education* 1:25–49.

Standage, T. 2007. *The Victorian Internet: The Remarkable Story of the Telegraph and the Nineteenth Century's On-line Pioneers*. New York: Walker & Company.

Stephenson, N. 1992. *Snow Crash*. New York: Bantam Books.

Steinkuehler, C. 2006. The Mangle of Play. *Games and Culture* 1(3):199–213.

Steinkuehler, C., and S. Duncan. 2008. Scientific Habits of Mind in Virtual Worlds. *Journal of Science Education and Technology* 17(6):530–543.

Stocking, G. 1987. *Victorian Anthropology*. New York: Free Press.

———. 1992. The Ethnographer's Magic: Fieldwork in British Anthropology from Tylor to Malinowski. In *The Ethnographer's Magic and Other Essays in the History of Anthropology*. Pp. 12–59. Madison: University of Wisconsin Press.

———. 1995. *After Tylor: British Social Anthropology, 1888–1951*. Madison: University of Wisconsin Press.

Stoler, A. 2002. *Carnal Knowledge and Imperial Power: Race and the Intimate in Colonial Rule*. Berkeley: University of California Press.

Stone, A. R. 1991. Will the Real Body Please Stand Up? In *Cyberspace: First Steps*. M. Benedikt, ed. Pp. 81–118. Cambridge: MIT Press.

Strathern, M. 2004. *Commons and Borderlands: Working Papers on Interdisciplinarity, Accountability, and the Flow of Knowledge*. Wantage, UK: Sean Kingston Publishing.

Suchman, L. 2000. Embodied Practices of Engineering Work. *Mind, Culture, and Activity* 7(1):4–18.

Suler, J. 1996. *The Psychology of Cyberspace*. http://users.rider.edu/~suler/psycyber/psycyber.html.

Sundén, J. 2003. *Material Virtualities: Approaching Online Textual Embodiment*. New York: Peter Lang.

Sveningsson, M. 2004. Ethics in Internet Ethnography. In *Readings in Virtual Research Ethics*. E. Buchanan, ed. Pp. 45–61. Hershey, PA: Information Science Publishing.

Taylor, T. L. 1999. Life in Virtual Worlds: Plural Existence, Multimodalities, and Other Online Research Challenges. *American Behavioral Scientist* 43(3):436–449.

———. 2002. Living Digitally: Embodiment in Virtual Worlds. In *The Social Life of Avatars: Presence and Interaction in Shared Virtual Environments*. R. Schroeder, ed. Pp. 40–62. London: Springer-Verlag.

———. 2003a. Intentional Bodies: Virtual Environments and the Designers Who Shape Them. *International Journal of Engineering Education* 19(1):25–34.

———. 2003b. Multiple Pleasures: Women and Online Gaming. *Convergence* 9(1):21–46.

———. 2004. The Social Design of Virtual Worlds: Constructing the User and Community through Code. In *Internet Research Annual Volume 1: Selected Papers from the Association of Internet Researchers Conferences 2000–2002*. M. Consalvo, N. Baym, J. Hunsinger, K. B. Jensen, J. Logie, M. Monero, and L. R. Shade, eds. Pp. 260–268. New York: Peter Lang.

Taylor, T. L. 2006a. *Play Between Worlds: Exploring Online Game Culture.* Cambridge: MIT Press.

———. 2006b. Beyond Management: Considering Participatory Design and Governance in Player Culture. *First Monday* Special Issue 7. http://firstmonday.org/.htbin/cgiwrap/bin/ojs/index.php/fm/article/view/1611/1526.

———. 2008. Becoming a Player: Networks, Structures, and Imagined Futures. In *Beyond Barbie and Mortal Kombat: New Perspectives on Gender, Games, and Computing.* Y. Kafai, C. Heeter, J. Denner, and J. Sun, eds. Pp. 50–65. Cambridge: MIT Press.

———. 2009. The Assemblage of Play. *Games and Culture* 4(4):331–339.

Thomas, D. 2009. In Praise of the Anecdote or Gaming for Columbine. *Television & New Media* 10(1):158–161.

Timmermans, S. 1999. *Sudden Death and the Myth of CPR.* Philadelphia: Temple University Press.

Tolkien, J.R.R. 1937. *The Hobbit.* London: Allen and Unwin.

———. 1954. *The Lord of the Rings.* London: Allen and Unwin.

Trotter, R., and J. Schensul. 1998. Methods in Applied Anthropology. In *Handbook of Methods in Cultural Anthropology.* H. R. Bernard., ed. Pp. 691–735. Walnut Creek, CA: Altamira Press.

Trouillot, M. 1991. Anthropology and the Savage Slot: The Poetics and Politics of Otherness. In *Recapturing Anthropology: Working in the Present.* R. G. Fox, ed. Pp. 17–44. Santa Fe: School of American Research Press.

Tsing, A. 1993. *In the Realm of the Diamond Queen: Marginality in an Out-of-the-Way Place.* Princeton: Princeton University Press.

Turkle, S. 1995. *Life on the Screen: Identity in the Age of the Internet.* New York: Simon and Schuster.

———. 2007. Introduction: The Things That Matter. In *Evocative Objects: Things We Think With.* Sherry Turkle, ed. Pp. 3–11. Cambridge: MIT Press.

Turner, V. 1982. *From Ritual to Theatre: The Human Seriousness of Play.* New York: PAJ Publications.

Tylor, E. B. 1871. *Primitive Culture, Volume 1: The Origins of Culture.* New York: Harper and Row.

Urry, J. 1972. "Notes and Queries on Anthropology" and the Development of Field Methods in British Anthropology, 1870–1920. *Proceedings of the Royal Anthropological Institute for 1972:* 45–57.

Ventrella, J. 2011. *Virtual Body Language.* Santa Cruz, CA: Eyebrain Books.

Vermeulen, H. 2008. The Early History of Ethnography and Ethnology in the German Enlightenment: Anthropological Discourse in Europe and Asia, 1710–1808. Ph.D. dissertation, University of Leiden/Proefschrift Universiteit Leiden.

Vinge, V. 1981. True Names. In *True Names by Vernor Vinge and the Opening of the Cyberspace Frontier.* James Frenkel, ed. Pp. 241–330. New York: Tom Doherty Associates, 2001.

Visweswaran, K. 1994. *Fictions of Feminist Ethnography*. Minneapolis: University of Minnesota Press.

Vitousek, P., A. Mooney, J. Lubchenco, and J. Melillo. 1997. Human Domination of Earth's Ecosystems. *Science* 277: 494–499.

Wacquant, L. 2004. *Body & Soul: Notebooks of an Apprentice Boxer*. Oxford: Oxford University Press.

Wardrip-Fruin, N. 2009. *Expressive Processing: Digital Fictions, Computer Games, and Software Studies*. Cambridge: MIT Press.

Waskul, D., and M. Douglass. 1996. Considering the Electronic Participant: Some Polemical Observations on the Ethics of On-Line Research. *The Information Society* 12(2):129–140.

Webb, B. 1926. *My Apprenticeship*. London: Longman.

Wellman, B., and C. Haythornthwaite. 2002. The Internet in Everyday Life: An Introduction. In *The Internet in Everyday Life*. B. Wellman and C. Haythornthwaite, eds. Pp. 3–44. London: Blackwell.

Westermarck, E. 1936. Methods in Social Anthropology. *Journal of the Royal Anthropological Institute* 66(2):223–248.

Wetherell, M. 1998. Positioning and Interpretative Repertoires: Conversation Analysis and Post-structuralism in Dialogue. *Discourse & Society* 9(2):387–412.

Whitehead J., B. McLemore, and M. Orlando. 2008. *World of Warcraft Programming*. New York: Wiley.

Whitney, S., and C. Schneider. 2009. Was the Institutional Review Board System a Mistake? *Clinical Infectious Diseases* 49(12):1957.

Whyte, W. 1943 [repr. 1993]. *Street Corner Society: The Social Structure of an Italian Slum*. 4th edition. Chicago: University of Chicago Press.

Wight, D. 1994. Boys' Thoughts and Talk about Sex in a Working-Class Locality of Glasgow. *Sociological Review* 42:702–737.

Williams, D. 2010. The Promises and Perils of Large-scale Data Extraction. Ms.

Williams, M. 2000. Interpretivism and Generalisation. *Sociology* 34(2):209–224.

Willis, P. 1977. *Learning to Labor: How Working Class Kids Get Working Class Jobs*. New York: Columbia University Press.

———. 1978. *Profane Culture*. London: Routledge.

Wimmer, A., and N. Glick Schiller. 2002. Methodological Nationalism and Beyond: Nation-State Building, Migration, and the Social Sciences. *Global Networks* 2(4):301–334.

Winnicott, D. W. 1971. *Playing and Reality*. London: Tavistock.

Wolcott, H. 2005. *The Art of Fieldwork*. 2nd edition. Walnut Creek, CA: Altamira Press.

Wolf, M. 1992. *A Thrice-Told Tale: Feminism, Postmodernism, and Ethnographic Responsibility*. Palo Alto: Stanford University Press.

World Medical Association (WMA). 1964. *The Declaration of Helsinki*. Ferney-Voltaire: WMA. http://www.wma.net/en/20activities/10ethics/10helsinki/.

Yanagisako, S., and C. Delaney. 1995. Introduction. In *Naturalizing Power: Essays in Feminist Cultural Analysis*. S. Yanagisako and C. Delaney, eds. Pp. 1–19. New York: Routledge.

Yee, N. 2001. *The Norrathian Scrolls: A Study of EverQuest* (version 2.5). http://www.nickyee.com/eqt/report.html.

———. 2006. The Labor of Fun: How Video Games Blur the Boundaries of Work and Play. *Games and Culture* 1(1):68–71.

Yee, N., and J. Bailenson. 2007. The Proteus Effect: The Effect of Transformed Self-Representation on Behavior. *Human Communication Research* 33(3):271–290.

Zhan, M. 2009. *Other-Worldly: Making Chinese Medicine through Transnational Frames*. Durham: Duke University Press.

Žižek, S. 1989. *The Sublime Object of Ideology*. London: Verso.

INDEX